All Sides of the Story

FOR

MY LATE MOTHER, MARIA NTOMBIZODWA, NEE NKAMBULE

MY FATHER, SILVERTON MANIKANI

MY BELOVED WIFE, GUGU

AND MY SON, ASHFORD NKULULEKO

All Sides of the Story

A grandstand view of
South Africa's
political transition

with a foreword by
Deputy President Thabo Mbeki

Kaizer M Nyatsumba

JONATHAN BALL PUBLISHERS · JOHANNESBURG

Published in 1997 by
Jonathan Ball Publishers (Pty) Ltd
PO Box 33977
Jeppestown 2043
ISBN 1 86842 038 8

Design by Michael Barnett, Johannesburg
Typesetting and Reproduction by Iskova Image Setting cc
Printed and bound by National Book Printers,
Drukkery Street, Goodwood, Western Cape

Contents

Foreword

By the Hon Thabo Mbeki

This book contains examples from the work of a South African African journalist and includes news reports, interviews, background pieces, colour stories and analyses. They cover the very interesting and critically important period in the history of South Africa spanning the years 1990 to 1995.

As I read through the various articles, I realised the importance of making such a publication available to the general public, both in South Africa and abroad. This derives from the fact that the items it includes will serve as a reminder of, and a point of reference with regard to, the important issues with which all of us had to contend during those eventful years; which seem to have passed so quickly. With its publication, there would be no need for anybody to plumb the depths of their memory to recall what were some of the important issues of the day.

This book, with all the inevitable overlaps of journalistic reportage and commentary, gives us Kaizer Nyatsumba's personal grandstand view of events. Throughout the book, the reader will come across the tension that is generated by the pressure to report and comment on today's events today, the simultaneous need to achieve a substantial understanding of the historical process to enable the writer correctly to report and interpret these events, and the urge to break loose from the 'herd response' – which unfortunately is reflected in so much of South African journalism.

All Sides of the Story is of significance in that it enables the diligent student of South African reality to understand some of the 'established truths', assumptions and norms that inform the practice of journalism in South Africa, yet it offers an interesting interpretation of the role of the media. It is also important to the extent that it provides – inevitably, sometimes, too fleetingly and occasionally – a picture of the mental and emotional framework that would inform the unique writing of a 'young South African African journalist'.

Introduction

Seldom do people, anywhere in the world, live through such an historic period as we have gone through in this country over the past six years, and *know* that they are part of history. We in South Africa have gone through just such a period in the last six years, and we have been extremely fortunate to have witnessed all the once-unthinkable changes which have taken place in the country. And I have been extremely privileged to have been so closely involved in our historic transition, albeit as an observer.

Once a pariah state among civilised nations, South Africa today speaks with moral authority on matters of human rights, and has taken her rightful place in the community of nations, whether it is in the Organisation of African Unity, the Commonwealth of Nations or the United Nations.

But our transition has not been entirely without hitches. There have been moments when we came dangerously close to a civil war, when it was doubtful if our founding democratic election in April 1994 would take place at all, and when there was so much sabre-rattling in and about KwaZulu-Natal that it may have looked like our transition was endangered. Yet, time after time, we pulled through most of the problems and emerged from them an even stronger democracy.

All of this has been documented in this book. The articles reproduced herein were first published in *The Star*, where I have worked with some of the finest, most professional and dedicated journalists. My thanks to them for their vicarious contributions to this book. My thanks also go to my wife, Gugu, whose support and assistance were invaluable; and to my secretary, Mrs Minnie Koekemoer, for having helped with this project without once complaining.

Contained in this book is a collection of some of the news reports I have written in the past six years – including stories I broke as 'scoops' at their time of publication – news backgrounders, colour stories, interviews, profiles and, of course, political analyses. This is not a definitive book on South African politics, but rather a grandstand view of our political drama as it has unfolded in the past six years, containing as it does vignettes of South African political life.

The interview with President Mandela was conducted with Shaun Johnson, Chris Whitfield and Esther Waugh. *Some* of the others were conducted with either Johnson or Patrick Bulger.

This is raw, or the first draft of, history, documenting for us where we have come from and what strides were made to get us where we are now.

Kaizer M Nyatsumba
Political Editor and Executive Editor: *The Star*
Johannesburg, January 1997

AUTHOR'S NOTE

This book does not contain every published article written by the author about South Africa's transition. The articles which do not appear in this book can be viewed in the library and archives of *The Star* newspaper, Johannesburg.

The Huge Weight on Mandela's Shoulders

2 February 1990

To most South Africans, the idea of a free Mr Nelson Mandela is no longer as unthinkable as it once was. The African National Congress leader may walk out of Victor Verster Prison as a free man any time now. What role, if any, will a free Mr Mandela play in the country's wide political field? Mr Mandela, writes *Time*'s South African bureau chief Scott MacLeod, will have on his shoulders a huge responsibility.

Unify

He will be expected to unify the different anti-apartheid organisations in this country and bring the Government and these extra-Parliamentary forces to the negotiating table.

MacLeod points out that the eyes of South Africans and the international community will focus on Mr Mandela who, on his release, will be expected to perform acrobatic political feats.

'Mandela,' MacLeod writes. 'The name reverberates like a mantra through South Africa these days, half in excitement, half in anxiety. Mandela will soon be free. Mandela will solve the problem. If Mandela can't do it, who can?'

In a report accompanied by portraits of Mr Mandela, MacLeod says the world-famous ANC leader's description of himself as a 'facilitator' indicates that he has accepted 'the job of wresting tangible results from this moment of opportunity'.

According to the report, for the past three years Mr Mandela has held a series of meetings with a team of Government officials and since last November has held meetings with cabinet ministers.

His unconditional release was widely regarded as the key to implementing the Government's promises of reform.

It was believed, MacLeod says, that if anyone could bridge the vast divide between whites and blacks, and among blacks themselves, Mr Mandela was the man to do it.

'The white Government looks on him as a born-again moderate, a man they can do business with. For blacks, Mandela may be the one who, as the personification of their long suffering, can help them transcend the disagreements over strategy and allegiance that have splintered their strength, and bargain on equal terms with the whites,' writes MacLeod.

He says that on his release Mr Mandela will walk out 'into a world vastly different from the strict apartheid society he vowed to overthrow'.

Healthy respect

The first meeting Mr Mandela held with State President F W de Klerk, at Tuynhuys, Cape Town, resulted in the two men having a healthy respect for each other, with each man thinking the other was someone he could 'do business with,' according to MacLeod's report.

He says Mr Mandela's biggest challenge may come from within the ranks of the ANC and the Mass Democratic Movement, 'where some in the new generation of leaders resent his automatic resumption of leadership and consider him too willing to compromise.'

MacLeod concludes: 'Mandela is the sole black leader in South Africa who has a chance to bring both sides (the Government and anti-apartheid forces) to compromise.

'Despite his advancing years and his near-fatal bout with tuberculosis in 1988, he was described by a visitor to Victor Verster as "very nimble, alert, self-confident, charismatic, not a mere symbolic leader but someone who is in touch with events."

'Few others possess the pragmatism that Mandela has honed over the years, which may enable him to grow from a facilitator of negotiations to a reconciler of men.'

ANC Military Supremo Strolls Around Johannesburg – Umkhonto Kingpin Unnoticed

20 June 1990

Chris Hani, once considered the Government's enemy number one, yesterday strolled around the streets of Johannesburg, unnoticed among the crowds. The chief of staff and deputy commander of the ANC's military wing, Umkhonto we Sizwe, was recognised only once – and on that occasion was urged by his bodyguard to leave the area.

When I was ushered into the ANC's office yesterday to meet Mr Hani, I was expecting to find a big, tough, serious-looking man. I was received by just such a man – but he turned out to be the diminutive Mr Hani's bodyguard and companion, Tokyo Sexwale.

In demand

Mr Hani himself, a 48-year-old who did not look as fearsome as the Government had painted him to be, was with colleagues in the ANC's boardroom, and just about everybody wanted to talk to him. It was the same when we later tried to leave the office with him, and we ended up conducting an interview in *The Star's* car, driving around Johannesburg. We drove down Fox Street next to the Carlton Hotel and mingled with black and white South Africans as *The Star* took pictures.

In Fox Street, no one recognised him. The Government's banning of the ANC and other organisations and the censorship of information on these organisations and their leaders has worked – South Africans knew the name, but not the face of Mr Hani and his Umkhonto colleagues. At the corner of Sauer and Pritchard Streets one man seemed to recognise Mr Hani as we stopped at the robots.

He raised a clenched fist and Mr Hani did likewise. Mr Sexwale was not impressed. 'Let's drive away from this place,' he said. 'We don't want people who will recognise you.'

Mr Hani joined Umkhonto we Sizwe at the age of 16. He spent a year in the Soviet Union doing military training, established an ANC camp in Tanzania, and became a commissar in Zimbabwe, fighting Rhodesian troops. When he and his comrades retreated to Botswana they were arrested and sentenced to six years' jail. He was released after two years.

In 1973 he returned to South Africa to organise for the ANC. He spent a few months in the country before going to Lesotho where he recruited 'hundreds of people' from the Free State. In 1975 he was appointed to the ANC's national executive committee (NEC) in absentia, becoming one of the youngest members of the organisation's NEC. He stayed in Lesotho until 1982 when he was appointed army commissar and was recalled to Angola where he fought against Unita.

Following Joe Slovo's resignation as MK chief of staff (in order to concentrate on his responsibilities as SA Communist Party general secretary), Mr Hani was appointed MK chief of staff and deputy commander.

Talks 'Another Field of Struggle'– Hani

21 June 1990

The African National Congress's military wing, Umkhonto we Sizwe (MK), is in full support of the ANC's position on negotiations and regards negotiations as yet another terrain of struggle, says Chris Hani, its chief of staff and deputy commander.

Mr Hani, who returned to South Africa on Monday, spoke about the armed struggle and negotiations. He said his home-coming was marred by the economic inequalities between whites and blacks.

While he was happy to come back home, Mr Hani (48) who left South Africa in 1963 at the age of 21 soon after obtaining his BA degree from the University of Fort Hare, said he was saddened by the fact that the National Party was still in power and blacks were still heavily deprived economically and politically.

Driving through the squatter camp of Mshenguville in Soweto on the first day of his arrival was 'like being hit with a sledgehammer'. This made him realise that coming home imposed 'extra demands on us to step up the struggle so that real freedom should be felt by the dwellers of the slums'.

'We cannot afford to have two South Africas, one very poor and one very rich.' The armed struggle, he said, would continue for as long as apartheid existed, and political prisoners remained incarcerated.

Incarcerated

'I am deeply aggrieved by the fact that fighters of Umkhonto are still in prison and on death row. I would like to see all my colleagues released without delay. In fact, I cannot see any reason for their continued incarceration.'

Mr Hani said all obstacles to negotiations had to be removed and once this had been done, the ANC would talk to the Government 'and hopefully arrive at a mutually acceptable ceasefire'.

Asked if talk of the armed struggle was now merely to strengthen the

ANC's hand in negotiations, Mr Hani said the armed struggle still existed. Although visible MK activities had declined since the unbanning of political organisations on February 2, the ANC's military wing was still functional and was busy recruiting and training cadres. Special attention had been paid, however, to make sure that whites did not feel themselves to be MK targets. Instead, they were called upon to join the ANC.

This contrasted sharply with Mr Hani's statement in 1987 that whites would not change until 'they experienced apartheid as bitter, very painful and costly in terms of human lives'. This was interpreted as a shift in ANC policy to make white civilians MK targets.

'I never advocated the attack of white civilians,' said Mr Hani. 'What I said then was that areas in which whites lived had to be attacked so that whites could feel our presence and know we were in a state of war.'

He admitted that some of the operations carried out by MK guerillas 'did not necessarily follow ANC guidelines and policies,' and he did not encourage such sporadic attacks on civilians. Similarly, he could not publicly denounce his fighters. He emphasised that these unauthorised operations did not, as it was suggested then, mean MK leaders had lost control of their soldiers.

'We certainly intervened and told our comrades making civilians targets was wrong, and pointed out to them that this would antagonise people and lose us international support. There is full conformity with our policies now, and our comrades carry out operations which reflect ANC policy,' he said.

The MK chief of staff denied reports that he was a hardliner who was initially opposed to negotiations and said the ANC had reached consensus that it would be proper to participate in 'talks abouts talks' which could lead to negotiations.

He said the South African Government had tried a number of times to assassinate him, mentioning the time he had narrowly escaped death in Maseru, Lesotho, during a raid by South African commandos. If he or other individuals in MK's leadership were assassinated, other leaders would take their positions, he said.

Mr Hani reiterated his demand that MK soldiers and members of the South African Defence Force (SADF) had to come together and hold talks of their own about a future defence force for the country.

It was important that 'the ordinary soldiers' were prepared for the political changes that were taking place so that the army would not block the negotiation process. He was therefore pained by Defence

Minister Magnus Malan's statements that MK fighters and the SADF would never be integrated. Although Umkhonto weSizwe was primarily a guerilla army, it was now in the process of undergoing a transformation into an orthodox army. What was now needed, Mr Hani said, was an army which would be committed to the defence of all the country's citizens.

It was for this reason that 'the de-racialisation of the SADF and police is an urgent matter'. Mr Hani said if negotiations broke down, MK forces, which were presently recruiting and training people inside and outside the country, would fight all over again 'with the firm conviction that ultimately victory is certainly ours'. He denied allegations that the ANC was involved in the murder of an ANC dissident in Transkei at the weekend, and that the organisation tortured its captives.

The ANC, he said, had a code of conduct which specifically forbade the torture of captured 'enemy agents', and where allegations of torture were founded decisive action was taken against those responsible. KwaZulu Chief Minister Mangosuthu Buthelezi, who has often accused the ANC of being out to assassinate him, was never on MK's target list, Mr Hani said.

'We will destroy Buthelezi politically. In fact, he is destroying himself. As far as we are concerned he is part of the South African regime and is not at all different from [Bophuthatswana president] Mangope'.

ANC to Spell Out its Views on Minute

9 August 1990

The African National congress publicity machinery went into top gear yesterday in an attempt to publicise and explain the accord signed between the Government and the ANC in Pretoria on Monday.

In a 'report-back to the people of South Africa', to be advertised in newspapers countrywide shortly, the ANC's Department of Information and Publicity has tried to put the Pretoria Minute into perspective from its point of view, pointing out 'the advances' in Monday's meeting.

In a preamble to the report, the ANC said its all-round offensive against apartheid had led South Africa to the beginning of a new and democratic era, noting that there was still some distance to cover before apartheid was replaced by a democratic institution. Although substantial advances had been made, some stumbling blocks still remained in place. The ANC said in view of the priority it gave to the peaceful solution of the country's problems, it had taken the initiative to suspend the armed struggle.

'This means that the ANC will not carry out any further armed actions and related activities such as the infiltration of armed cadres and weaponry. The ANC will participate in monitoring the activity of the SAP and the SADF', it said.

The organisation was quick to point out, however, that the armed struggle had not been abandoned, Umkhonto weSizwe was not dissolved and the ANC had not forfeited its right to self-defence. Continued suspension of the armed struggle depended on the behaviour of the SAP and the SADF.

Gains made

Mass struggles, according to the ANC, would continue 'in all spheres of our lives' and the Government would have to heed the people's demands. The ANC said before Monday's meeting political prisoners and detainees had not been released, political trials were still continuing, security legislation was used against the people and the state of emergency in Natal was still in force. Gains made in Monday's meeting at the Presidensie in Pretoria were that:

- A timetable for the release of political prisoners and the return of exiles had been agreed upon. The release of political prisoners will begin on September 1 and is expected to end by December 31. During that period all political trials would have ceased, political detainees been released and most exiles would have returned home indemnified from prosecution.
- The Government has committed itself to amending existing security legislation at the next session of Parliament. It will also give immediate consideration to repealing all provisions of the Internal Security Act which prohibits the furtherance of communism, provides for the listing of banned people and required newspapers to pay a deposit before registering.
- Although the state of emergency in Natal was still in force, both the ANC and the Government had committed themselves 'to search for peace and stability in the spirit of mutual trust'.
- The South African Youth Congress (Sayco) has warned that the suspension of armed actions by the ANC did not remove the people's right to defend themselves against aggressors.

Meeting of Black Groups May Halt or Fan Violence

19 September 1990

When leaders of the country's major black political and church organisations sit down today to discuss ways of halting the present wave of township violence, many South Africans will be hoping for an agreement which could defuse tensions and help restore peace in the war-torn areas.

The meeting, scheduled to begin at 9am at Funda Centre, Diepkloof, Soweto, was hastily convened by the Azanian People's Organisation. Azapo said it hoped the meeting would result in a joint commitment by the organisations to a concrete programme of action to stem the violence permanently, according to Azapo president Itumeleng Mosala.

The meeting would also afford the different organisations' leaders, who have often publicly criticised each other, an occasion to condemn the violence unanimously. Azapo was therefore asking the entire nation to commit itself to the agreements emerging from the meeting.

Making the announcement for the first time in Azapo's national council in Pietersburg at the weekend, Professor Mosala said the time had come for leaders of the various factions of the black community to analyse the many facets of the recent bloody violence. Azapo publicity secretary Strini Moodley this week said it was no longer enough for leaders of the different political groups to issue press statements condemning the violence; it was time something concrete was done about it.

The meeting, he said, would deal specifically with the question of violence and it was hoped that the organisations would agree to appoint a co-ordinating committee which would set up joint defence and monitoring structures. Mr Moodley said the meeting would look into the possibilities of the different organisations holding and addressing joint rallies in the townships.

Invited to the meeting are all the major extra-parliamentary political organisations such as the ANC, the Pan Africanist Congress, the New Unity Movement, the Workers' Organisation for Socialist Action, the

Congress of South African Trade Unions and the National Council of Trade Unions.

Influential

Religious and professional bodies, including the South African Council of Churches and the South African Black Social Workers' Association, have also been invited.

Influential individuals who have been invited are Archbishop Desmond Tutu; Methodist Church presiding bishop, the Rev Stanley Mogoba; and newspaper editors Khulu Sibiya (*City Press*) and Aggrey Klaaste (*Sowetan*).

Whether the meeting, whose importance lies in the fact that Azapo has asked the different organisations to send their top leadership, will attain all the goals envisaged by its conveners is hard to tell.

Both Azapo and the PAC have attacked the ANC for holding talks with the Government, accusing it of having sold out in 'the struggle'. The two organisations have also been critical of the ANC's handling of the violence and have consequently urged the ANC to cast aside its differences with Chief Mangosuthu Buthelezi, the president of the Inkatha Freedom Party (IFP) – which has not been invited to the meeting – and meet him.

Mr Moodley pointed out that the fact that these organisations' top leadership would be behind closed doors together could have great psychological effects 'and signify to the people that we are serious about the need to end the violence'. The meeting could also serve to register the point that although these organisations differ in ideologies adopted and strategies used, they are united by the fact that they are all against apartheid and the mindless violence.

The ANC will send a low-level delegation to the meeting because its leaders are engaged in a two-day national executive committee meeting to discuss their response to the Government's plan to end the violence. The meeting's major flaw, however, is that one of the key players in the violence, the IFP, has not been invited.

Azapo has said that had the IFP been invited, the other organisations would have refused to take part. The question of the IFP's exclusion could mean that Chief Buthelezi's party will not feel bound by whatever agreement is reached today. There is also the danger that Chief Buthelezi could present the IFP's exclusion as exclusion of the Zulu people, thus perpetuating the feeling that the ANC and its allies are ganging up against Zulus.

There is also a danger of the meeting ending in a deadlock if the various organisations emphasise their ideological differences at the expense of compromise. Given the already high degree of political intolerance in the townships, this prospect would be very dangerous – if these organisations' leaders cannot talk to one another, then expecting their followers to be tolerant of opposing views would be a tall order.

A Struggle that Defies Unity

3 December 1990

Calls for the formation of a broad united front of South African liberation movements or anti-apartheid organisations have come and gone unheeded countless times in the past decade. The calls, which tended to originate mainly from bodies such as the Organisation of African Unity (OAU) and some African countries, were directed mostly at the two oldest liberation movements, the African National Congress (ANC) and the Pan Africanist Congress (PAC), in the foreign capitals from which they operated.

The calls for a united front have been seen as a wise strategic move to enable the liberation movements to speak with one voice on black aspirations and exert maximum pressure on Pretoria to ditch apartheid and give way to a new democratic order. Various African leaders, including Zimbabwean President Robert Mugabe, have expressed support for such a front.

These presidents' calls, however, have largely been ignored by the two organisations, and accusations and counter-accusations have abounded as to which organisation has constantly scuttled the calls, thus effectively ensuring that the front was still-born. Top PAC leaders interviewed in Harare in September pointed accusing fingers at the pre-February 2 ANC leadership, which was based in Lusaka, saying it has constantly poured cold water on plans to form a united front. This, the PAC leaders said, was because the ANC believed itself invincible at the polls and therefore saw no reason for a united front.

ANC leaders have denied these allegations, and since his release on February 11 this year, ANC deputy president Nelson Mandela has been consistent in his calls for the formation of a broad front to speak with one voice at the negotiating table. Mr Mandela, who paid a tribute to PAC acting president Clarence Makwetu, made this call again before African heads of state in Swaziland last month.

Mr Mandela told the Swaziland conference that since Mr Makwetu took over from the late Zephania Mothopeng last month, prospects for unity between the two organisations had never been brighter. Mr Makwetu rose to the occasion, telling the conference he was in favour of a joint approach with the ANC to President de Klerk's reform initiatives and that the PAC would decide at its second national congress in Johannesburg next month whether or not to join the ANC in a united front.

But until calls for a united front emanate not only from the leaders but also from the different organisations' members themselves, the proposed united front will not take off. Significantly, while Mr Mandela's position in the ANC is quite secure and he is quite likely to assume the ANC presidency when Oliver Tambo bows out of active politics next year, the same cannot be said with certainty about Mr Makwetu.

The PAC leader stands on shaky ground, and there is the December 7–9 PAC national congress, which will determine whether to confirm Mr Makwetu in office. In spite of the uncertainties, the leaders of the different organisations, including the Azanian People's Organisation (Azapo), are optimistic that such a front will get off the ground. The ANC's Gill Marcus said her organisation had repeatedly stated that 'to move forward, we have to get the oppressed together'. It was for this reason the ANC had held talks with a variety of organisations, including homeland leaders.

Miss Marcus said all organisations which stood for peace, democracy and 'the transfer of power to the majority' would be welcome in such a front, and this did not exclude the ANC's arch enemy, the Inkatha Freedom Party (IFP), if it subscribed to the same ideals. PAC general secretary Philemon Tefu was equally optimistic. The PAC, he said, had always stood for 'unity in action' among the oppressed, and it now welcomed Mr Mandela's pronouncements on the need for a constituent assembly and an interim government.

Like Mr Tefu, Azapo president Professor Itumeleng Mosala said his organisation had 'always been pushing for unity among the oppressed'. This was the reason Azapo had constantly called for a consultative conference of all the liberation movements, and he hoped the foundation for the formation of the united front would be laid at the meeting convened last week by Archbishop Desmond Tutu in Cape Town. The successful outcome of that meeting will strengthen those hopes.

Despite the optimism expressed by the leaders, the united front's success will depend on its acceptance at grass-roots level. The three organisations are all aware of this, and have pledged themselves to selling the idea vigorously to their followers. The other serious issue presently dividing the potential partners is the question of negotiations with the Government. The ANC fully endorses negotiations and takes pride in having initiated the 'peace process', but Azapo has rejected the Government's invitation to enter into exploratory talks, and the PAC has yet to announce its response to the invitation. Unless these organisations adopt the same position on negotiations, the planned united front could be short-lived.

The ANC's recent insistence on the need for a constituent assembly and an interim government is the only thing the three organisations now have in common. What unifies these organisations, however, immediately puts them in direct confrontation with Inkatha, which argues that the situation in South Africa is different from that in the pre-independent Namibia and consequently rejects both a constituent assembly and an interim government. But if all these organisations indeed establish a united front, the National Party is unlikely to cherish the prospect of sitting opposite a sea of black faces at the negotiating table.

Big welcome for Tambo

3 December 1990

Thousands of jubilant ANC supporters thronged the concourse outside Jan Smuts Airport this morning to welcome their organisation's president, Oliver Reginald Tambo (73), as he returned home after 30 years in exile. Airport security was tight and police manned roadblocks and searched vehicles.

When ANC deputy president Nelson Mandela and his wife Winnie arrived shortly after 10.30, the huge crowd, which until then had been singing and toyi-toying, surged forward, trying to touch the couple. Police used dogs to maintain order until the Mandelas entered the airport building.

Bus-loads of supporters began arriving early this morning and, although buses were not allowed on to airport premises because of parking problems, ANC supporters were allowed to disembark a few metres away and walk to the concourse. Transkei military leader Major-General Bantu Holomisa was one of the first dignitaries to arrive. Inside the airport confusion reigned as scores of local and foreign media representatives were told they would not be allowed on to the tarmac and that Mr Tambo would not enter the airport building.

ANC spokesman Gill Marcus said police were being 'very obstructionist' and would allow only the ANC's national executive committee and a few dignitaries on to the tarmac when Mr Tambo's private plane touched down. His flight from Lusaka via Harare was delayed by more than two hours. At midday the national reception committee and police were locked in a meeting to discuss arrangements for the arrival.

Miss Marcus said police would not allow Mr Tambo to address the thousands of supporters outside the airport building. Reception committee member Cyril Ramaphosa was also not allowed to explain to supporters why Mr Tambo had been delayed.

'Already a few people have been bitten by dogs. The police don't want any media around. No speeches are to be made', Miss Marcus said.

Mr Tambo is scheduled to address the ANC's National Consultative Conference at Nasrec, south of Johannesburg, this weekend. The ANC president is reported to have recovered considerably since suffering a stroke last year.

Accompanying the Mandelas were internal ANC chairman Walter Sisulu and his wife Albertina, ANC secretary-general Alfred Nzo and NEC member Aziz Pahad. They were later joined by the NEC's Steve Tshwete.

The crowds chanted 'ANC! ANC! ANC!' as the ANC leaders entered the airport building. A few others shouted 'Mother of the Nation' to Mrs Mandela. Other dignitaries to arrive included Lebowa Chief Minister Nelson Ramodike and former South African Council of Churches general secretary Rev Beyers Naude.

Sapa reported earlier from Harare that Mr Tambo received a tumultuous welcome there.

Accompanied by a 15-member delegation, he was met at the airport by Foreign Minister Nathan Shamuyarira, his deputy Stephen Nkomo and hundreds of chanting and dancing ANC supporters waving banners. Walking with a slight limp, Mr Tambo shook hands with Father Michael Llapsley, who was seriously injured in a 'South African bomb raid in Harare', Zimbabwe's news agency Ziana reported.

Mr Tambo, Mr Shamuyarira and Mr Nkomo had talks in the airport VIP lounge with President Robert Mugabe. President Mugabe said there could be no going back on the elimination of apartheid. There had been a lot of political changes in South Africa since he and Mr Tambo last met, he said, adding that the outlook was very optimistic.

Youthful Saboteur who Became a Leading Advocate

2 February 1991

When a 15-year-old boy appeared before Pretoria Supreme Court judge Mr Justice Celliers on a charge of sabotage about 28 years ago, nobody believed he would one day be a leading advocate. Nor did they think he would rise to the second top position in the hierarchy of the organisation for whose activities he was about to be sent to jail.

He had been arrested during a morning raid at his Atteridgeville, Pretoria, home early in 1963 and was standing trial with a number of other Pan Africanist Congress (PAC) activists, including incumbent PAC projects co-ordinator Mark Shinners, the late Jeff Masemola and former assistant general secretary Philemon Tefu.

When his advocate withdrew after a disagreement with the judge, the boy conducted his own defence. Later he vowed: 'One day I will return to this court not as an accused, but as an advocate'.

He did. Exactly 20 years later he was admitted to the Pretoria Bar and became the first black advocate in the capital city. That boy was Ernest Dikgang Moseneke, now aged 43, who will on Monday appear at the Rand Supreme Court as one of three advocates in Winnie Mandela's defence team in the Stompie Seipei case. The other two are advocate George Bizos SC and Pius Langa of the Durban Bar. The briefing attorney is Ismail Ayob.

About two months ago Mr Moseneke was unanimously elected second deputy president of the PAC, which makes him Nelson Mandela's equivalent in his organisation. He has now been called upon to defend his ANC counterpart's wife in an important trial. In the short period that Mr Moseneke has held the office of deputy president in the PAC he has brought dynamism and respect to the PAC leadership.

Born in Atteridgeville – a township he describes as 'an outstanding place to live in' – in December 1941, he was the first of four sons.

He went to school 'around the age of six or so' in Atteridgeville before proceeding to 'a very outstanding missionary school', Kilnerton, in Pretoria. In 1962 he was involved in a strike at the school and was expelled at the end of that year when he was in Std 7. The following year he moved on to Hofmeyr High School and two months later was arrested for sabotage during a countrywide raid on PAC and ANC activists. He was detained for 90 days before appearing before Mr Justice Celliers at the synagogue building in Pretoria on a charge of sabotage. He was found guilty, sentenced to 10 years' jail and went to Robben Island, where he was the youngest prisoner.

'In Robben Island I had the single advantage of being exposed to the leadership of both the PAC and the ANC at an early stage. There I met the big names in black South African politics. Robben Island was an exciting place'.

Mr Moseneke continued his studies on the island and passed Stds 8, 9 and 10, a BA degree in English and political science and a B Juris degree with the University of South Africa (Unisa). He was already doing his LLB degree when his sentence expired. But on his release he was banned for five years, which meant he was restricted to his home and was required to be home between 6 am and 6 pm and never to be in the company of more than one person at any time. In the mean time Mr Moseneke continued studying. He finished his LLB with Unisa, became the first black attorney to do articles of clerkship with a white law firm in Pretoria, and worked for a popular black law firm in the city.

'We immediately got down to the business of defending a large number of people who had been arrested during the 1978 riots. We also offered clerkships to many black lawyers,' he said.

Mr Moseneke practised as an attorney for five years before being admitted to the Pretoria Bar as an advocate after taking and passing the Bar exam, thus becoming the first black advocate in the city. He has since defended many political activists.

He said: 'It's a very rich and rewarding career I have had, having defended activists from the ANC, the PAC and the Black Consciousness Movement'.

How was he attracted to Africanist politics when the PAC was only a few years old when he went to jail for its activities?

The PAC leader said the PAC's anti-pass campaign in 1960 resulted in one of the biggest marches this country had ever seen. Its impact on Africanism was 'quite pronounced'.

'The PAC was clearly the movement of the moment and it was very popular among young people; it went out there to challenge the system. Young as I was, I was very much alive – my own father was a PAC activist,' he said.

Although Mr Moseneke's appointment to the deputy presidency of the PAC has given substance to the organisation's leadership, Mr Moseneke is regarded by some as too gentle, a political leader who relies heavily on diplomacy in his dealing with his rough-and-tumble political opponents. Responding to this 'complimentary criticism', Mr Moseneke said he had been through a 'baptism of fire' and knew what adversity and suffering were. Nevertheless, he did not believe the struggle was about destroying one another.

Asked how he felt about having been asked to be in Mrs Mandela's defence team, Mr Moseneke said he would comment once the trial was over.

Mr Moseneke is married and has two sons aged 12 and 14. When he is not in court or attending to his duties as PAC deputy president, he 'runs a lot'. He has travelled extensively abroad, has delivered academic papers at many international legal conferences and was a visiting law professor at the University of Columbia in the US in 1987.

Far too Many Empty Seats

24 May 1991

Seating at President de Klerk's multi-party peace conference in Pretoria today and tomorrow must surely have had to be rearranged as a number of organisations – political and religious – this week announced one after another that they would not attend. When Mr De Klerk opens what could have been an historically important peace summit to deal with widespread violence in the townships he will do so with a heavy heart. The seats which would have been allocated to his Government's main negotiating partner, the ANC, will be empty.

Empty, too, will be those seats which would have been allocated to delegates from the Pan Africanist Congress, the Azanian People's Organisation (Azapo), the Workers' Organisation for Socialist Action (Wosa), the New Unity Movement (NUM), the Civic Associations of Northern Transvaal, the South African Council of Churches, KaNgwane's ruling Inyandza National Movement, the Transkei military government, the Lebowa government, the Boerestaat Party, the Conservative Party and a number of other extra-parliamentary organisations at the left and right of the political spectrum.

Present will be Government representatives, the Democratic Party, the Inkatha Freedom Party, business leaders, some homeland leaders and parties operating within the tricameral Parliament. The two-day conference, therefore, gets under way amid widespread perceptions that it has been a failure before it even began. The organisations which have refused to attend the conference have given a number of reasons – the main one being that it will not achieve its purposes of ending the violence.

The liberation movements – the ANC, the PAC, Azapo, Wosa and NUM – have accused Mr De Klerk of having decided on the conference unilaterally. Their main contention, however, has been that the Government is not only party to the conflict, but is also responsible for it. These organisations have expressed their preference for a conference convened by a neutral body such as church leaders, where all attending parties – including the Government – would be there as equals.

The ANC and the CP were swift in their reaction to the announcement of the peace summit in Parliament by Mr De Klerk last month. CP leader Dr Andries Treurnicht said the conference was meant for those who were involved in violence. The CP, he said, was not involved and would therefore not attend the summit. He also dismissed the summit as 'a panic reaction' by the Government.

The ANC, on the other hand, said from the outset it would not attend the government-convened peace conference, which was a mere public relations exercise. The Government, the ANC said, had failed to take decisive steps to end the violence. All that can reasonably be expected from this conference is a joint statement denouncing violence as a political strategy and pledging to work for political tolerance.

Given the fact that those organisations not attending the conference, both on the left and on the right – and they are the ones that matter – will probably outnumber those attending the meeting, the wisdom of continuing with the conference has been questioned in certain quarters. However, the conference will continue largely because Pretoria cannot afford to be seen to be allowing itself to be dictated to, albeit indirectly, by the ANC and its allies as well as by other extra-parliamentary organisations.

Disconcerted Huddleston Recalls Sophiatown

28 June 1991

Archbishop Trevor Huddleston took a drive down memory lane yesterday when he visited Triomf – a place where he defiantly posed for local and international photographers more than three decades ago as bulldozers moved in to demolish Sophiatown.

For Father Huddleston, who arrived in South Africa on Sunday to open the ANC's national congress in Durban next week, Sophiatown was not only his parish. It was also his home, and among his neighbours were prominent ANC leaders such as the late Dr A B Xuma. Father Huddleston, who at 78 now heads the British Anti-Apartheid Movement, yesterday spoke with fondness about his home on 74 Meyer Street, which has been an open piece of ground since the demolition of his house many years ago.

Standing outside the Pinkster Protestante Kerk, which used to be called the Church of Christ the King, Father Huddleston spoke with emotion about the place, its people and those who declared the area a 'black spot' and moved its inhabitants to several townships in Soweto. Sophiatown, he said, was 'culturally immensely alive', with numerous talented artists, writers and musicians. He lamented the loss of the place's vitality. Looking at the church in front of him, the archbishop told how his sermons were translated into seven different languages.

'It's very disconcerting', he said when asked how he felt to be back after so many years. 'The only thing that is still recognisable is the church'.

Although the place's name was changed to Triomf, the street names remain the same.

One of apartheid's fiercest critics, Father Huddleston yesterday spoke only with affection about the Sophiatown he loved, and indulged in politics only when responding to questions from the press. He was asked if he would like to spend his last years in the area and be buried there.

'As a first step,' he said as ANC spokesman Saki Macozoma led him to his car, 'I would like to have the place called Sophiatown again.'

Head of Azapo has Loads of Experience

22 October 1991

President F W De Klerk must certainly have had no idea when he opened Parliament on February 2 last year and made his 'New South Africa' speech that he was about to give Pandelani Nefolovhodwe a memorable birthday present.

For Mr Nefolovhodwe ('Nev' to his friends) – the charismatic Azanian People's Organisation president for whom 'the black experience' has held a special fascination from his student days at the University of the North – February 2 1990 was a day to remember for at least two reasons.

It was his 43rd birthday and his organisation was among many others which had been declared un-restricted. For a man who was once a barefoot herdboy in the rural northern Transvaal, Mr Nefolovhodwe has made great strides. Not only is he president of Azapo, but he is also the labour co-ordinator and personnel officer of the Roodepoort-based Ubuntu Social Development Institute.

A member of a royal family in the tiny village of Folovhodwe in Venda, Mr Nefolovhodwe left home in 1982 for Pietersburg when the Venda government tried to lure him to serve in the homeland government. As the son of a chief, he had a seat for the taking in the Venda Legislative Assembly, but he turned it down. This was shortly after he had served a six-year prison term on Robben Island for his political activities as president of the South African Students Organisation (Saso).

Mr Nefolovhodwe was elected Azapo president at its congress in Cape Town last December. He was also one of the key players in the formation of the National Council of Trade Unions and, before it, the Azanian Council of Trade Unions. Previously he was Azapo's general secretary. The Azapo leader was educated at schools in Venda, including the then Vendaland Training Institute, before registering for a BSc degree in zoology and botany at the University of the North.

It was there that he cut his teeth in serious politics, holding, among others, the positions of Students' Representative Council publicity secretary and later president. A founding member of Saso, he was chosen as its president in July 1974. In that position, the Azapo leader played a leading role in organising the 'Viva Frelimo!' rally in the same year. He and a number of his comrades were subsequently arrested, tried and jailed on Robben Island.

A former general secretary of the Black Allied Mining and Construction Workers Union, Mr Nefolovhodwe is a qualified quality controller, holding diplomas in datametrix as well as management and administration of community projects from the University of South Africa and the University of the Witwatersrand respectively. He is now finishing a degree in operation research and management science with Unisa.

United PF Seeks Swift Government Action

28 October 1991

Durban – The newly formed Patriotic Front (PF) of forces opposed to the Government yesterday called for an all-party congress to be held as soon as possible to set in motion a process leading to a democratically elected constituent assembly which would effect the transfer of power.

In a unanimously adopted declaration issued at the end of the historic three-day conference, the 92 attending organisations said the all-party congress – which the Pan Africanist Congress calls a meeting – should be convened by independent and neutral conveners as a matter of urgency.

Yesterday's declaration came after an earlier joint statement by co-conveners, the ANC and the PAC, saying a meeting should be held with the Government and other interested parties 'within the next few weeks' to discuss the date, venue and convener of the all-party congress.

The ANC and the PAC, which said the transfer of power 'from the minority regime to the people' was the main objective of 'the struggle', said the all-party congress's duties would be to work out the procedures of setting up a constituent assembly; work towards the creation of an interim government or transitional authority with sovereign powers; ensure the re-incorporation of homelands into South Africa; define the role of the international community in the transitional process and agree on the time frame to bring about a democratic order.

Control

The PF declaration said the interim government or transitional authority would, at the very least, control areas of major concern such as security forces and related matters, the electoral process, State media, and defined areas of budget and finance. It would also secure international participation in the process. The PF pledged itself to ensure that the Government's unilateral re-structuring of the economy was defeated. All the organisations vowed to create mechanisms for harmonising their approach to socio-economic transformation.

Condemning the introduction of VAT, the PF called on all South Africans to join the anti-VAT general strike on November 4 and 5. Other resolutions passed at the conference included calls for:

- The Government to stop violence in the country and expel all 'foreign mercenaries'.
- The people to refuse 'to become tools of the regime' in violence and a pledge that all peace initiatives, including the recently signed National Peace Accord, are fully exploited and implemented.
- The normalisation of relations between the people and traditional chiefs.
- The release of remaining political prisoners and the granting of general amnesty to all exiles.

It was also resolved that the joint ANC-PAC liaison committee, which handled preparations for the conference, be maintained to co-ordinate the PF and convene another PF conference afterwards. PAC and ANC leaders said they would fully brief the Azanian People's Organisation – expelled as co-convener last weekend – on the proceedings and resolutions of the conference. They said efforts would be made to bring Azapo back to the PF.

PAC deputy president Dikgang Moseneke told the press conference that the Inkatha Freedom Party, which was not invited because of its known rejection of a PF as 'a ganging-up against whites', was welcome to join forces with the other organisations in the PF if it could endorse demands for a constituent assembly and an interim government. Mr Moseneke and his ANC counterpart Walter Sisulu said the conference had succeeded beyond expectations.

Out in the Political Wilderness

29 October 1991

While for many South Africans the main political game in 1992 will be negotiations, the immediate challenge facing organisations to the left of the African National Congress (ANC) will be survival and relevance. The organisations thus affected would be the Pan Africanist Congress (PAC), which last year hesitantly knocked at the door of negotiations, and the Azanian People's Organisation (Azapo), which is nowhere near engaging in tête-à-tête.

Throughout 1991 Azapo has, by and large, remained faithful to its principles and dogmas, and showed neither ideological flexibility nor willingness to adapt to changing times. Predictably, Azapo and its sister organisation, the Black Consciousness Movement of Azania (BCMA), have consistently refused to talk to the Government, insisting instead that a consultative conference of 'the oppressed' had to be held first. The PAC, on the other hand, began to take the question of negotiations seriously last year.

Although the Africanist organisation had initially criticised the ANC when it first engaged in detente with Pretoria in 1990, accusing it of 'selling out', there were unmistakable signs during 1991 that the PAC leadership was looking for a dignified way of entering into negotiations. If the success of Codesa is anything to go by, the PAC and Azapo – like the right wing – will have to present viable alternatives to negotiations if they are to be taken seriously in a country which is war-weary and yearning for a peaceful settlement.

These organisations' main hope is that Codesa will fail – they have vowed to make it fail – and that the ANC will emerge either too bruised to pose a serious threat or that it will be sufficiently weakened to seek a pact. However, the PAC has not given up on the possibility of influencing the ANC to put the question of a constituent assembly and an interim government or transitional authority back higher up on the agenda. It is on these issues that the PAC believes the ANC has gone soft, and that it has reached a secret deal with Pretoria to be co-opted into a farcical transitional government which will not be time-bound.

It is for this reason, one suspects, that the PAC has asked frontline states to call the ANC to a meeting early this year so that it can explain its position on negotiations. But if Codesa succeeds – and there is a good chance it will succeed in spite of attempts by both the extreme left wing and extreme right wing to sabotage it – the prospects facing Azapo and the PAC this year are not bright. The organisations will find themselves sidelined and consequently marginalised, or they will have to redouble their efforts to stop the process. Indications are that they do not have the capacity to do the latter.

However, the dominant view was that Azapo had erred by writing a letter to invited parliamentary parties and homeland governments and organisations demanding that they resign from Government-created structures where they serve before attending the conference. Azapo, like the marginalised Workers' Organisation for Socialist Action (Wosa), could have used the PF platform to articulate its views against parliamentary parties and homeland governments. Wosa made full use of the PF platform, even distributing various anti-talks statements during breaks at the conference.

The formal launch of the PF, then, heralds real negotiations where component organisations will participate individually both at the all-party congress and within an elected constituent assembly. And the 'bonsella' is that the holding of the conference had ensured the early beginning of negotiations.

Visible Black Unity will Spur all Parties to the Table

29 October 1991

The three-day Patriotic Front conference held at the weekend has come and gone, leaving in its wake a vision of unprecedented black unity. Now that the controversy that has surrounded the PF has died down and the conference has finalised its deliberations, it might be in order to assess the conference's success and implications. In doing so, one will have to consider the conference's objectives and whether these were met.

The ideal of black unity is as old as the African National Congress, one of the co-convenors of the conference. The late Pixley ka-Izaka Seme, uncle to Inkatha Freedom Party leader Chief Mangosuthu Buthelezi, was the one who was most instrumental in the formation of the ANC in 1912, then known as the South African Native National Congress.

Educated at the University of Columbia and Oxford University, Mr Seme, a lawyer, wanted to bring together all blacks from the different tribes and ethnic groups. A year before the formation of the congress he declared: 'We are one people. Let us forget the differences between Xhosa-Fingo, Zulus and Tsongas, Basothos and other Natives.'

Many years after the formation of the ANC, the dividing lines Mr Seme wanted expunged were no longer as tribal as they were political and ideological, beginning with the formation of the Pan Africanist Congress by disgruntled former ANC members in 1959 – four years after the adoption of the Freedom Charter.

Steve Biko, widely regarded as the father of Black Consciousness, also discouraged divisions, ethnic or political, and strongly advocated black unity. And so it is in the light of all these attempts at unity that the formation of the PF in Durban at the weekend should be seen.

The conference's success first became apparent on Saturday when the two co-convening organisations, the PAC and the ANC, jointly issued a statement saying a meeting had to be held 'within the next few weeks' with the Government and other interested parties to make arrangements for an all-party congress, a pre-constituent assembly conference or a multi-party conference. (The different terminologies are used by the ANC, the PAC and the Government respectively).

In a unanimously adopted declaration at the end of the conference on Sunday, the different organisations took this issue further, resolving that the all-party talks be held 'as soon as possible' to set into motion the process leading to a democratically elected constituent assembly 'which shall effect the transfer of power'.

While the component organisations will remain independent, they will nevertheless act in unison and speak with one voice on those issues they agreed upon, such as on a constituent assembly and an interim government or transitional authority. Conference delegates were under no illusion that the Front would be able to grow on its own, and they therefore undertook to engage in joint campaigns and inform their respective members fully about the agreement.

Significantly, another PF conference is scheduled to be held within six months to involve the organisations which attended the conference in 'closer consultation, joint action and the drawing in of formations that are still outside this process'. The entire conference was open to the media, and proceedings were impressively democratic. The various delegates made substantial inputs into the debate, such as the PAC's Maxwell Nemadzivhanani who enjoined delegates to 'be like the fingers of a hand, separate but able to strike like a fist against the common enemy'.

Participation ranged from that by members of various political parties and organisations, through to that of professional and non-political organisations. By resolving to call for the immediate holding of all-party talks, the PF has in effect given a new impetus to negotiations. Not only has the PAC, for the first time, publicly committed itself to holding talks with Pretoria to discuss the modalities of setting up a constituent assembly, but it has got aboard the negotiations train.

The only major organisation on the left still left out of the process is Azapo.

In their opening speeches at the conference on Friday morning, PAC president Mlamli Makwetu and ANC deputy president Walter Sisulu again laid stress on unity, briefly sketching out the kind of role they envisaged for the PF. The aim of the PF, Mr Makwetu said, was 'to rally all those who have a contradiction with the regime behind the call for a constituent assembly' and to consult as broadly as possible on strategies and means of speeding up 'the liberation of the oppressed.'

Mr Sisulu, accusing President De Klerk of wanting 'to be referee, player, linesman and write the score' during the negotiation process, said the PF's responsibility would be to find common ground 'so that while preserving the distinct identity and integrity of each one of the organisations represented here, we are able to march in step.' It seems, on this basis, that the PF conference was a success 'beyond our expectations and the expectations of our detractors', as Mr Sisulu and Mr Makwetu said in their closing addresses.

Azapo 'Just Marking Time in the Wings'

6 June 1992

Conventional wisdom among some political observers has it that organisations such as the Azanian People's Organisation and the Pan Africanist Congress, which have refused to take part in negotiations going on in the Convention for a Democratic South Africa, have effectively marginalised themselves.

The question is often asked whether these organisations, which apparently have no viable alternative to Codesa and are incapable of applying brakes to the negotiations process, would be able to muster a modest showing in polls when the first all-in elections are held. One opinion poll after another has shown the ANC to be ahead in the popularity stakes followed closely by the National Party and then, a distant third, by the Inkatha Freedom Party. Azapo and the PAC, which are often lumped under the heading 'the others', get the thumbs-up from about 10 percent of the country's population.

But the two organisations believe their potential has been grossly underestimated. While the PAC considers itself to be a major player in black politics – with some people in the PAC leadership even believing the organisation could surprise everybody in an election and beat the ANC, like Robert Mugabe's Zanu-PF trounced Joshua Nkomo's more popular Zapu in Zimbabwe in 1980 – the Azapo leadership has accepted the ANC's apparent invincibility in a first election, but believes it will be a major player in opposition politics after the first election.

This view was expressed first by former Azapo president Professor Itumeleng Mosala in an interview in London two weeks ago, and by incumbent Azapo president Pandelani Nefolovhodwe in an interview in Johannesburg this week. Azapo's view, as enunciated by Professor Mosala – who is now a lecturer at Cambridge University – is that the mystique surrounding the ANC as the main liberation movement will wear off once that organisation is in power either alone or in partnership with the NP.

It is then, said Professor Mosala, that the ANC would be judged on issues and on its ability to deliver on its election promises. Azapo, Professor Mosala said, would then emerge as 'the people's organisation', articulating their grievances and disillusionment with the new government and outlining its own policies. Mr Nefolovhodwe agreed, saying Azapo's alternative to Codesa as it was currently constituted was the formation of a solidarity front with the PAC and other organisations outside the negotiations forum.

Though quite influential, Azapo is a small organisation whose members are mostly black intellectuals. Compared with the other major organisations, Azapo's following is minuscule, and not much has been heard of the BCMA's activities in the country. The PAC, on the other hand, is a somewhat bigger organisation, with branches in most parts of the country. Its military wing, the Azanian People's Liberation Army (Apla), has recently taken responsibility for a number of attacks on police which will engender a reign of terror, but they are unlikely to sabotage Codesa.

The best scenario for the PAC and Azapo is one that might be good for South Africa but not necessarily for these organisations themselves. They might remain an outspoken pressure group, forever breathing down the ANC's neck and making it difficult for the organisation to accept a deal which will be less than fair. Another possibility which should not be discounted is that the PAC might, once the ANC has put the issue of a constituent assembly at the top of the agenda in the next round of talks, return to Codesa to make a contribution.

That way the PAC would benefit from agreements reached in the earlier rounds of talks without having been party to them, just as it benefited indirectly from the release of political prisoners, the return of exiles, and the granting of indemnity to prisoners, without first engaging in talks-about-talks with the Government.

ANC-bashing – But No Pacts

19 June 1992

KwaZulu Chief Minister and Inkatha Freedom Party (IFP) president Chief Mangosuthu Buthelezi might not admit it readily, but he and his followers gained precious little from President de Klerk's controversial visit to the KwaZulu capital of Ulundi this week.

The visit – surprisingly scheduled on the 16th anniversary of the Soweto uprising – was ostensibly meant to afford the State President an opportunity of addressing the KwaZulu Legislative Assembly on the exclusion of KwaZulu and Zulu King Goodwill Zwelithini from the Convention for a Democratic South Africa (Codesa). Although Chief Buthelezi spent the second half of his speech on the 'main issue' – the first half having been devoted to excoriating the ANC for its mass action and 'total dishonesty' – Mr De Klerk barely mentioned it.

In a six-page speech, he devoted a mere paragraph to King Zwelithini's exclusion from Codesa. And when he did deviate from his speech to respond directly to Chief Buthelezi's emotional appeal, he stated that 'the Zulu nation', like other 'nations' in South Africa, had an important role to play and had to be accommodated in a future dispensation. Consummate politician that he is, Mr de Klerk, who also used the platform to spell out his party's constitutional views once again, left his listeners feeling happy without actually giving them anything concrete to be happy about.

Much of the day's proceedings were taken up by an issue on which both sides did agree: the need to attack the ANC. In his opening address to the assembly, meant to welcome the State President, Chief Buthelezi lambasted the ANC for its mass action, saying it was 'totally irresponsible' of the organisation to call for mass action 'which will be backed by harsh intimidation at this time when there is an upward spiralling of violence'.

Chief Buthelezi said the National Party leader was 'a man of integrity and political honour'. He said it was 'a hideous distortion of the negotiation process' to suggest that the Government was responsible for the deadlock in Codesa 2, and stoutly defended the NP team's performance there. On these issues Chief Buthelezi and President De Klerk were speaking the same language, mutually patting each other's backs. When he stood up to talk, President De Klerk thanked Chief Buthelezi for putting the Codesa deadlock 'in its right perspective', called on all leaders to stand against violence, outlined the actions his Government has taken to deal with violence, and went on to extol regionalism/federalism.

But on the question of King Zwelithini, subtle differences began to emerge. Chief Buthelezi had accused the Government of giving in to ANC demands far too easily, and said it had been naive in the bilateral discussions held with the ANC before Codesa 1 last year. He called on Mr De Klerk to 'act as State President' and tell the ANC and other Codesa delegates that, willy-nilly, KwaZulu, King Zwelithini and the IFP would be allowed to send three separate delegations to Codesa.

The Chief Minister alluded to a long-standing friendship between Zulus and Afrikaners, and referred to his own co-operation with the Government in the past – at the risk of being called 'a stooge'. He expressed the wish that these good relations might yet again be revived. Here he was merely giving expression to what many political observers had long believed would happen: that the IFP and the NP would sooner or later enter into an alliance of some kind against the ANC-SACP-Cosatu axis. Mr De Klerk did not respond enthusiastically to this implied request, suggesting that – at least for now – the long-expected formal *toenadering* is not on the cards.

Mr De Klerk said the question of King Zwelithini's participation in Codesa would have to be addressed by the multi-party negotiating forum. He and his Government did not need to be convinced of the importance of Zulus, he said, nor of the contribution they could make. But just as Zulus and their king had to be involved in negotiations that affected them, so too did other 'nations' and their traditional leaders.

The President said: 'It is regrettable that Codesa was unable to reach agreement on the inclusion of His Majesty the King of the Zulus, and his own delegation, as participants in their own right.

'Notwithstanding all our efforts, including my own constructive involvement, the matter remains un-resolved.'

The best he promised to do was to redouble his and his Government's efforts in working for King Zwelithini's inclusion. This will not have been welcome news to Chief Buthelezi. But while the De Klerk visit did not have all the desired results, it demonstrated most lucidly – if such a demonstration were needed – the convergence of views between the NP and the IFP. Moreover, many believe that for Chief Buthelezi to have scheduled a sitting of the KwaZulu Legislative Assembly on June 16 – a day widely revered in the black community for its historical significance – is one thing, but for him to have chosen that day to invite President De Klerk to Ulundi, and for President De Klerk to have accepted, amount to little less than frightening callousness.

To make matters worse, not once did either man refer to the day, apart from observing that it had been chosen by the ANC-led alliance for the launch of its mass action campaign.

Waiting in Vain in the Wings

24 June 1992

The ANC's decision to withdraw from the Convention for a Democratic South Africa (Codesa) has been greeted with mixed reactions here and abroad. Although some foreign governments have expressed understanding for the ANC's frustrations as a result of the ongoing violence and Pretoria's apparent inability – some even say reluctance – to deal with it satisfactorily, they have nevertheless urged the organisation to return to the table.

For the Pan Africanist Congress (PAC) and the Azanian People's Organisation (Azapo), the ANC decision should come as a boon and, consequently, go a long way towards enabling these organisations to attract to themselves disgruntled ANC supporters.

The two organisations have so far refused to participate in Codesa, pointing to a number of inadequacies with the negotiating forum's structure. Predictably, they have reacted to the ANC's decision with glee, saying it had vindicated their views that Codesa, as presently structured, was heavily flawed and could not lead to 'the transfer of power to the oppressed'. But there seems to be no reason to believe a large-scale exodus of disgruntled ANC supporters will take place.

At best, the two organisations could hope for a trickle of support from the embattled ANC. If that trickle should materialise at all, there is no precedent suggesting that the PAC and Azapo can turn it into a flood. Azapo and the PAC have been very critical of the ANC for its involvement in 'exploratory talks' with the Government in May and August 1990 to pave the way for negotiations and accused it of having 'sold out' in the struggle for majority rule.

The criticism grew louder after the ANC's suspension of the armed struggle as a result of the Pretoria Minute, and relations between the ANC and the PAC were severely strained when the then South African Communist Party general secretary Joe Slovo, speaking for the ANC-SACP-Cosatu alliance, said the PAC's armed struggle had existed in name only. It was around this time that a new slogan 'One negotiator one bullet!', was heard chanted with the same enthusiasm at PAC rallies as the familiar 'One settler one bullet!' Commentators believed then that the two organisations to the left of the ANC, especially the PAC, would gain support at the expense of the ANC if negotiations ever floundered.

The PAC, it was argued, would mobilise vigorously in the black community and present itself as the 'real' liberation movement which had not rushed into talks with Pretoria to conclude deals which fell short of meeting blacks' aspirations. The ANC has since suffered a number of embarrassments, but the PAC and Azapo have, through lack of either organisational skill or the requisite will, failed to take advantage of those situations.

Shortly after the signing of the Pretoria Minute, violence – until then confined to Natal – spilled over into Transvaal townships. Whole communities, including ANC members and sympathisers, were affected and the ANC appeared vulnerable to the PAC. But neither the PAC nor Azapo made any major inroads into ANC constituencies. Since the first tête-à-tête between the ANC and the Government at Groote Schuur in 1990, there has been a widespread perception in the black community that Pretoria has out-smarted and outmanoeuvred the ANC all the way. And where the Government has made concessions, it has been slow to implement them.

Throughout this period, however, there is no evidence that the ANC has lost some of its support – even among the radical elements in its ranks – to Azapo and the PAC. There is no reason, therefore, to believe now that last week's killings in Boipatong, and the ANC's subsequent decision to pull out of Codesa temporarily, will give the PAC and Azapo any significant advantage.

For a change, it can be argued that by pulling out of Codesa, the ANC is responding to sentiments expressed by its general membership on the ground and therefore wisely eschews any erosion of its support. That does not, however, explain why organisations to its left have failed to capitalise on the situations. At least two reasons can be advanced: the PAC and Azapo are not as organised as the ANC – whose sophisticated propaganda machine they lack – and they take for granted that they will be able to mobilise vigorously when the right time comes.

Although its own and Nelson Mandela's allure is no longer what it used to be, the ANC can still attract crowds to its rallies and protest marches, and can count on a huge contingent of the local and international media to attend and cover its activities. Not so Azapo and the PAC, whose crowd-pulling does not compare to the ANC's.

And if time will ever be right for Azapo and the PAC, it is now. Azapo has spoken of a nationwide 'village to village, township to township' recruitment campaign, evidence of which has yet to be seen. The best the PAC could hope for, then, is the revival of the Patriotic Front (PF) formed in Durban last year, so that it and the ANC would confront the Government with similar demands.

But the ANC, which is likely to return to Codesa shortly once President De Klerk's Government has addressed some of the demands it made last week, does not share the PAC's enthusiasm for the PF. Nowhere in the ANC NEC's statement was reference made to the PF and the need for its revitalisation. Indeed, the ANC, whose main intention appears to be to jolt the Government and rid it of its complacency in negotiations, has left the door wide open for its imminent return to Codesa.

White Hostility can Resurface

1 July 1992

Just when many years of general white antipathy towards it appeared to be giving way to a grudging acceptance of its credentials as a legitimate political organisation which was a serious contender for power, the African National Congress (ANC) stands to alienate its new sympathisers in the white community and once again turn them into enemies.

For while the ANC has taken major strides since its unbanning on February 2 1990 and has successfully reversed the then widespread perception in the white community that it was a blood-thirsty organisation intent on seizing power for power's sake, it still has a long way to go towards converting those in the white community whose opinion of it remains, at best, low. The organisation's standing in the eyes of both conservative and liberal whites has not been helped much by its rock-solid alliance with the South African Communist Party (SACP). It is this alliance with the SACP, rather than its oft-criticised economic policy or lack of it, that hangs like an albatross around the ANC's neck.

It is this alliance which last year triggered ANC Western Cape regional chairman Dr Allan Boesak's attack on the ANC, which has driven many 'coloureds' and Indians to the bosom of the National Party, as the outcome of last week's Diamant by-election has shown, and which has continued to serve as ready ammunition against the ANC for the Government and its allies, not least the Inkatha Freedom Party (IFP).

The alliance notwithstanding, the ANC has nevertheless attained some respectability in politically informed quarters in the white community. Even those whites who shudder at the prospect of living under an ANC-dominated government – and there are many – have for some time now appeared to have accepted an ANC government as a *fait accompli*. More than any ANC leader, it is Steve Tshwete who has done much to change white attitudes towards the organisation. Perhaps the most popular ANC leader in the white community, Mr Tshwete was largely instrumental in gaining South Africa's re-admission into international sport.

The ANC, which was losing the fight against the lifting of the cultural boycott and 'people-to-people' sanctions, wisely decided to manage this process and preside over South Africa's re-entry into international sport. This move, which gave the appearance that South African sport was at the ANC's mercy for its re-admission, won the organisation plaudits and widespread acclaim in the white community, albeit grudgingly. Now all the goodwill engendered by South Africa's participation in international sport appears to be at risk. The organisation's mass action campaign, which kicked off with the June 16 national stayaway, will again harden whites' attitude towards the ANC.

As the British Labour Party discovered in the April 9 election in that country, political parties can win or lose elections on the basis of perceptions of how they would manage the economy. Show disregard for the economy, and threaten people with high taxes, and you have a sure-fire recipe for losing an election. The ANC has a very strong case for mass action: it is its only remaining leverage in the negotiation process.

It has suspended the armed struggle and cannot easily go back to it without bringing upon itself the wrath and censure of the international community, unless Pretoria does something stupid such as once again banning political organisations and imprisoning their leaders. Whites and the business community – and, indeed, many blacks – worry about the possibility of further harm being done to the country's already shaky economy.

Threats that the sport moratorium might be reintroduced in the aftermath of the Boipatong massacre on June 17 again sent shock waves through the sports-crazy white community last week. For them – and for many black South Africans who eagerly look forward to the South African Football Association's readmission into the soccer world body FIFA this week – the reimposition of the sports moratorium would amount to unforgivable betrayal.

The question might be asked: Why should the ANC worry about whites when they form a small minority in the country? If the organisation's hopes of being the next government of the country are to be realised, it should worry about whites and their feelings. It will need them when it matters most – when it wants their votes in the not-too-distant future. While the ANC may be the single biggest political organisation in the country – political analyst Eugene Nyati believes it could easily take 55 percent of the popular vote if an election were to be held now – it is by no means guaranteed universal black support.

It is because the organisation is aware of the threat posed by the NP in an election that it has so far made it difficult for the former whites-only party to canvass in the townships. One calls to mind here the protests masterminded by the ANC when President De Klerk recently visited the Western Cape. If the ANC is to get the two-thirds majority it needs to consolidate its position in any elected constituent assembly, it will have to do so with the support of whites, 'coloureds' and Indians in addition to that which it already enjoys in the black community.

Any actions it embarks on now, which might further alienate these communities which it has so far had difficulties penetrating, might later backfire badly and the organisation might pay heavily for them.

The Rickety Negotiations Track

7 August 1992

While the international community and many South Africans watched with satisfaction the proceedings of Codesa 1 on December 20–21 last year, marvelling at the camaraderie among delegates, on May 15–16 this year they watched in disbelief as Codesa – dubbed a 'Tower of Babel' by its detractors – dithered and floundered.

Therein lie the seeds of the ANC's mass action campaign. As preparations for Codesa 2 continued, May began with a great sense of optimism. Came the eve of Codesa 2 and things started to look different. Some politicians tried to present smiling faces at the end of Codesa 2 but ANC president Nelson Mandela warned that a potentially serious deadlock had occurred. At issue was the percentage needed for decisions to be taken by an interim government, although the impasse went much deeper.

A bitter slanging match between the ANC and the Government followed, with Mr Mandela blaming Mr De Klerk for violence in the townships, and even likening the killing of blacks to the holocaust in Nazi Germany. Posters calling Mr De Klerk and some Cabinet ministers 'murderers' were displayed, and in a mock trial in Cape Town the State President was 'tried, found guilty and sentenced to many years' imprisonment' for human rights abuses. It was a wounded and embittered ANC that met at Nasrec, south of Johannesburg, for its national policy conference on May 28–31, and emerged with a tough stance on negotiations.

The organisation also endorsed 'unprecedented, rolling mass action'. On June 1 Codesa management committee chairman Pravin Gordhan said subcommittees dealing with matters in working groups 1 (creating a climate for free political activity), 3 (interim arrangements) and 4 (TBVC states) would resume talks on June 8.

The Government started pushing through Parliament legislation on issues being negotiated at Codesa, such as unilateral amendments to electoral procedures in the Referendum Bill and the Electoral Bill. The ANC expressed outrage at the moves, saying they revealed the Government's 'utter contempt' for the negotiations process. The last meeting of Codesa's management committee was on June 15. ANC secretary-general Cyril Ramaphosa denied any progress had been made, but Constitutional Development Minister Roelf Meyer said negotiations were proceeding favourably and constructively.

Further developments came thick and fast:

- On June 16 Mr De Klerk addressed the KwaZulu Legislative Assembly in Ulundi and was accused of siding with the Inkatha Freedom Party.
- After the June 17 Boipatong massacre an outraged Mr Mandela suspended bilateral talks and the ANC later withdrew from Codesa – listing 14 demands to be met before it resumed negotiations.
- On June 17 Mr De Klerk announced that Parliament would reconvene for a second short session in October to implement transitional arrangements. The ANC describes the announcement as 'a ruse' to give the impression that progress had been made at Codesa.

The ANC and the Government resorted to an exchange of memoranda, with the former flatly refusing to meet Pretoria. The ANC asked the Organisation of African Unity to call for an urgent meeting of the United Nations Security Council.

- On July 2 Mr De Klerk softened the Government's demands for minority protection in a transitional government. He called the ANC an 'unreliable negotiating partner'.
- On July 15 the Security Council met in special session on South Africa, addressed by a number of South African leaders. UN special envoy Cyrus Vance was sent to investigate the violence and to help get negotiations back on track.
- On July 30 the Government ordered 5000 policemen and troops into Reef townships in a 'peace and stabilisation' operation as the ANC-SACP-Cosatu alliance geared up for the August 3–4 stayaway. The stayaway was followed by marches around the country.

In the immediate aftermath of the mass action, voices were heard expressing optimism about the prospects for re-starting negotiations.

The formal position is that the ANC still insists that the Government meets its 14 demands, but olive branches were being held out tentatively by both sides. A reversion to something like the pre-Codesa 2 atmosphere seems possible, although by no means certain.

Talks Mark Milestone on Rocky Road

12 August 1992

When a six-man Pan Africanist Congress delegation and senior Government ministers sat down to talk at the Airport Sun Hotel last night, a milestone was reached on a long and rocky path towards negotiations. The meeting effectively eased the PAC's entry into the negotiations process.

For although rumours have abounded that Pretoria and the Africanist organisation were holding secret talks – denied by the PAC leadership – yesterday's was the first official meeting between the two inside the country. Not much of practical import can be expected from the talks, but it allowed the PAC to make a quiet entry into negotiations, largely on its own terms. More importantly, it established a precedent: from now on, the insistence that talks be held 'at a neutral venue' does not necessarily mean outside the country.

In spite of its rhetoric, the PAC has knocked on the negotiations door before. Not only was it a co-convenor of the Patriotic Front (PF) conference in Durban last year – which called for an immediate meeting with the Government – but it also took part in the multi-party preparatory meeting which led to Codesa 1 on December 20–21.

The PF conference, observers pointed out then, offered the PAC a strategic way of jumping on to the negotiations band-wagon without losing face. Announcing its decision to pull out of talks, the PAC cited its reasons as the forum's rejection of some of the organisation's important proposals and alleged collusion between the Government and the ANC.

What the PAC leadership did not concede, however, was that it was facing considerable opposition and dissent within its ranks. The leadership had to consolidate support on the ground. If it is taking time for some rank-and-file PAC members to accept the inevitability of negotiations, this reality had long dawned on the PAC leadership. Hence the resolution adopted at the organisation's second national congress in December 1990, declining the Government's invitation to talks while tactically leaving open the possibility of contact.

Wisely, the PAC set itself four goals for yesterday's meeting, all of which are now attainable. These are ensuring that the Government agrees to a sovereign constituent assembly; the re-structuring of the flawed Codesa as a negotiating forum; the continued involvement of the international community 'in the resolution of violence and mediation in negotiations'; and to arrange a top-level summit with the Government 'in a neutral venue under a neutral chairman'.

If these can be achieved to the PAC's satisfaction, we might see the emergence of an important new player inside negotiations.

Hard-line ANC Tail Beginning to Wag the Dog

13 August 1992

In his response to the ANC's memorandum in June listing 14 demands before negotiations could resume, President De Klerk made a point he and some members of his Government have made frequently. The ANC, he said, was allowing itself to be dictated to by its alliance partners, the South African Communist Party (SACP) and the Congress of South African Trade Unions (Cosatu).

In a letter to ANC president Nelson Mandela, Mr De Klerk let slip that the Government was obtaining secret information from the top echelons of the ANC, and said 'hardline communists' were largely responsible for the organisation's withdrawal from the Convention for a Democratic South Africa (Codesa) in the wake of the June 17 Boipatong massacre.

Mr De Klerk said the decision to suspend negotiations had been taken despite opposition within the ANC national executive committee (NEC). This point, made many times in the past in the Government's attempt to drive a wedge between the ANC and its allies – especially the SACP – got lost in the political wrangling and point-scoring which ensued, and the press accorded it no special attention.

But were Mr De Klerk's allegations as far-fetched as they sounded then? Subsequent developments suggest otherwise. To start with, the ANC's Department of Information and Publicity (DIP) took the unprecedented step of issuing a statement to the press saying no ANC member – including NEC and National Working Committee heavyweights – was *authorised* to comment on behalf of the organisation on Mr De Klerk's letter. Unless official comment came from the DIP itself, anything else was to be taken as a personal view from whoever would have made it.

If there had been consensus on the decision to suspend negotiations and withdraw from Codesa, why the injunction against otherwise respected members of the ANC-SACP-Cosatu alliance leadership commenting publicly on Mr De Klerk's response? Was the public show of unity, perhaps, nothing more than a facade?

Considering the DIP's handling of the matter, observers can be forgiven for concluding that cracks were beginning to emerge in ANC ranks and that the alliance was beginning to operate more like a three-headed snake. Even if one were to make allowance for the fact that the ANC leadership, like that of any other organisation, will sometimes differ on matters of strategy and policy – a healthy development, indeed – recent events support the observation that all is not well.

These differences became somewhat magnified for all to see in the build-up to last week's two-day stayaway. Perhaps the most salient example of the tail beginning to wag the dog was provided by the ANC-aligned South African National Civic Organisation (Sanco), which recently publicly differed with the ANC on a proposed boycott of bond repayments.

Sanco, whose president Moses Mayekiso is a luminary figure in both the ANC and the SACP, as well as a trade unionist of considerable stature, called for the boycott. The idea, he explained, was to get banks to put pressure on the Government 'to accede to democratic demands and stop violence'.

At a press conference in Johannesburg after his return from Barcelona, Mr Mandela took issue with the proposed bond repayment boycott, saying it was ill-advised and would lead to financial institutions refusing to extend home loans to blacks. Civic organisations, Mr Mandela said, were not in a position to call for a bond boycott without the ANC.

To which Mr Mayekiso swiftly responded: 'The civics don't take orders from anybody. The policy of the civics is independent and accountable to its membership.' (Ironically, as a Johannesburg daily recently revealed, Mr Mayekiso's rent for his Hillbrow flat has been paid for him by the International Confederation of Free Trade Unions since his release from prison in 1988).

Also in the week before the stayaway, the South African Students' Congress (Sasco) publicly differed with the ANC's education desk on students' role in mass action, saying it reserved the right to determine its own programme. While the ANC wanted students to be exempt from the stayaway, Sasco called for a shut-down of all tertiary institutions on Monday and Tuesday, saying students were 'primarily members of society before they are students'.

The ANC later backed down, and said after 'extensive consultations' with students' and teachers' organisations it accepted their decision to participate in the stayaway. Lastly, in a briefing with black journalists and editors two weeks ago, Mr Mandela differed with Cosatu secretary-general Jay Naidoo, saying he was opposed to the occupation of factories as then proposed by the Cosatu leader. Mr Mandela said he would prefer the occupation of Government buildings instead.

So while the ANC presents the picture of a monolithic alliance pulling harmoniously in one direction, it is becoming increasingly obvious that various components of the organisation – including students' and civic organisations and, at times, even the ANC Youth League – are beginning to assert their independence.

It seems reasonable to conclude, then, that while allegations of division within the ANC and its allies might be greatly exaggerated by the Government in its propaganda warfare, they are not entirely without foundation.

As the frantic pulling in the political tug-of-war intensifies, more cracks in the ANC-led alliance are likely to surface, with more and more formerly aligned structures asserting their independence on some issues, and seeking to influence ANC policy.

What They Don't Say Out Loud

31 August 1992

Like many others before it, the latest debate on federalism as an option for South Africa has so far elicited different reactions from various political players.

There are those, like the National Party and the Inkatha Freedom Party, whose strong pro-federalism stance is almost an obsession. And there are others, like the African National Congress, who are sceptical of the concept and see it as an attempt to emasculate a new – and, presumably, ANC-dominated – government and leave it politically impotent.

What the debate has sadly lacked so far is depth and a calm, rational approach from federalism's proponents and critics alike, and this is largely attributable to the different players' secret agendas. It is no accident that the NP, the IFP and the ANC have taken the positions they have so far adopted on the issue. Stripped of all the niceties such as the commendable rhetoric about the need to establish 'a participatory democracy' and 'bring government to the people', the NP and the IFP see federalism simply as a means to safeguard their interests and guarantee regional spheres of influence for themselves. Their hope, quite clearly, is to be able to influence national political developments from their pockets of power, KwaZulu being the obvious such region for the IFP.

But the IFP and the NP will not admit these are their motives for insisting on federalism – and no political observer can seriously expect them to do so. The ANC's opposition to the concept, on the other hand, stems from the organisation's belief in a strong central government which will freely intervene in the private sector if and when it believes the need exists. Similarly, the ANC will not admit this is the reason for its opposition to federalism – and nobody expects it to do so.

The debate is neither helped nor advanced by white liberal commentators who have taken to extolling the virtues of federalism and liberally drawing on 'the lessons' of the former Soviet Union and conflict-ridden Yugoslavia to paint scenarios of doom and gloom if federalism were not adopted in South Africa.

What these interventions – which many in the black community see to be proliferating on the eve of a majority government – manage to achieve is to create the impression that whites would like the new government to be so weak that it cannot effectively address the historic imbalances which are a legacy of apartheid.

It further muddies the debate, thereby ensuring that federalism continues to be a controversial and emotive issue which will not be judged on its merit or lack thereof. In a commendable move, the Institute for Multi-Party Democracy and the Centre for Policy Studies last week arranged a three-day workshop in Cape Town on 'The Politics and Economics of Federalism: A South African Debate'. Here, too, delegates got locked into long-standing ideological positions, much to the detriment of the debate.

Those who opposed federalism – and there were many – did so primarily because it has the support of the NP and the IFP, whose motives they find questionable. While developments of the past two years in the Soviet Union and Yugoslavia are no doubt instructive – not more so than the lessons of apartheid in our own backyard – there are some differences with the situation here. In South Africa apartheid has tried for years through the homeland system to keep blacks apart from one another on the basis of ethnicity, and people in the urban areas have *consciously* reacted to that policy by emphasising oneness among blacks.

Federalism no doubt has its advantages. To give any government untrammelled powers in the new South Africa would be inadvisable, but to weaken it so much that it cannot function properly is equally undesirable.

The argument for provision to be made for some form of 'participatory democracy', including the delegation of some powers to regions, is one which enjoys considerable support across the political spectrum. How such regions are to be defined, and how much power they should have, are issues to be debated.

But the debate needs to be approached with caution, for it would be a pity if it were to be still-born because of the different players' hidden agendas and selfish interests.

Buthelezi Warns of Civil War, Secession

15 September 1992

Any march on Ulundi by the ANC-led tripartite alliance would be 'the opening salvo of the commencement of a South African civil war', KwaZulu Chief Minister and Inkatha Freedom Party leader Chief Mangosuthu Buthelezi warned yesterday. Addressing KwaZulu civil servants in Ulundi, Chief Buthelezi gave notice for the first time that KwaZulu would seriously consider seceding from the country if it could not become part of a federal South Africa. In a meeting called to deal with the distribution in Ulundi last week of pamphlets linking some KwaZulu civil servants to the ANC, Chief Buthelezi said South Africa and the international community had to be 'timeously warned that the ANC's march towards the seizure of power will be stopped in its tracks'.

He said the first-ever march on Ulundi was on July 4 1879 when the British army defeated the Zulu impi. He challenged KwaZulu civil servants to rally around his administration or 'consider the option of resigning if you have any conscience at all. If KwaZulu is attacked, it will be defended. I expect every KwaZulu civil servant to either accept the legality of the KwaZulu government or get out. If you accept the legality of the KwaZulu government, you must pledge your undivided loyalty to it.'

Chief Buthelezi said KwaZulu, which was 'a sovereign kingdom' until 1879, had been 'dragged' into the Union of South Africa in 1910 without consultation and there was no reason why it had to 'feel morally bound to what was decided' regarding its future. He said he would be calling for 'the recognition of KwaZulu's mandate' to decide under what circumstances it would remain part of a new South Africa, but he was not sure whether that would be done through a referendum or through meetings in the Natal/KwaZulu region. He said last week's pamphlets, coupled with Pretoria's bowing to pressure 'to leave self-governing territories like Ciskei in the lurch', made the whole matter serious.

'If that is done to KwaZulu we will be faced with a civil war situation on a large scale', he warned.

Strange Bedfellows at Indaba

8 October 1992

Ciskei military ruler Brigadier Oupa Gqozo was deep in conversation with Bophuthatswana President Lucas Mangope when Conservative Party leader Dr Andries Treurnicht walked towards them.

The diminutive brigadier – who, a day earlier, had met the Afrikaner Weerstandsbeweging's Eugene TerreBlanche – stood up, shook hands with Treurnicht and hugged him like an old friend. Press photographers kept clicking their cameras as the two men, later joined by CP deputy leader Dr Ferdi Hartzenberg, engaged in animated discussion.

It was the same with the leadership of the newly formed Afrikaner Volksunie, headed by Potchefstroom MP Andries Beyers. There was no language problem: as Gqozo had already demonstrated on the SABC's 'Agenda' programme, he speaks *suiwer* Afrikaans.

The 'Conference for Concerned South Africans', held at the Indaba Hotel, outside Johannesburg, on Tuesday, was full of such politically incongruous sights. One of the odder alliances to be thrown up by the new South Africa was on display.

At the conference Gqozo clearly felt he was among friends. On his arrival, he said it was normal among Africans for neighbours to rally around one another when one of them was in trouble. The meeting, he said, was such an exercise. The headmaster-like Mangope was not as visibly excited about the cross-cultural indaba. He had been sitting on the sofa quietly chatting to Gqozo before the CP leaders came their way.

There was, it seemed, a lot on his mind. But he, too, exchanged pleasantries with Treurnicht. Sitting alone in a corner were two National People's Party delegates, talking quietly to each other. Fraternising or socialising was not for them – and neither, it seemed, were other delegates eager to strike up a conversation with them.

Then, to complete the mosaic, there was Chamber of Mines president Bobby Godsell, an observer rather than a delegate, who looked fairly uncomfortable. Already in the conference hall was a delegation from the SA Chamber of Commerce, led by director-general Raymond Parsons.

Godsell was overheard asking Inkatha Freedom Party central committee member Suzanne Vos: 'Where is your leader?'

Chief Mangosuthu Buthelezi, clearly the man of the moment, was not there. His guests – including conference co-conveners Gqozo and Mangope – had arrived at 9 am, but he did not make an appearance until 10 am.

Buthelezi launched a scathing attack on the ANC and the Government, but the more vicious personal attack on President De Klerk came, somewhat surprisingly, from IFP national chairman Dr Frank Mdlalose. Mdlalose, who said the different leaders had gathered 'to strike a blow for democracy in South Africa', said De Klerk was 'becoming a threat to the negotiations process', and that he and his Government had 'turned to political expendiency in bowing to ANC demands'.

'We now see that he was trading on the support that we were giving to whatever he did right. He basked in the warmth of applause for what he did that was right, and when it came to opposing the ANC, he always claimed that he was in good company, and pointed to us and other black parties who opposed the ANC.

'When the ANC was at its worst, President De Klerk was at his conciliatory best. Our experience leads us to the conclusion that we have to prepare for a negotiating future in which Mr De Klerk will not be able to cross back where he was before when he opposed having to deal with him protected by the ANC,' Mdlalose said.

His message was well received by the new allies. Although they met and talked to many people, the CP and Afrikaner Volksunie delegations appeared purposely to avoid one another. This was just one of the day's oddities: former rightwing white colleagues finding it easier to chat to black South Africans than each other.

Asked if he had exchanged pleasantries with his former leader Treurnicht, Afrikaner Volksunie leader Beyers gave a curious answer: 'We have no problem.' It was that kind of day.

Fingers that Couldn't Form a Fist

26 October 1992

A year ago this week, more than 500 delegates representing 92 political, social and professional organisations gathered at the Malibu Hotel in Durban to form a Patriotic Front (PF) which, it was said, would confront the Government as a monolithic entity in negotiations.

The October 25–27 PF conference, co-convened by the ANC and the Pan Africanist Congress – after the expulsion a week earlier of the Azanian People's Organisation as third co-convenor – raised fears in Government circles of a ganging-up against Pretoria.

The words of the PAC's Maxwell Nemadzivhanani echoed long after the conference was over: 'We have to be like the fingers of a hand, separate but able to strike like a fist against the common enemy'. To many observers, however, it was a watershed development in our extra-Parliamentary politics.

Some even speculated, prematurely it soon turned out, that the move could in time mark the healing of a rift which existed between the ANC and the PAC since the Africanist organisation's formation in 1959, after its founder and first leader Robert Sobukwe and others had broken away. That rift later widened further in exile, when some members of the two organisations would not even talk to one another.

As things turned out, the PF ran into trouble soon after its launch. The organisations which had attended the launch had resolved that a meeting be held with the Government to discuss the need for a constituent assembly. The PAC wanted the PF to confront the Government as a monolithic unit in negotiations, but the ANC wanted to retain its independence and flexibility.

The compromise agreement was that the ANC, the PAC and other organisations which were members of the PF would speak with one voice on those issues on which they agreed, but operate separately on those issues on which they did not agree.

That compromise agreement was to be the reason for the first main strain on the PF. In the run-up to the multi-party preparatory meeting – which the ANC then called the all-party congress and the PAC called the pre-constituent assembly conference meeting – cracks between the two organisations reappeared. Reluctant to enter negotiations with its hands tied as a result of a prior agreement with the PAC, the ANC wanted the organisations to attend the preparatory meeting as different entities. The PAC later pulled out of the December 19–20 meeting in Kempton Park, alleging ANC-Government collusion.

From then onwards relations between the two liberation movements were to remain strained, and the PF has been in the throes of death since then. The ANC shifted its gaze to its allies – mostly homelands favourably disposed towards it – in the Convention for a Democratic South Africa (Codesa), and began using the words 'patriotic front' to refer to them.

But just as there is no Codesa without either the ANC or the Government, so too, is there no PF without either the PAC or the ANC, its main co-convenors. While the ANC has since made it clear that it does not care about the revival of the PF – whose meeting should have been re-convened in April this year, according to the agreement reached at the PF conference in Durban – the PAC continues to chase after the illusion that the front could still be saved.

Indeed, various PAC leaders have even hinted at the possibility of having their organisation and the ANC fighting elections jointly within the PF à la Robert Mugabe's and Joshua Nkomo's parties in Zimbabwe in 1980. They have expended their energies in an attempt to revive the front, and have lately muted their criticism of the ANC out of the fear of further jeopardising the chances of the front's revival.

The ANC, on the other hand, sees the PAC as a noisy little brother who seeks to ride on its shoulders. Some of them argue that the PF was formed to demand the establishment of a democratically elected constituent assembly, and say, now that the Government has given in to that demand – at least in principle – there is no need for the PF's revival.

They say that they are a big enough organisation and therefore do not need the PAC. Others within the ANC are more than slightly irritated with the PAC at the moment, and see it as an opportunistic organisation which seeks to give an appearance of reasonableness compared to the ANC in order to score propaganda points. They cite at least three steps as evidence.

Although most of the people killed in Boipatong on June 17 were ANC members, the PAC later contributed R1 000 to each family of the 32 victims. After the Bisho massacre on September 7, PAC president Clarence Makwetu held talks with Ciskei military ruler Brigadier Oupa Gqozo.

And the PAC has now – for the second time since 1990 – offered itself as a possible mediator between the ANC and the Inkatha Freedom Party. For its own sake, the PAC leadership needs to realise that the PF – as it was formed in Durban last year – is dead. It now needs to channel its energies to more deserving programmes and issues instead of chasing after what increasingly looks like a mirage.

PAC, Government Encounter 'A Draw'

27 October 1992

As is often the case after such encounters, the Government and the Pan Africanist Congress (PAC) will each claim victory after their historic two-day summit in Gaborone, Botswana at the weekend. And the reason is not hard to find.

Both the Government and the PAC have constituencies to answer to, hence the temptation to present the October 23–24 meeting as having been in their favour. Granted, Pretoria would like to get the PAC involved in negotiations, but it is also worried about attacks on security forces by people claiming to be cadres of the Azanian People's Liberation Army (Apla), armed wing of the PAC. It failed to persuade the PAC to suspend the armed struggle.

After the Government has accommodated the PAC by agreeing to meet it outside the country, the Africanist organisation will now find it difficult to maintain its organisation's stance, which was that of denouncing the ANC as a 'sellout' when the latter first entered into talks with Pretoria in 1990.

Indeed, that the PAC will take part in negotiations when they resume in a new multi-party forum – not unlike the much-maligned Codesa – is now a certainty. The organisation needs, therefore, to sell its position to its members and persuade them that a major victory was scored in Botswana at the weekend.

The truth, however, is that neither the Government nor the PAC can claim outright victory. Pragmatism, and mutual accommodation, characterised the meeting. Its importance lay more in its symbolic value than in any substance that emerged from it.

The first official meeting between the Government and the PAC in Kempton Park in August was an exploratory, 'get-to-know-you' exercise. It was at the next meeting, in Pretoria two weeks later, that substantive issues began to be discussed, and differences between the two parties became pronounced.

The major point of disagreement, then as now, was the PAC's armed wing, Apla, and its alleged attacks on the police. This issue, clearly, was of concern to the Government, and had been raised at the first meeting in Kempton Park. The PAC's rejoinder was that it would consider the Government's concerns.

After the Pretoria meeting, the PAC and the Government presented two points of agreement: that South Africa's new constitution would be written by a democratically elected constitution-making body – which the PAC called a constituent assembly – and that the registration of voters had to begin as soon as possible.

Though it was a significant concession, the Government's position on a constituent assembly, which was reiterated when President De Klerk met ANC President Nelson Mandela at the World Trade Centre on September 26, was not new. Neither are the 'agreements' reached in Gaborone at the weekend.

In a meeting chaired by Botswana's Foreign Affairs Minister Dr G K Chiepe, the Government and the PAC found 'common ground' on the following:

- that South Africa's problems should be resolved 'through peaceful negotiations',
- that all parties should bring an end to violence,
- that a new constitution should be written by 'an elected body on a common voters roll', and
- that an inclusive and more representative negotiating forum should be established to decide on transitional arrangements.

None of this was new. The only main concession the PAC appears to have extracted from the Government, judging by the joint statement issued after the meeting, was Pretoria's acceptance that once established, the new negotiating forum 'should be managed impartially'.

This could mean that the Government now accepts the PAC's long-standing demand that negotiations should be presided over by 'a neutral chairman' in the form of a representative of the UN, the Organisation of African Unity or even the Commonwealth.

For its part, the PAC seems to have given in to the Government's oft-repeated demand that a constitutional vacuum should not be allowed to develop during the negotiation process. The two parties agreed that 'constitutionality should be maintained during the transitional period'. On this issue, then, the PAC, the Government and the ANC – which has proposed the Transition to Democracy Act to prevent such a constitutional vacuum – are finally at one.

And so the importance of the Botswana safari lies in the fact that from now on the PAC's involvement in negotiations is almost a *fait accompli.* An important new player is joining the negotiations process, and Pretoria can only hope that it will one day prevail in persuading the PAC leadership to suspend the armed struggle.

Indeed, it is possible that from now on Apla operative Karl Zimbiri will make fewer telephone calls to newspapers claiming responsibility on behalf of Apla for attacks on security forces.

The meeting's importance also lies in the development of what looked like rapport and mutual respect between Foreign Affairs Minister Pik Botha and PAC second deputy president Dikgang Moseneke, who led their respective delegations.

At the end of the summit, Botha complimented Moseneke 'for the spirit, style and tone in which the discussions took place'. Moseneke paid Botha a similar compliment, saying 'the spirit, manner and tone' of the deliberations had led to 'better understanding'.

It is Time to Re-cross Rubicon

23 November 1992

Two years ago President De Klerk appeared poised to make history as the only National Party leader who had managed to rise above being a parochial white South African president and come close to being a leader of South Africans of all hues.

Unlike his predecessors, De Klerk was received with open arms in a number of townships, including Soweto. When he visited Baragwanath Hospital in the sprawling Johannesburg township and King Edward Hospital in Durban in 1990, these hospitals came to a standstill. Black patients, nurses and doctors surged forward and surrounded him, all seeking to shake his hand.

For a fleeting moment he was their leader and they were proud of him. He was a messiah. He had done what no other Afrikaner leader in this country's chequered history had done. Even some battle-hardened activists then called him 'Comrade De Klerk', and his Government was no longer 'the regime'. The extent of goodwill towards him was amazing.

Around this time I took part in a round-table discussion of senior black journalists in Johannesburg, and my colleagues and I were unanimous in the view that, if a one-person, one-vote general election were held, De Klerk's NP would trounce the ANC, which was still battling to re-establish itself in the country after almost three decades in exile.

Foreign governments were also singing De Klerk's praises, saying what a different Afrikaner leader he was. A few months earlier, on February 2 to be exact, De Klerk had surprised everybody by unbanning political organisations such as the ANC, the South African Communist Party and the PAC, and announcing the release of Nelson Mandela, who became a free man nine days later.

Even sceptics in the black community grudgingly admitted he had truly crossed the Rubicon. Sadly, all that has changed. All the goodwill blacks who did not hold strong political views had towards him has since been squandered. Like his predecessors, he is now no more than a leader of white South Africa.

De Klerk dithered when he should have gone the whole hog in the process he had begun. He has recently introduced many preconditions that his chief negotiating partner, the ANC, has to meet before he can sit in an interim government with it, and it is becoming increasingly clear that his definition of democracy is, at best, terribly flawed.

By democracy and 'power-sharing' he seems to mean the retention of white privilege and the granting to whites of powers way out of proportion to their numbers in the country. In slightly more than two years he has moved from being a South African leader to being first a white leader and now to being an Afrikaner leader. And all this at a time when the NP desperately needs black support if it is to be the main player De Klerk and his colleagues believe it will be in future.

A confidential NP document, entitled 'Expansion of the NP in the Transvaal', makes the telling point that blacks – who have been targeted for the party's recruitment campaign – constitute the majority in the province, with whites making up only 16,8 percent. The document sets out an ambitious NP strategy for 'winning the hearts and minds' of the black populace through the 'use of propaganda and information', protection of new Nationalists in the townships, and the combating of tension, suspicion and negative perceptions in the communities'. It is not clear how this is to be done.

This is indeed a tall order, given the fact that the NP's credibility in the townships at the moment is at its lowest since February 1990. Damaging revelations are made about the security forces and corruption in high places, and Pretoria does precious little about them. As part of its strategy to canvass black support, the NP intends to approach 'well-intentioned ministers, teachers, business leaders and other leading figures [in the townships] and make them part of the NP's activities'. Again, it is doubtful whether the NP in its present guise will find people willing to be used in this regard.

De Klerk has himself to blame for his ruthless fall from grace. Unbridled corruption continues apace in his Government and its satellites in the homelands, as one commission of inquiry after another has shown. His security forces have done little to stem the on-going carnage in the townships, and he has continued to align himself with discredited homeland leaders like KwaZulu Chief Minister Chief Mangosuthu Buthelezi, Ciskei military dictator Brigadier Oupa Gqozo and Bophuthatswana leader Chief Lucas Mangope.

De Klerk, like the general white public, fails to understand that almost three years since his historic 'New South Africa' address in Parliament in 1990, the average black South African has seen little change in his standard of living, and is apprehensive about the future. Blacks look at the Government and at the power structures of the companies where they work and they see that power, both economic and political, still resides firmly in white hands.

Foreign Affairs Minister Pik Botha has come to the surprising conclusion that the NP can win the first all-in election, but even he must know that this is nothing more than a dream.

The homeland leaders the Government has in mind as potential allies are totally discredited in black eyes and, except for Chief Buthelezi, have no support worth talking about in their own areas. They will not deliver any significant support to the NP.

Fortunately for Botha and De Klerk, the NP can still improve its tattered image in the black community before elections are held some time next year. De Klerk can still redeem his erstwhile popularity by doing at least two things: taking decisive steps to end township violence once and for all, and distancing the NP from the IFP, Gqozo and Mangope.

If De Klerk were to do this, there are many non-political blacks in the townships who, in the secrecy provided by the ballot box, would cast their historic votes for the NP. The question now is whether De Klerk and his scandal-weary Government have any vision and courage left to do the only thing essential for their survival.

Moseneke Resigns from PAC

17 December 1992

Pan Africanist Congress (PAC) second deputy president Dikgang Moseneke yesterday resigned from the leadership of the organisation, saying he wanted to dedicate himself to his legal practice and do some writing.

A Pretoria advocate, Moseneke resigned both his position as second deputy president and as a member of the PAC's national executive committee. In a letter to PAC president Clarence Makwetu, Moseneke said he had neither political ambitions nor a desire to hold political office in any future government.

'I do intend retaining my professional practice through which I hope to continue making some modest contribution in the process of the transformation of our country from an illegitimate, settler minority regime to a non-racial democracy'.

Moseneke, who joined the PAC at the age of 14 and began a 10-year sentence for PAC-related activities on Robben Island when he was 15, also served a 3-year banning and house-arrest order from 1973 to 1975. He was first elected PAC second deputy president in December 1990.

At the time of going to press last night, the PAC leadership could not be reached for comment. Moseneke's secretary said he was away on holiday until early January.

Political Cake Must be Shared

14 January 1993

The African National Congress has often complained bitterly – and with justification – about the manifest lack of free political activity in certain parts of the country, especially in some of the homelands.

The organisation has pointed accusing fingers at Chief Mangosuthu Buthelezi's KwaZulu, Brigadier Oupa Gqozo's Ciskei and Chief Lucas Mangope's Bophuthatswana, claiming it cannot hold its meetings openly and organise freely.

It was for this reason that the ANC targeted these homelands during its 'unprecedented rolling mass action' last year, and planned marches on their capitals. The mass campaign was put on hold after the savage shooting of unarmed marchers by the Ciskei Defence Force on September 7, but the motivating principle behind the campaign still holds true in ANC circles.

The ANC was correct to insist on its right to be able to organise and canvass for support anywhere in South Africa. It makes little sense to talk of a possible free and fair election where some political bullies have declared parts of the country no-go areas for their opponents. But is the ANC's position wholly consistent, in the light of the break-up of a Democratic Party meeting in a Peninsula township this week?

The question of free political activity is of paramount importance now in the run-up to the first all-in general election – probably early next year – which will finally close the curtain on the old South Africa and usher in a truly new South Africa.

If that election is to reflect the will of the people, then surely no political organisation can be allowed to regard any area in the country as its private fiefdom. Every square inch of the country has to be open to all political organisations to contest in peace. This makes the position of the ANC a difficult one – for it can be accused of engaging in the same sorts of practice for which it criticises the homeland regimes.

This week ANC supporters joined followers of the PAC and Azapo in disrupting a DP meeting in a Cape Town township. Previously, various National Party (NP) events – including a safari into Mitchell's Plain by President De Klerk to canvass for support in the coloured township – were disrupted. The ANC's response has been confusing. Some spokesmen at the national level have unequivocally condemned the disruptions, but others at branch and regional levels have tried unconvincingly to justify them, saying parties like the DP have to understand the 'deep hostility' prevalent in the townships against 'parties operating within the tricameral parliamentary system'.

After the disruption of a DP meeting in Khayelitsha in mid-December, ANC western Cape regional executive committee member Nomatyala Hangana said while the party had the right to speak in the township, it had to first 'settle the white areas'. This prompted DP national chairman Ken Andrew to retort: 'Perhaps she (Hangana) is sorry the Improper Political Interference Act was repealed so that political parties are not required to be racially exclusive'.

After the disruption of a DP Youth meeting in Gugulethu at the weekend by alleged members of the ANC, the PAC and Azapo, DP Western Cape regional chairman Jasper Walsh said these sad events' wider implication was that 'there can be little hope of free and fair elections in the future'. To dismiss his statement merely as a sign of desperation would be irresponsible.

Political intolerance has been displayed on all sides, and this gives cause for concern. After Mitchell's Plain last year there was Boipatong where De Klerk was prevented from expressing his condolences to families of the victims of the June 17 massacre in that Vaal Triangle township. Granted, there was groundswell anger in Boipatong directed at De Klerk, whose security forces were alleged to be in cahoots with the alleged murderers. It is also true that had De Klerk been able to pay such a high-profile visit to the strife-torn township in the glare of the local and international media, he would have scored a major propaganda coup.

Nevertheless, the ANC's post-Boipatong strategy – to portray De Klerk as a murderer and even sentence him and his Cabinet Ministers to 'death' during a mock trial in Cape Town – was ill-considered in this era of negotiations. The odd logic behind the disruption of other parties' meetings seems to be that predominantly white parties such as the DP and the NP are not supposed to sell their policies to people in the townships. They are, as Hangana suggested, to 'first settle the white areas' and leave the townships to the ANC and its allies.

This kind of thinking is as dangerous for the country as it is for democracy. Until all organisations accept that their rivals have a right not only to exist but also to compete with them for support *anywhere* in the country, we may as well forget about democracy and free and fair elections. For the underlying tenet of democracy is that people – and organisations – have a right to exist and to hold and express views as long as in exercising that right they do not harm others or interfere with their rights.

If the ANC makes some parts of the country no-go areas for the NP and the DP, then it must accept that others – like the IFP in KwaZulu and Gqozo's African Democratic Movement in Ciskei – will make their areas no-go zones for it.

To stretch this logic, there will similarly be PAC/Azapo areas, NP/DP areas, and even Afrikaner Weerstandsbeweging/Wit Wolwe zones which will be out of bounds to others. The irony is that the DP is a relatively small party which poses no real threat to the ANC-led tripartite alliance. For years it has spoken against apartheid and has called for the release of political prisoners and the unbanning of political organisation.

DP leaders – and, indeed, South Africans of all hues – could be forgiven for saying they deserve better. The ANC and all other organisations and parties have to learn that the rights they want for themselves have also to be extended to their opponents if the democracy we all yearn for is to have any meaning.

Disarm Sanctions Weapon Now

26 January 1993

For some months there have been indications of a feeling in a powerful section of the African National Congress that South Africa's economy will continue to bleed unless a political settlement, leading to stability, is reached quickly.

It is this realisation, which both big business and the Government worked hard to promote, that is largely responsible for the new resolve in the ANC to get multi-party negotiations resumed and to speed up the transition to democracy. ANC president Nelson Mandela, more than any of his colleagues in the leadership, has in recent months shown an appreciation of the country's perilous economic state and has repeatedly urged that a political settlement will have to be reached expeditiously so that the economy can start to grow.

In Washington last week, he also said he would be willing to call for the lifting of the remaining sanctions if business strove to increase employment and if agreement was reached on the need for elections for a constituent assembly to be held before the end of this year. While one can understand the ANC's wish to use sanctions as a bargaining chip to keep Pretoria moving towards an interim government and elections, South Africans can, in fact, no longer afford the luxury of arguing about whether or not sanctions should go. Millions of our fellow citizens, mostly blacks, are unemployed and do not know from where their next meal will come.

Sanctions, once a powerful weapon used effectively to bring Pretoria face-to-face with the consequences of the lunacy of apartheid, are as anachronistic today as are the Azanian People's Liberation Army's attack on whites. *Sanctions must go now* – and reasons for this are legion.

South Africa is experiencing one of the worst economic meltdowns in its history. More people are being retrenched by the day. With no hope of getting jobs, some returning exiles – that is, those who were brave enough to come back – turn to crime for survival.

The crime rate has soared to the extent that felony is now almost a national pastime – and more criminals are spewed *out* of jails which, we are told, are bursting at the seams. The police, discredited and overworked, no longer have any motivation for making arrests because they know the people they apprehend today are likely to be out on the streets tomorrow, plying their trades again.

As more and more people retire to bed on empty stomachs and feel they have no stake in the much-vaunted 'new South Africa', they become susceptible to accepting cash – anything from R200 to R1 000 appears to be the going rate – in exchange for committing murder. The violence spirals.

The rand, once stronger than the US dollar, continues to shrink, white collar crime proliferates and corruption in the public sector becomes the order of the day. Financial sanctions must go, and go now, before South Africa becomes 'a typical African country' and slides at supersonic speed towards mob rule – thus becoming ripe for *coups d'état* African-style. What the country needs desperately is immediate access to the World Bank and the International Monetary Fund, and massive investment to create jobs.

The lifting of sanctions alone, of course, will not be a panacea. The initial benefit of such a move will be more psychological than material, both in South Africa and abroad. More important than the lifting of sanctions will be the reaching of a political settlement and the creation of stability in the country to engender investor confidence – but the end of sanctions is an important step on this path. All political players need to realise that the political and the economic situations are inextricably linked.

The sooner a political settlement is reached and stability attained, the sooner the economy will begin to turn around as investment starts to pour in. That, however, does not mean that preparations for that economic turnaround should not be made now, with the lifting of remaining sanctions being the first move. The problem with some people in the ANC leadership is that, unlike their followers on the ground, they live in luxury in formerly white suburbs and are assured of ANC cheques at the end of the month from foreign governments favourably disposed to the organisation.

The South African Council of Churches, the Pan Africanist Congress and the Azanian People's Organisation argue that the lifting of sanctions now would be premature, with Azapo and the PAC saying it is widespread corruption and mismanagement – not sanctions – which have so ruined our economy. A white minority government, they say, is still comfortably in power and apartheid remains intact. Until these two are gone, they contend, sanctions remain a necessity.

But it is now increasingly probable that elections for a constituent assembly will be held within the next 18 months, and that some form of new government will be in office before the end of 1994. To say preparations for economic growth should begin when that happens seems shortsighted to this writer.

But then Azapo and the PAC have been opposed to just about anything else that has happened so far – the relaxation of the cultural boycott and the subsequent visits to South Africa by foreign musicians, suspension of the armed struggle by the ANC and Codesa-style negotiations, etc.

The lifting of remaining sanctions will have to take place despite their vociferous objections.

Slackening their Grip on Power

6 February 1993

I present myself to the security guard at the main entrance of the parliamentary premises, and as a matter of courtesy inform him that I am going to the press gallery in the House of Assembly.

At first he tries to point out to me one of the three huge buildings in front of me, and then he offers to walk me there. He stops in front of an imposing, white and new-looking building and says: 'Walk right in there, sir, and they will help you'.

Sir. That was the form of address I was to hear from the police, security guards and messengers, all white, throughout my week-long visit to Parliament in Cape Town.

I walk in, pass through a security metal detector and inform the pleasant police officer there that my colleagues are expecting me at the press gallery. The man looks at his watch – it is 7.30 am. No, he tells me, it is still too early for anyone to be in the press gallery.

I explain again that my colleagues and I have an agreement to meet there at that time, and assure him they should be there. Would he perhaps want to phone them in their office? I ask. No, he doesn't need to do that. Instead, he will have me taken to the office as soon as someone becomes available to walk me there. In the meantime, would 'sir' be kind enough to take a seat?

While I am waiting here some important-looking man, no doubt a politician, strolls in and starts chatting with the police officers. The 'big action' this year, he tells them conspiratorially, will not take place in the hallowed chambers of Parliament, but outside them. Parliament as they knew it, he tells them, is about to be a thing of the past.

I was later to sense again and again this all-pervasive uneasiness about the future, this acute awareness that *this* is probably the last 'white' Parliament. Although many MPs tried to look carefree, it was obvious that uppermost in their minds was the nagging thought that they might not be back there at the same time next year.

Half an hour later the ever-pleasant policeman says one of his colleagues is now available to walk me to the press gallery. One more security gate is negotiated, and I am then told the building I am in is the wrong one. I am in the Chamber of Parliament, and the building I want is the brownish one on the right-hand side. Once there, passage into the press gallery is fairly easy.

Shaun Johnson, *The Star's* Political Editor, takes me into the House of Assembly where the formality of announcing that President De Klerk will open a joint sitting of Parliament at 11 am has to be gone through.

He points out the chair on which Dr Hendrik Frensch Verwoerd sat when Dimitri Tsafendas stabbed him to death those many years ago. The irony of my sitting in this House hits me smack in the face. It is here that so many ruthless laws were made, aimed at curbing every facet of blacks' lives.

It is here that infamous laws such as the Group Areas Act, the Population Registration Act, the Reservation of Separate Amenities Act, the Land Acts, the Influx Control Act, the Mixed Marriages Act, the Immorality Act, the Bantu Education Act, the Extension of University Education Act, and many others, were debated and enacted.

It occurs to me that the most important people in this Parliament were not the people who sat inside it and made laws, but rather the voteless majority out there against whom they legislated. The House's entire *raison d'être* was me, the black person who was never represented in it. I did not feel sad as the Conservative Party staged a walk-out when the Speaker called the names of five National Party nominated MPs to fill the posts of MPs who had resigned. In many ways the CP is an anachronism in South African politics. Major changes have taken place right in front of it, but it continues to live in a time-warp.

And when I heard former CP MP and Afrikaner Volksunie leader Andries Beyers explain his new party's policies at a press briefing a few days later, it became obvious that the CP was fast becoming a dinosaur in local politics. Unless the CP drops racism and adopts pragmatism as the Afrikaner Volksunie has done, it is in danger of becoming nothing more than a footnote in the history of the new South Africa that many believe is around the corner.

De Klerk makes his entry into the Chamber of Parliament at exactly 11 am. No surprises were expected, and he delivers none. The man is simply no longer the all-powerful leader he was when he delivered his epoch-making address on February 2 1990. He has to keep looking over his shoulder to make sure he does not alienate his negotiating partners and lay himself open to accusations of acting unilaterally on matters which have to be negotiated.

He is in a terrible dilemma: he has to continue making the right noises to show his white supporters he is still in control, and to constantly guard against offending his negotiating partners – chiefly the ANC. I raise my eyes to look at the people in the public gallery. It looks like a flower-garden: MPs' wives, most wearing hats, are dressed in bright colours – red, pink, green, yellow and white.

Pervasive throughout my stay in Parliament was the awareness among many MPs that they are yesterday's men. As they took part in the no-confidence debate last week, at times looking like children at a high school debate – with the Speaker being the headmaster figure – it was apparent they were merely going through the motions.

One of the highlights of my visit to the citadel of power was when colleagues and I were given an off-the-record briefing by a senior cabinet minister. The man was like a breath of fresh air, and one could tell he was not pretending to be something he was not. He had no patience for his colleagues from Natal, who wanted the NP to have a working relationship with the IFP. He was not interested in the protection of group rights or privileges, and said his bottom line was nothing more than a truly democratic South Africa with a justiciable Bill of Rights.

As we left his office, I thought: This is a very different Nationalist politician. I can well see many blacks voting for this man, as opposed to his party.

Apla Sits Down with 'Murderers'

6 March 1993

Romero Daniels stands up from his chair in his colleague's hotel room and offers his hand as PAC political affairs secretary Jaki Seroke introduces us.

The formalities having been disposed of, he sits down again. Dressed in a grey suit, he looks somewhat tired. It has been a long day for him. He has been locked in long and frustrating discussions with the Government over the PAC's armed struggle and the activities of the Azanian People's Liberation Army (Apla), and has already given a number of interviews.

It is about 10.15 pm when my chance to talk to him finally comes, and he has been subjected to a 30-minute grilling from the SABC's Leslie Mashokwe. When I ask him whether he is tired, he concedes it has been a long day, and that he is indeed exhausted. But he has a few more interviews to go through.

Although he is not the highest authority in Apla, Daniels (37), as chief commissar, is one of the top leaders of the guerilla army. Not only is he a member of the Apla high command, but he also serves in the organisation's military commission, which decides on Apla's operations and gives instructions to cadres.

Daniels makes it plain there are things he will not talk about: himself – the only personal detail he will give is his age – and the three-man Apla delegation's contributions in the meeting with the Government. He reiterates the view expressed earlier by PAC delegation leader Willie Seriti that there was only one PAC delegation at the talks, not two – political and military.

Daniels proceeds to pronounce on Apla's relationship with the PAC leadership, on the controversial Karl Zimbiri, who often calls the press to make statements on behalf of Apla, and on Congo Jibril, who claimed in December that Apla would launch indiscriminate attacks against whites. First, however, he wants to put permanently to rest the widespread belief that Apla is opposed to the PAC leadership's involvement in negotiations, and staged last year's attacks on whites in King William's Town and Queenstown to scupper the negotiations which were going on then.

Apla leaders and cadres, he says, are fully behind the PAC leadership's involvement in negotiations, are loyal to the PAC leaders and would like to see a political solution to South Africa's problems. Apla would, therefore, abide by any agreement the organisation might enter into.

'The whole thing is political; it is not war for the sake of war. If an agreement is reached, the armed struggle will just have to go. We are not warmongers'.

On Jibril's statement that Apla would target whites indiscriminately, Daniels says the PAC and Apla are 'not fighting a racial war'. Statements made by Zimbiri since about June last year have to be taken with a grain of salt, according to Daniels. He says Apla leaders gave instructions to cadres that no one was to telephone the press on Apla's behalf and use the *nom de guerre* Karl Zimbiri any more. Daniels also denies that Apla has, or once had, bases in Transkei, but says it is operating 'everywhere in Azania, including in Transkei'.

And the armed struggle is far from over, warns Daniels. Apla will continue 'to hit the enemy' until an agreement is reached. Apla is a formidable force to be reckoned with, and the fact that Law and Order Minister Hernus Kriel led a delegation to Gaborone to discuss Apla confirmed this.

How did he feel sitting opposite Kriel, SAP chief General Johann van der Merwe and the SADF's General Jan Erasmus? He replies: 'It was quite interesting to sit down with murderers and criminals, people who basically slaughtered our people. But there is a need, regardless of our different backgrounds, to sit down and talk. Whether we like it or not, in the final analysis we will have to work together'.

Not All is Well with the Front

26 March 1993

For a while in the past two weeks it looked as though the Patriotic Front conference scheduled for Lenasia, south of Johannesburg, tomorrow, might go some way towards healing the rift which opened between the ANC and the Pan Africanist Congress late last year.

This would have injected a new lease of life into the PF, formed in Durban 17 months ago. For the first time since October 27 1991, the two co-conveners of the Durban conference, the PAC and the ANC, were going to bring together the other 90 members of the PF to assess political developments since then.

This should have taken place six months after the launch of the PF, at the end of last April, according to a resolution adopted at the time of the launch. Since then the PF – which has tottered on the brink of collapse – has by and large existed only in name. And when the PF has been mentioned in the media, it has been in reference to the ANC's coterie of allies within Codesa, mostly homeland governments and tricameral parliamentary parties.

But when the PAC accepted an invitation to a caucus meeting of the ANC's 'Codesa allies' during the recent multi-party preparatory conference at the World Trade Centre, observers were quick to suggest that perhaps the PF – called the Patriotic United Front by the PAC – was not dead after all. For, once the PAC was part of the 'Codesa PF', the point could be made fairly convincingly that the Durban PF was finally up and running.

After all, as the ANC has often pointed out, those it considered its allies within Codesa had also attended the launch, and consequently were members of the PF. And when it was later announced that the 'broad PF' – to distinguish it from the 'Codesa PF' – would meet in Lenasia to discuss a range of issues, including common strategies to be used in negotiations, speculation grew bolder.

Some observers suggested this broad alliance, now including the PAC and possibly the Azanian People's Organisation (Azapo) – which was expelled from co-convenership of the PF only days before the launch – could enter into some kind of an election pact 'to avoid dividing the black vote'. These observers were running way ahead of developments. As unpublished events this week confirm, much arguing and arm-twisting remained to be done, and controversy continued to embroil the PF as late as yesterday.

Only 48 hours before the conference, the PAC had still not ironed out its differences with the ANC, and was unsure whether or not it would attend. At the centre of the row is the status of the organisations attending the conference, and the role of these organisations in arranging the conference.

The PAC feels the ANC has excluded it in organising the conference, in sending out invitations and in drawing up the agenda. Most of the decisions regarding the conference were taken at an hotel in Johannesburg last week, at a meeting attended only by the ANC and its 'Codesa allies'.

It was that meeting which decided, among other things, that ANC president Nelson Mandela should deliver the keynote address – and the PAC is aggrieved. Mandela can do that, says the Africanist organisation, but PAC president Clarence Makwetu should be accorded an opportunity to address the gathering.

And to this the ANC says no, according to PAC sources. Although the PAC was still frothing at the mouth yesterday, its national executive committee decided at its meeting in Umtata, Transkei, last weekend to send a delegation to the conference. Should the organisation reconsider that position, the Lenasia conference will be nothing more than yet another gathering of the ANC and its allies.

While it could be argued that that alliance has a better-than-average chance of entering into an election pact without the PAC, it is also true that the Africanist organisation – and Azapo when it finally joins negotiations – will make stronger allies for the ANC in a multi-party forum.

With the new forum divided into three distinct groups – the Concerned South Africans Group led by the Inkatha Freedom Party, the 'Codesa alliance' led by the ANC, and the Government standing on its own – the ANC would no doubt be happy to have a voice such as the PAC's on its side.

Not only would that eliminate for the ANC the worry about sniping from the touchlines by the PAC and Azapo, but it would also strengthen the ANC's hand on some issues on which these three organisations agree – and there are many such issues, despite the well-known differences.

This explains the ANC's insistence that the PAC should be allowed to attend multi-party negotiations, regardless of the activities of its armed wing, the Azanian People's Liberation Army. And so the success of the Lenasia conference will be gauged not only by the resolutions adopted there, but also by the quality of the organisations attending it.

For it matters little to have an array of insignificant groups coming out with fine-sounding resolutions, if they lack the capacity to help implement them or their voices do not add weight to the debate.

A meaningful unity or front is not one which involves already like-minded organisations trying to curry the favour of the big one in their midst who might one day be in a position to dish out goodies to those who stood by it when it needed allies.

Instead, it is the one which involves adversaries or organisations which differ with one another but who, for some greater common cause, agree to put their differences aside and co-operate. Such a front would include social, professional, church and sports organisations, but, more importantly, it would also involve the important political players on the left, notably the ANC, the PAC and Azapo.

It's Time to Get Off the Fence

31 March 1993

More than a week after the latest spate of attacks on whites in Eikenhof, south of Johannesburg, the leadership of the Pan Africanist Congress continues to equivocate on the issue. Except for publicity secretary Barney Desai, the PAC's leaders have yet to condemn such attacks, or those responsible for them.

The organisation's explanation until now has been that it does not have sufficient information to make authoritative comment possible, and that the high command of the Azanian People's Liberation Army has also not commented.

Reports have Apla chief spokesman Johnny Majozi saying the guerilla army's cadres inside South Africa had not yet contacted Apla's headquarters in Dar-es-Salaam to claim responsibility for the terror attacks. It is pointed out that all there is to link Apla to the apparently racially motivated acts, at this stage, is a telephone call to the South African Press Association from an anonymous caller claiming to be an Apla cadre.

However, the situation remains murky because although PAC leaders insist anybody could have telephoned the press to claim responsibility on Apla's behalf, they have not ruled out the possibility that Apla might in fact have been responsible. Indeed, the PAC has tactically left the door wide open for this possibility, and as a direct consequence appears to condone the murders and their perpetrators.

The furthest it has gone is to say that the PAC adhered to no policy which involved killing women and children. But that, as PAC leaders should know, is cold comfort to the families of those whom faceless gunmen have mown down in cold blood in the past two weeks.

At a media conference, PAC president Clarence Makwetu was twice asked if he condemned the attacks. Twice he evaded the question, saying only: 'We regret any killing, irrespective of colour'. Told by the journalist who had posed the question that he had not answered it,

Makwetu replied acidly: 'Unfortunately we are not here to be tried by the media.'

Ah, the media. The PAC leader – like most of his colleagues in the PAC leadership – has an aversion to the media matched by few of his counterparts in the country. The average PAC leader and member believes the organisation has had a raw deal from the press over the years. As a consequence, they say repeatedly that the Africanist organisation was 'not built by the press' and therefore 'will not be destroyed by it'.

Instead of cultivating good relations with the press, some PAC leaders have regarded the institution with scepticism, and have not made themselves readily available for interviews or briefings. Because of the PAC leadership's prevarication on the recent attacks, theories have abounded. There are those who say the attacks were staged by a disgruntled wing of Apla, which is intent on getting the PAC leadership to quit negotiations.

Others, including people in the ANC, say Apla is not responsible for the barbaric murders, and lay the blame on a nebulous 'third force' which seeks to sow racial hatred and in the process derail negotiations. Whatever the truth is, the PAC leadership must now state categorically and unequivocally where it stands on the attacks. Could it be that it knows Apla is not responsible but does not want to admit this because the perception that it is 'a defender of the people' would be jeopardised?

Does it perhaps know that Apla carried out the heinous deeds, but will not say so publicly because of the local and international censure which will inevitably follow? Or could it be that Makwetu and his colleagues really do not know, and are reluctant to admit their ignorance? We do not know, because of the organisation's ambivalence. Let us consider what the attacks mean for the PAC.

Undeniably, the attacks do have some grisly short-term benefit for the organisation, especially while violence continues in the country. PAC secretary-general Benny Alexander is not alone in his belief that the Government has not done enough to stop the spiral of violence in the country, and that this is because most of the victims are black.

There are many in the black community who, while they might not say so publicly, hold the view that Pretoria would take the violence seriously and embark on effective initiatives to end it if whites were also primary victims. Unfortunately, the Government's reaction so far has merely reinforced the widespread perception that it indeed values white life more than it does black life. This is a view that ANC President

Nelson Mandela has expressed a number of times, both here and abroad.

Moreover, PAC leaders say more than 20 000 people have joined their organisation since the eastern Cape attacks – for which Apla claimed responsibility – in December last year. But the acts of terror have also brought local and international condemnation of the PAC, and have severely embarrassed many PAC leaders. Whatever support the organisation gains in the short-term as a result of the attacks has to be weighed against the embarrassment they cause to it.

There is another disturbing dimension to these racial killings, and that is that they further polarise South Africans along racial lines, and trigger retaliatory attacks on blacks by rightwingers.

This is a chilling prospect, and one which could make eventual reconciliation well-nigh impossible if the situation runs out of control. The PAC leadership could play its part in staving off this doomsday scenario by categorically and unequivocally distancing itself from the murders, and strongly denouncing those who perpetrate the acts of terror.

To this end, it might also remove the poster at its head office's board room, where it holds its press conferences, which seems to condone Apla's alleged attacks. The poster reads: 'Each bullet takes us forward. Viva Apla. Year of Great Storm. Apla by day, Apla by night'.

Picking Up the Glove in Elections Challenge

7 April 1993

Stocky former United Democratic Front's Popo Simon Molefe might not be hogging newspaper headlines, but he has been hard at work – as a back room boy preparing the African National Congress for South Africa's first all-in elections, expected within a year.

Molefe, who heads the ANC's election commission, is quite aware of the responsibility that lies on his shoulders, and those of colleague Patrick 'Terror' Lekota. But he says he welcomes the challenge. He is eager to talk about his work, but has to keep an eye on his watch because not only does he have another meeting after the interview, but he is also leaving for Switzerland in the evening to raise funds for the ANC.

Precisely how well the ANC performs in the elections will depend to a great extent on Molefe and his colleagues. The organisation expects, as the oldest anti-apartheid standard-bearer, to reap the voting benefits of having struggled against the hated system for so long. But Molefe also concedes another obvious truth – that thanks to apartheid, the overwhelming majority of South Africans have no experience in voting or campaigning for elections. It is his job to see that the ANC's structures are developed for the robust campaigning that lies ahead.

It is one thing to enjoy emotional support; entirely another to translate that into crosses on ballot papers. ANC organisational infrastructures are inadequate, says Molefe – and money is too tight to mention. Molefe estimates the ANC will need between R168 million to R200 million for the elections, and he is cautiously optimistic that that amount will be raised before the elections.

The budget will go towards voter education training, the production of propaganda literature, transport, and the setting up of organisational infrastructures in 94 ANC sub-regions, in addition to the 14 existing regions. He says R5 million is in the bag so far, and the ANC expects to raise at least 20 percent of the targeted figure locally.

'This is because we rely heavily on the poor, and business has not been a friend of the ANC,' Molefe says.

The bulk of the money will be raised internationally, where the ANC has numerous fundraising structures. Methodically, Molefe explains that the work for the election has already begun, and says he believes the problems which lie ahead are by no means insurmountable. The ANC, he says, is putting the finishing touches to its campaign plans, and has begun training people who will implement it.

So far the organisation has held 17 workshops, 14 of them in the PWV area and only one in the coloured community. The organisation has also held one national seminar and four regional ones to discuss implementation of strategy. This, Molefe says, involves the training of election co-ordinators at local level. Workshops have so far covered 10 of the ANC's 14 regions and he is confident this initial process will have been completed nationwide by the end of this month.

But a vast amount of work still awaits. His commission plans to train at least five people to be 'specialist co-ordinators' in every branch of the ANC, and would like to have three trained monitors at each polling station. He estimates there will be between 7 000 and 10 000 polling stations for the historic elections for a constituent assembly and Government of National Unity and Reconciliation.

The ambition of Molefe and his colleagues is breathtaking. They plan to have 180 000 election volunteers who will serve as 'foot soldiers' – and to have one volunteer for every 100 voters.

To this end, the ANC is engaged in 'an intensive voter education campaign', and is using the services of 'neutral organisations' such as Matla Trust, the Centre for Policy Studies and the Institute for a Democratic Alternative for South Africa for voter education.

Molefe estimates that 4,5 million black South Africans do not have identity documents. He hopes that by the time the elections are held the ANC will have persuaded most of them to obtain ID documents, but says those who will still be without them would have to be given uniform voter cards to be issued by an independent election commission.

That said, the busy Molefe looks at his watch and says: 'I have only one political statement to make. For us, the coming elections are a continuation of the struggle to end apartheid and to transform our society so that we can deliver a better life to the majority of the disadvantaged. They are also about the establishment of the legitimacy of the new government. It is absolutely essential that we register no less than a 90 percent poll in the election. This is the surest way to ensure that the majority consider this process of transition as their own. It is also important for the creation of political stability which will engender investor confidence. It is, therefore, key for us to ensure that ordinary people understand voting procedures, the secrecy of the ballot, that they are sufficiently motivated to vote, and that on the day of election they will go out to vote, and that television and radio will be open to all.'

These are statements that – as he well knows – might well come back to haunt him unless he does an extraordinary job.

Assassin's Bullets Put Paid to Our Lunch Date

12 April 1993

Chris Thembisile Hani and I were in deep conversation as we walked into the international arrival terminal at Jan Smuts Airport a month ago, when an elderly white woman tapped him on the shoulder from behind and greeted him.

It was around 4 pm on Monday, March 22, and our Transkei Airways flight from Umtata had just landed. I had gone to Transkei on a special assignment, and Hani had travelled there to address March 21 rallies and to inform ANC and South African Communist Party followers in the area about the latest developments in the negotiations.

'Chris, oh how nice to meet you. I wish you luck in your efforts to bring peace in this country,' the white woman said as she shook Hani's hand. The SACP general secretary's bodyguard studied the situation but kept his distance.

The woman, who said she was born and bred in Butterworth, and described herself as a Transkeian, invited him to stop by at her home when next he was in the area.

Inconvenient

As Hani and I walked out of the arrivals hall, we were making arrangements to have lunch together as soon as time allowed. In the nature of the current political scene in South Africa, that week was out for both of us, the following week was equally inconvenient – because of the multi-party negotiations – and we finally settled on last Thursday. As fate would have it, he had to cancel at the last moment. It would have to be this week ...

I happen to have been the first South African journalist to interview Hani on his return to South African soil in 1990. The interview was conducted in *The Star's* car, and for an hour we drove up and down the streets of Johannesburg and Braamfontein. I took Hani and Tokyo Sexwale to Fox Street, next to Carlton Hotel, where they mingled freely with people – unrecognised.

Hani savoured every minute of his first walk in the streets of Johannesburg in years, and it was a special interlude to share with him. I will not be able to repeat it, and nor will the unexpected lady from Butterworth receive her visitor.

DP Believes it Can Do Well in Election

15 April 1993

Democratic Party (DP) national chairman Ken Andrew is not the type one could expect to be doing the macabre toyi-toyi dance, and the appellation 'comrade' would no doubt not sit comfortably on him.

Just like his opponents in South Africa's historic non-racial election to be held some time next year, he is acutely aware of the need for his party to reach out to the millions of South Africans who will be casting their votes for the first time.

For years the DP – and its predecessors, the Progressive Federal Party before it – has been seen as a white, predominantly English, middle-class party spouting liberal values. Andrew readily acknowledges this and attributes it to apartheid, which decreed that blacks would not be members of 'white' political parties.

The challenge now confronting the DP is to extend its appeal to South Africans of all hues if it is to continue to be a significant player in the much-touted new South Africa – and Andrew is convinced the party is equal to the task.

'There are not that many places where (political) intimidation is low.' Says Andrew: 'Obviously there are many communities in which the DP is unknown or relatively unknown, but we are encouraged by the response we have received so far.'

Although Andrew is reluctant to use racial tags, he lets slip that the coloured community is the most receptive to the DP's message of a liberal democracy based on a German-type mixed economy. He says the DP had 14 branches in the coloured community – mostly in the Cape – last year, and now boasts no less than 55 branches.

Like Pik Botha, who surprised many last year when he said the NP could win a non-racial election, Andrew has also done his arithmetic: he believes the DP will win about 16 percent of the popular vote, enough to book it a place in the government of national unity and in the constituent assembly.

The Cape Town Gardens MP estimates that the DP will win 25 percent of the white vote, 14 percent of the coloured and Indian vote, and 10 percent of the African vote. This, he says, will add up to 16 percent of the overall plebiscite.

He believes the DP can become kingmakers and co-governors of the country – like Count Lambsdorff's Free Democratic Party which has ruled Germany with Chancellor Helmut Kohl's Social Democratic Union for over a decade.

Andrew says for the DP to get the 16 percent it wants it will need at least R15 million for the election compared to the ANC's R168 million to R200 million. He will not say how much the party has raised so far, but only reveals that it is now 'in a much stronger position financially than we were a year ago'.

The DP, he says, is still 'very tight on money', and has a long way to go before it could be satisfied with its coffers. However, where the party's fundraising campaign is at an advanced stage it has been 'very successful'.

Contrary to popular belief, Andrew says, the DP does not depend on big business for its funding. Instead, it relies heavily on pledges and debit orders from its members, who give donations ranging from R20 to R2 000 a month.

The party is also looking abroad for additional financial support now that the restriction on political parties receiving foreign funding has been rescinded. 'Therefore, for people who want true democracy to survive in this country, for people who want stability in South Africa and are not happy that the other parties will guarantee that, the DP would be a natural party to support', he says.

Like the ANC, the DP is engaged in a voter-education campaign, and is presently drawing up programmes and proposals on preparing the electorate for the election. Andrew believes the DP has the potential to grow further after the election 'if we do everything right'.

SA Owes Thanks to ANC

22 April 1993

All South Africa ought to be grateful to the leadership of the ANC for the way it handled the aftermath of the assassination of South African Communist Party leader and ANC national executive committee member Chris Hani.

That may seem to some like an exaggeration, but South Africa would have slipped into civil war and anarchy over the past few days had it not been for the statesmanship of ANC president Nelson Mandela and colleagues.

The cold-blooded murder of the charismatic Hani, who was arguably the second most popular political leader in the country after Mandela, could have been just the spark to ignite violence on a scale never before seen in this country. Hani, it must be remembered, polled the highest number of votes at the ANC's national congress in Durban in July 1991 and had earlier pulled out of the race for the ANC's vice-presidency in favour of the ageing Walter Sisulu to avoid a showdown with international affairs director Thabo Mbeki.

He had a huge personal following in townships all over South Africa, but was not hesitant to chide and chastise those within the alliance who terrorised some townships and tried to become a law unto themselves. Hani could take on errant self-defence unit members as fearlessly as he criticised the Pan Africanist Congress's Azanian People's Liberation Army's declaration of 1993 as the 'Year of Great Storm'.

Hani's main weakness, as he told me in his first interview conducted on South African soil in June 1990, was that he lacked diplomacy. He spoke directly from the heart and never pulled any punches. That is what made him so popular among the country's youth, and his assassination had the potential to plunge the country into chaos.

There is no doubt, therefore, that the deaths, burnings and lootings that occurred last week could have been worse had it not been for the ANC leadership's powerful calls for restraint. To their credit, ANC leaders Gill Marcus and Mosima 'Tokyo' Sexwale were the first to call on black South Africans to remain calm and not take the law into their own hands.

Made at the scene of the assassination soon after the crime had been committed, with Hani's body still lying in his driveway in Dawn Park, this call was particularly important. Millions of South Africans heard the appeals on the radio throughout the day and saw them repeated on television during the evening.

Mandela, who was holidaying in Transkei, rushed back to Johannesburg and went on television to make an emotional plea for peace.

'With all the authority at my command, I appeal to all our people to remain calm and to honour the memory of Chris Hani by remaining a disciplined force for peace,' Mandela said.

It was a moving gesture, it was a statesmanlike act which, unfortunately, President De Klerk and his Cabinet Ministers would neither match nor reciprocate.

It was a move which saw Mandela grow in stature as he put the nation's interest before those of his seething supporters. The calls for peace were to be echoed over and over again by Mandela's colleagues. After its emergency meeting on Sunday morning, the ANC-SACP-Cosatu alliance reiterated Mandela's calls and re-affirmed its commitment to negotiations.

Last Thursday Mandela again addressed the nation on television and repeated his mantra of peace, calm and restraint. This powerful message was delivered many times between Thursday and Hani's funeral on Monday, with Mandela again exhorting his followers to be 'radical and militant activists for peace'.

Yes, a number of deaths did take place during the week of mourning and some young hotheads took advantage of the situation to engage in violence, wholesale looting and the burning of vehicles and people's homes. In Dawn Park on Monday I saw recalcitrant youths raiding a nearby maizefield and setting a house on fire. Clearly, they were an aberration, and would not listen to anyone – not even Mandela.

But I also saw the majority of people gathered there behaving most impressively, taking orders from tired marshals who had toiled diligently since Sunday. And what was de Klerk's response throughout? A predictable pandering to his white constituency and the right wing, which he continues to handle with gloves.

Only towards the end of the week did he begin to show some

understanding of the wrath which was threatening to rip this country apart, and to grudgingly acknowledge the ANC leadership's efforts to channel that anger effectively, while reining in its radical elements.

Hani's assassination was the biggest challenge Mandela had to deal with since he was out of Victor Verster Prison a free man on February 11 1990. He handled it with finesse, putting his own leadership and popularity on the line in the process.

It was a challenge Mandela passed with flying colours, and De Klerk would do well to walk the extra mile to meet the ANC. I believe South Africa owes Mandela and his colleagues in the alliance a big 'thank you'.

World Pays Tribute to Oliver Tambo

26 April 1993

Tributes for the late ANC national chairman Oliver Tambo have been pouring in since his death was announced at the weekend.

Tambo (75), who returned to South Africa in June 1991 after spending three decades in exile, died of a stroke at Milpark Hospital at 3.10 am on Saturday. The ANC said Tambo, who had been admitted to hospital on April 23 for observation in connection with a chest infection, had been in no pain.

Tributes have come from political organisations in South Africa, as well as from foreign governments and international bodies. ANC president Nelson Mandela, Tambo's friend and one-time legal partner, told a press conference in Johannesburg on Saturday that Tambo had done more than any individual to build the ANC through hard years in exile.

'He was my brother, my comrade, my friend and my colleague,' an emotional Mandela told the press conference.

President F W de Klerk said Tambo, whom he had met only once when they had 'a very constructive discussion', had always been supportive of the peace process in the country and was an example worthy of being followed.

In a letter to Tambo's wife Adelaide, United Nations secretary-general Boutros Boutros-Ghali described Tambo as a 'remarkable political leader whose impact was felt far beyond his own country'. Boutros-Ghali said the ANC leader had a deep understanding of international relations. He added: 'South Africa has lost a great leader who not only championed the struggle against apartheid, but also made a significant contribution towards the establishment of a democratic, non-racial and united South Africa'.

Commonwealth secretary-general Chief Emeka Anyaoku said there could be no more fitting tribute to Tambo than that South Africans of all races worked with more vigour to achieve the ideals to which he had devoted his life. The British government said South Africa had lost 'a great national leader' who had dedicated his life to ending apartheid and attaining democracy.

The Nigerian military government said Tambo's death two weeks after Chris Hani's assassination was 'a major set-back in the struggle for majority rule in South Africa'. The ANC Youth League appealed to young people to pay tribute to the former ANC president by emulating his 'outstanding attributes' of humility, discipline and selflessness. The ANC Women's League commended Tambo for being a strong supporter of women in their struggle 'for women's emancipation and empowerment'.

Afrikaner Volksunie leader Andries Beyers said it was a pity that Tambo, who had exerted himself for peaceful negotiations since his return from exile, had not lived to witness a settlement.

Archbishop Desmond Tutu said Tambo, 'a man of deep spirituality', would be remembered for his sacrifices for the sake of others, as well as 'for his forbearance, his gentleness and his lack of bitterness'.

Tributes have also come from Inkatha Freedom Party president Chief Mangosuthu Buthelezi, the Pan Africanist Congress, the Azanian People's Organisation and the National Council of Trade Unions (Nactu).

Struggle's Strategist

26 April 1993

On his first official visit to the United States in January 1987, when he travelled to Washington DC to hold talks with the then Secretary of State George Schultz, Oliver Reginald Tambo also paid a lightning visit to Georgetown University to address a select gathering of students and members of the academic staff.

Tambo, then president of an organisation which the American government had until then described as a terrorist organisation, was accompanied by ANC international affairs director Thabo Mbeki. Although the fact that Washington had finally agreed to give the ANC leader a hearing was a major milestone, Tambo's visit was not without its share of controversy.

Members of President Ronald Reagan's Republican Party and some rightwingers mounted demonstrations outside the State Debarment, protesting against Tambo's official presence in Washington. They carried cardboard coffins to draw attention to the necklacing by South African 'comrades' of people regarded as sellouts.

Near the State Department, at Georgetown University – where I happened to be studying at the time – Tambo impressed his huge audience. Although he was a Christian, and with his long-time friend Nelson Mandela had been against collaboration with communists in their youth, Tambo refused to respond when a Republican student asked him whether he was a communist.

At a reception after the address, I was invited to sit at the table where he, Mbeki and Georgetown University authorities were sitting. Upon being told that I was a South African, Tambo engaged me in conversation, and told me that his other name was 'Kaizer'. In September that year ANC cadre Tladi Ditshego – now employed in ANC President Nelson Mandela's office in Johannesburg – enrolled at the same university. When I told him Tambo had said his other name was 'Kaizer', Ditshego laughed.

Tambo, he said, had told him his other name was 'Tladi' when they first met in Zambia years before. 'That is the kind of man he is,' Ditshego said.

Tambo, more than anyone else, is credited with having single-handedly built up the external wing of the ANC and its military wing, Umkhonto weSizwe (MK), in exile.

Soft-spoken and mild-mannered, Tambo was a respected strategist, and is credited with having masterminded the 1989 Harare Declaration that paved the way for negotiations with the South African Government.

Born the son of a peasant farmer in Bizana in eastern Pondoland on October 27 1917, Tambo attended mission schools in the region before going on to the Anglican-run St Peter's Secondary School in Johannesburg in 1933 – to which he later returned as a science teacher.

Expelled

It was at the University of Fort Hare, a cradle of African leadership, that Tambo became politically active. It was there that he met Mandela. A long-time friendship, which later saw them becoming partners in the first black law firm in Johannesburg in 1952, began.

Tambo obtained his BSc degree from Fort Hare, and later enrolled for an education diploma at the same university. He was not to complete that diploma: he was expelled a month before his final exams for organising a student protest. Together with Mandela, Anton Lembede and others, Tambo was a founder member of the ANC Youth League in 1944, and the following year he was appointed its vice-president. He went on to become a member of the ANC's Transvaal executive committee, and in 1949 was elected to the ANC national executive committee.

From there his rise in the ANC was rapid, and like his colleagues in the leadership he had his fair share of arrests and bannings, until he slipped out of the country in 1960 – just before the ANC and the PAC were banned – to rally international support against Pretoria and to form the ANC's underground.

In 1956 he married Adelaide Tsukudu, with whom he had three children. While he was outside the country he heard about the arrest of Mandela and many others in South Africa. He remained abroad, building the ANC and turning it into some kind of government in exile, and did not return home until December 1990 to attend the ANC's first consultative conference inside the country.

Over the years Tambo became a major international figure, and was received as a head of state in many countries. He had succeeded in isolating the Government internationally, and by 1989 the ANC had more diplomatic representatives abroad than the Government.

He had built MK into a formidable guerilla army, and whenever bombs exploded in the country, Pretoria was quick to blame the ANC even before there was any shred of evidence or ANC headquarters in Lusaka had claimed responsibility. In August 1989 Tambo suffered a major stroke which left him partly paralysed, with his speech impaired. He returned home permanently on June 23 1991, and the following month was succeeded by Mandela as ANC president. Tambo, however, was appointed national chairman.

Before handing over the reins, he urged the ANC to adhere to the suspension of the armed struggle. 'To go back means defeat and it would also be a tragedy because it would also mean the destruction of a new South Africa'.

At the time of his death Tambo was chancellor of the University of Fort Hare, and had been awarded an honorary doctorate in law by the University of the Western Cape.

Courtesy Surprise at Treurnicht Funeral

28 April 1993

Yesterday I was one of a few blacks who attended Conservative Party leader Dr Andries Treurnicht's funeral at the Bosman Street NGK in Pretoria.

I went to Pretoria expecting to be given a rude reception, but that did not happen. Instead, I was treated most courteously by the mourners, with some of them even making way for me at the end of the church service as I walked towards my car and they walked towards the Church Street West cemetery, where the CP leader was laid to rest.

I did not go to the cemetery, however, because I did not feel that would be a safe thing for me to do. I thought there would be people there – to the right of the CP in the political spectrum – who might not take too kindly to my presence.

But inside the church I was safe. CP acting leader Dr Ferdi Hartzenberg and his fellow MPs were in attendance, and so were some foreign government representatives. For the record, Ciskei military ruler Brigadier Oupa Gqozo was one of the mourners and guests of honour. And so was the Inkatha Freedom Party's western-Transvaal-based Humphrey Ndlovu.

According to the official invitation list, which I saw, the governments of Bophuthatswana and Qwaqwa had also been invited. The names of Afrikaner Weerstandsbeweging leader Eugene TerreBlanche and the Herstigte Nasionale Party's Jaap Marais were on the list. Treurnicht's few black friends who attended the funeral all belong to organisations which are part of the Concerned South Africans Group, which slowed down the pace of negotiations at the World Trade Centre on Monday.

Correctional Services Minister Adriaan Vlok represented the National Party, and the Government was represented by Public Enterprises Minister Dr Dawie de Villiers. A relaxed Rev J E Potgieter conducted the service, showered Treurnicht – whom he said had 'fought the good fight' – with praise, and preached about Abraham's willingness to kill his son Isaac as a sacrifice to God after he had been asked to do so.

Unlike slain South African Communist Party leader Chris Hani's expensive and colourful coffin last week, which was draped in ANC and SACP colours, Treurnicht's casket was modest. On top of it was the South African flag.

Hartzenberg paid a glowing tribute to Treurnicht, and said he was confident that the late CP leader would say, like Paul in the Bible (2 Timothy 4:7–8): 'I have done my best in the race, I have run the full distance, and I have kept the faith. And now there is waiting for me the victory prize of being put right with God.'

Three Power Blocs in Struggle for Future SA

30 April 1993

When negotiations began at the World Trade Centre outside Kempton Park this week, many believed the negotiators would move with speed towards an agreement.

This would lead to a Transitional Executive Council (TEC), elections for a constituent assembly and, eventually, a government of national unity and reconstruction. Expectations were high before Monday's Negotiating Council meeting, which proved to be a failure. The two parties which matter most, the Government and the ANC, had told South Africans the next six weeks would be the most crucial in the country's history.

Not only would agreement on a TEC be reached, but a date for the watershed one-person one-vote election would also be set. They had pointed out that the country continues to bleed economically, that the violence is scaring off potential investors, and that millions of South Africans are beginning to lose confidence in a negotiations process which has yet to yield meaningful results since it began three years ago.

After Monday's meeting, however, hopes began to fade. Earlier, the Inkatha Freedom Party's Joe Mathews had told other negotiators: 'I am not impressed by talks of urgency ... They leave me stone-cold'.

The 104-member Negotiating Council – each of the 26 organisations and parties has two delegates and two advisers – convenes again today. Will it do better this time?

It is important to understand that there are three power blocs in the negotiations, and to know what they each want out of the process. Until the collapse of Codesa 2 in May last year, there were two strong power blocs: the ANC and its allies on the one hand, and the Government and its cohorts on the other hand.

Siding with Pretoria on a number of issues were the IFP, the governments of Bophuthatswana, Ciskei and Qwaqwa, and some minor tricameral parliamentary parties. The ANC could count on the support of the South African Communist Party, the Transvaal/Natal Indian Congress, the Labour Party and the governments of Transkei, KaNgwane, Lebowa, KwaNdebele and Venda.

And so 'sufficient consensus' meant an issue had to have the support of both the Government and the ANC, who would each sell it to their allies. This explains why negotiations broke down in Codesa 2 when the ANC and the Government failed to reach agreement on the percentages needed for decisions to be taken in an elected constituent assembly.

This situation changed, however, when on September 26 last year ANC president Nelson Mandela and President F W De Klerk signed a Record of Understanding, which included the fencing-in of hostels identified as flashpoints of violence, and a ban on the carrying of weapons, including 'cultural weapons'.

The agreement so angered IFP leader Chief Mangosuthu Buthelezi that he consulted fellow homeland leaders Brigadier Oupa Gqozo of Ciskei and Chief Lucas Mangope of Bophuthatswana, as well as right-wing groups such as the Conservative Party and the Afrikaner Volksunie.

Together they formed the Concerned Southern Africans Group (Cosag). What they had in common then was fierce opposition to Pretoria and the ANC, whom they accused of entering into secret deals. What binds them together now is their commitment to federalism – some say confederalism. And so there are now at least three power blocs in the talks, comprising the ANC and its allies, the small but vociferous Cosag group, and the Government/National Party delegations. For 'sufficient consensus' to obtain, an issue must now have the support of each of these blocs. Not belonging to any of these groups are the Pan Africanist Congress and the Democratic Party, which fall somewhere between the Government and the ANC groups.

For the ANC and its allies, urgency is the name of the game. The Government shares this concern but, as the IFP's Matthews said on Monday, talk of urgency leaves the Cosag group 'stone-cold'.

Concessions

Observers believe the Cosag group wants to slow down the process until it can extract concessions on regional powers in a future dispensation, and have the constitution written by the multi-party forum as opposed to an elected constituent assembly.

Except for the IFP, Cosag members are small parties, and they realise that by themselves they do not stand much chance of making it into the constituent assembly, which the Government calls a constitution-making body. If, as some observers fear, filibustering is indeed Cosag's strategy, it might further delay the negotiations process.

The problem is complicated by the fact that each of the parties represented in the Council, regardless of its size, has the same status.

National Party Ready to Take on All Comers

5 May 1993

The National Party's chief director of information, Springs MP Piet Coetzer, has done his homework.

As the person in charge of the NP's propaganda machinery for South Africa's forthcoming watershed election, he is only too well aware of the fact that the NP will have to rely on more than just its traditional white support-base if it is to be the dominant force it hopes to be in the 'new South Africa'.

Although his party has ruled this country for more than 40 years, and he himself has been closely involved in election campaigns since 1977, Coetzer knows that the coming election will not be like any other the NP has ever fought since its formation in 1914.

For the first time in history, the NP will have to face those who have been victims of its racial policies over years and ask them to cast their votes for it. The irony of the situation does not escape Coetzer (46), but he insists the NP, led by President F W de Klerk, is new – and completely different from the party which gave the world 'apartheid' in 1948.

A few minutes earlier, Manpower Minister Leon Wessels and Public Enterprises Minister Dr Dawie de Villiers had been in the office with their new colleagues who form part of the NP's delegation to the Negotiating Council: two Indian women.

According to Coetzer, the NP started preparing for the forthcoming election shortly after last year's March 17 referendum which, he says, was the NP's 'last all-out campaign aimed at whites'.

The preparations, he says, have been low key, and have involved planning, conducting research, appointing personnel and establishing the necessary infrastructure for what will be the mother of all elections.

'We are convinced that the majority of South Africans at this stage long for co-operation between the bigger parties in the interest of peace and stability', says Coetzer.

But Coetzer is insistent: while the situation might change later, as of now the NP will contest the election alone, and not in an alliance with any other party or organisation.

He says not much significance should be given to surveys and opinion polls giving the NP a low percentage of the vote, because it is not possible to measure support for a governing party between elections. Only during the election time is there what he calls 'a single-minded proposition' which exercises people's minds.

This, he says, was illustrated by the fact that only six weeks after the NP had suffered a crushing defeat at the Potchefstroom by-election early last year, it won the referendum so convincingly. For the coming election, Coetzer believes the 'single-minded proposition', to which the electorate will have to respond, is who is going to govern and who is going to have a major say in the writing of the country's constitution in the constituent assembly.

The kind of economic system South Africa will have, and internal security and stability, he says, are 'side-issues' which will also feature strongly in debates in the election campaign. Then, of course, there is the 'incumbency factor', which usually works in favour of ruling parties during elections.

Does he think the fact that the NP is the Government will help the party?

Coetzer says there are two aspects to this: the fact that the NP has been in power for so long – and therefore has experience as a ruling party – could count in its favour, but the fact that it also carried 'the baggage of apartheid' could count against it.

The NP, he says, would be ready to start its election campaign at 'fairly short notice', and could be ready to contest an election before the end of this year. However, it does not expect an election to be held until around the first quarter of next year.

According to Coetzer, a lot of work remains to be done in preparation for an election.

Cosag Tries to Flex Negotiating Muscles

10 May 1993

They have leap-frogged to the top of television news bulletins over the past few weeks and have had more than their share of newspaper headlines.

And last week spokesmen for the newly formed 'Committee of Generals', which seeks to unite the right wing, gave as one of their reasons for existence the bolstering of Cosag in multi-party negotiations at the World Trade Centre.

They call themselves the Concerned Southern Africans Group (Cosag) – because some of them cherish their territories' 'independence' and therefore do not see themselves as South Africans – and seek to strengthen one another's position in negotiations.

But who are they, and how did they come to be allies, these members of Cosag? Theirs is a strange political marriage of convenience, and political observers expect it to go the way of all such marriages when the relationship among them sours and the chemistry ceases to exist.

Cosag was formed in Sandton in October following the signing of the September 26 Record of Understanding by President F W De Klerk and ANC president Nelson Mandela.

That agreement, which included the fencing in of hostels regarded as violence flashpoints and the banning of the carrying of all dangerous weapons – including 'traditional' or 'cultural' weapons – angered Inkatha Freedom Party (IFP) leader and KwaZulu Chief Minister Chief Mangosuthu Buthelezi.

He immediately suspended contact with the Government, accusing Pretoria and the ANC of having embarked on an 'ethnic cleansing' campaign against Zulus. He said while he was not against the holding of bilateral meetings between the Government and the ANC, he was opposed to agreements reached in such meetings if they had implications for people and parties not represented in the meetings.

Buthelezi, whose relationship with De Klerk's Government was gradually cooling off, met in Mmabatho with Bophuthatswana President Chief Lucas Mangope and Ciskei military strongman Brigadier Oupa Gqozo. The three met again a week later in Sandton and extended an invitation to right-wing and homeland groups which shared their antipathy to the ANC and the Government.

Present at that meeting were Buthelezi and his party, Mangope and some members of his government, Gqozo and members of his government, the late Conservative Party (CP) leader Dr Andries Treurnicht and his delegation, Afrikaner Volksunie (AVU) leader Andries Beyers and his delegation, as well as delegations from other lesser-known groups such as the Afrikaner Vryheid Stigting (Avstig) and the Transvaal Hostel Residents' Association.

Except for the IFP, none of the organisations and parties present could claim that the Record of Understanding had any direct implications for it and its members. And so Cosag was born, and its first public statement was a call for a multi-party conference which would review both the Record of Understanding and agreements reached in the moribund Convention for a Democratic South Africa.

The group seems to be functioning only at leadership level – Gqozo and IFP western Transvaal leader Humphrey Ndlovu attended Treurnicht's funeral in Pretoria two weeks ago – but one can hardly imagine any camaraderie between, say, IFP members with their CP counterparts on the ground.

Asked what binds them together, Cosag secretary Johan Ferreira told *The Star* what they had in common was their opposition to a unitary state in favour of a federal/confederal state providing for self-determination. Although its KwaZulu-Natal constitution adopted by the KwaZulu Legislative Assembly in December last year is more confederal than federal, the IFP insists it wants a federal system for South Africa.

Gqozo and Mangope do not want to relinquish the power they now enjoy in their respective territories, and would like a confederal system for South Africa. Unlike Buthelezi, they have little support in their own backyards. Gqozo is extremely unpopular in Ciskei, and there was jubilation and excitement on the streets of Mmabatho when Mangope was ousted in a coup in February 1988 – before the then President P W Botha stepped in to restore him to office.

The CP and the AVU have support in the Afrikaner community, and both want a confederation. The difference between them is that while the CP remains racist in outlook, the AVU has doffed racism and also embraces 'brown Afrikaners' – coloureds – in its vision for an Afrikaner state.

All Cosag members are opposed to the holding of elections for a constituent assembly, and maintain that the multi-party negotiations forum will have to write the country's new constitution before presenting it to the populace for approval through a referendum. Only then, they contend, should elections be held.

While the IFP, Bophuthatswana, Ciskei, the CP and the AVU may be better known Cosag members – being involved in negotiations – they are by no means the only ones. With them are Professor Carel Boshoff's Avstig, the Transvaal Hostel Residents' Association, Action Save South Africa, the Volkseenheid Komitee, Gqozo's African Democratic Movement, KaNgwane's Insika Party, Natal's Reform Party, Kwa-Ndebele's Sindawonye Party and Transvaal Member of the Executive Council John Mavuso's National Forum.

Buthelezi's Joe Has It All Tied Up

13 May 1993

Joe Matthews is a warm and likeable man and, unlike many of his colleagues in the leadership of the Inkatha Freedom Party (IFP), enjoys the respect of some of his political adversaries.

Some people on the Left, especially in the ANC, may not like him, and may even accuse him of opportunism, but they will grudgingly concede that he has an impressive record in struggle politics.

For not only was he once a prominent member of the ANC in exile many moons ago, but he is also the son of the legendary Z K Matthews, a writer and academic who was a luminary in the ANC until his death.

That Joe Matthews fell out with the ANC and subsequently left the organisation is now history, and that he returned to South Africa in 1990 – after an illustrious legal career in Botswana – to join his old friend, Chief Mangosuthu Buthelezi, in the IFP is also well documented. Extremely knowledgeable in African politics, Matthews's rise in the IFP, like that of his many white colleagues whose initial association with Buthelezi was as advisers, was meteoric.

As the man in charge of the party's election strategy and campaign, Matthews knows that the fate of the IFP in South Africa's first all-in election may just lie in his hands. He is not at all unnerved by the responsibility, and believes he will be equal to the task.

The IFP, he says, will do well in the following areas, even though it does not expect to win in all of them: KwaZulu-Natal, PWV (he expects the ANC to win here), northern-western Cape, western Cape and northern Transvaal. He says the IFP has more non-Zulu members in the PWV than it does Zulu members, and says this proves that the party is not an ethnic regional entity as many believe.

However, Matthews singles out the eastern Cape, Ciskei and Transkei as areas where the IFP has no presence and enjoys no support. According to Matthews, the IFP, which wants South Africa to become a federation, has three objectives in the forthcoming election. These are:

- To win 'sufficient support' nationally so that the party can be 'an essential partner in the proposed government of national unity'. First, he refuses to give the percentage poll the IFP hopes to get nationally, and later he reluctantly lets slip that the IFP aims to win only a few votes among coloureds in Port Elizabeth, and 'little support' among Indians in the country. However, the party plans to embark on a massive recruiting campaign. A scientific poll is under way to determine the extent of support the party enjoys in the country.
- For the purpose of the election, the IFP has divided South Africa into 30 regions, and has appointed teams in the different regions. A 'massive army of volunteers', whose job will be to establish an IFP presence throughout the country, is also being mobilised.
- 'We are assuming that the electorate will be between 21 million and 22 million. It has been established through research that the first all-inclusive election in a country has a turn-out as high as 80 percent', Matthews says.
- He says the IFP plans to fight the election alone, but quickly adds that some of the party's allies might be prepared to contest the election under the IFP banner.

Adamant

Matthews is adamant that the exercise will not be 'a bread-and-butter one', and contends that the issue confronting the electorate will be the economic system to be adopted in the country, jobs, investment and housing.

According to Matthews, the IFP is preparing for an election early next year, but will not be caught flat-footed if the election were to be held around November this year.

Matthews says the IFP will need between R160 million and R170 million to adequately fight the election, R40 million of which will be for head office expenses.

This contrasts with the ANC's R168 million to R200 million, the NP's R100 million and the Democratic Party's R15 million.

PAC Gearing Up for D-day

26 May 1993

The mention of Pan Africanist Congress secretary-general Benny Alexander's name in sections of the white community evokes anger and hatred, but among his people in the PAC the outspoken Alexander is something of a hero.

He it was who appeared on television last December to comment on attacks on whites in the eastern Cape by alleged operatives of the PAC's military wing, the Azanian People's Liberation Army. The sentence which stuck in the public mind long after that interview was that 'the hullabaloo' which greeted the attacks was because 'only four whites' had been killed.

It was a statement which earned the amiable Alexander the attention of Afrikaner Weerstandsbeweging leader Eugene TerreBlanche, who threatened publicly that the AWB would annihilate the PAC leader and his followers if he declared war on whites. But there is another side to Alexander, not known to many.

As they are discovering at the World Trade Centre since the PAC entered negotiations, he is also a thoughtful and shrewd negotiator who will seek compromise as much as possible and studiously avoid ruffling feathers unnecessarily. He is, at 38, the youngest member of the 10-person negotiations planning committee.

He believes that the PAC will, like a dark horse, bolt to the finishing line ahead of all its competitors, including the high-profile ANC. Unlike the ANC, the PAC has not yet embarked on 'a hard campaign', but has so far been engaged in a 'soft-sell' election campaign, which will gradually peak as the day of reckoning approaches, Alexander says.

'We are still working on a campaign slogan, but it will have to take into consideration the fact that the PAC will give the oppressed the best deal they can ever have, and that the PAC will not compromise them. We believe that the field is wide open, and there is no need for us to go on a hard campaign now.'

But Alexander will have you know the PAC began preparing long ago for the election. The PAC, he says, has engaged a black agency to handle research. White agencies, he says, are not as knowledgeable as they might appear about the way blacks will vote, and sometimes even subcontract the black agencies to help with certain aspects of their research.

The PAC wants 'a factual picture' of the electorate and of who it should target in its election campaign. Other questions are what message the PAC will need 'to secure the vote', how that message will be communicated to the electorate, what resources will be needed for the organisation to attain its 'desired performance', and how the plan to 'turn the strategy into reality' will be implemented.

He says the organisation will have more than 900 'precinct commanders' working in each township, and that an estimated 190 000 volunteers will be needed for door-to-door canvassing. To do all this, of course, will cost lots of money, and Alexander is confident the PAC will tackle the enormous financial challenges head-on.

He believes that to accomplish its goals in the election, the PAC will need R190 million – similar to the ANC's election budget of between R169 million and R200 million – 60 percent of which will be used on election day itself.

The PAC, he says, prefers a two-day election, during which the organisation's election budget will be used to pay lawyers, who will be on standby throughout the country 'so that we can challenge any irregularities immediately'; to transport voters to the polling stations; and to feed the army.

Alexander says the PAC has already started raising funds, and that trips to Africa and overseas have been lined up for PAC president Clarence Makwetu. According to Alexander, the PAC is happy to leave voter education to 'the independent Matla Trust', which provides nonpartisan education about voting. The PAC secretary-general will not say how much the Africanist organisation has raised so far, but reveals only that the road ahead is still long and arduous. However, he is confident that by election day the PAC will be quite close to its financial target.

He says that although the PAC, which expects the election to be held towards the end of March next year, plans to fight the election alone, it will nevertheless consult with the National Council of Trade Unions and traditional leaders.

'Ironically', says Alexander, 'the first election will have nothing to do with the purpose of the election, which is writing the new constitution. It will have to do with party positions on various issues and people's perceptions as to who can deliver the goods.'

Azapo has 'No Preoccupation' with Election

8 June 1993

Lybon Tiyani Mabasa's name may not be one of the most readily recognisable in certain circles in the country, but the long-serving Azanian People's Organisation (Azapo) leader takes solace in the knowledge that among what he calls 'the oppressed and exploited', his name does more than just ring a bell.

Mabasa, like many other political activists in the country in the 1970s and the 1980s, has seen the inside of prison walls more times than he cares to remember, but he remains doggedly committed to the philosophy of Black Consciousness (BC) which he first embraced years ago as a young man.

A former president of Azapo, Mabasa has seen more of his close comrades and associates leaving the BC fold to join organisations like the ANC and its allies – many of whom have since risen to positions of authority in those organisations – but his faith in BC remains as unshakeable now as it was before Steve Biko's death in 1977.

And like his comrades in Azapo, Mabasa is very sceptical of the multi-party negotiations taking place at the World Trade Centre (WTC), and calls some of those deliberating on the country's future in that forum nothing but 'puppets and stooges of the regime'. But Mabasa and his colleagues have been keeping a watchful eye on the goings-on at the WTC, and they know that the negotiators have set the date of the country's first all-in election as April 27 next year. Will they participate in the election?

Mabasa, now Azapo's deputy secretary-general, hesitates. His president, Professor Itumeleng Mosala, recently told a press conference in Johannesburg that the question of elections 'does not arise' for Azapo. But two weeks later, does that question still 'not arise'? Azapo, Mabasa says, has no 'preoccupation with an election being an instrument for the transfer of power'.

However, the organisation would contest the election if it were satisfied that an elected constituent assembly would not be 'constrained' by constituent principles still to be adopted by negotiators at the WTC.

'As an organisation, we would not fear that our people would not support us in an election, but we would also not want our people to be dragged into an election if that election will not deliver', he says.

And so one thing is established: Azapo's participation in the election will depend on 'whether the WTC will not completely emasculate an elected constituent assembly'. Azapo's participation, says Mabasa, might just 'save South Africa from heading for a neo-colonial system'.

But has Azapo already started preparing for the election? Yes, says Mabasa. Like other organisations and parties, Azapo has begun mobilising people throughout the country and telling them about its position on the election. It has also been conducting voter-education seminars and has participated in other programmes dealing with elections.

Azapo's main handicap, Mabasa says, is its lack of funds. He says Azapo, probably the poorest national political organisation in the country, has always prided itself in its record of never having been 'beggars' abroad. However, the organisation has no illusion about the role money can play in an election. 'Money plays a major role in influencing, controlling and directing the manner in which elections are held and who wins them. Between you and me, only rich people win elections in America, for instance,' he says. Mabasa says the obvious – that Azapo has no money – and reveals that he is not at all confident about the organisation's prospects of raising money for the election.

Confiscated

Azapo, he says, will rely on its members and supporters for its election budget, and expects to collect about R1 million from them. The Government, says Mabasa, confiscated R1 million from the Black People's Convention and other BC groupings when they were banned in 1977, and Azapo will want the money returned to it. In addition, Azapo will also demand that Pretoria gives it money from the public purse to enable it to contest the election effectively.

And like leaders of the other organisations, Mabasa is confident Azapo will do 'very well' in the election. He says the majority of black South Africans will vote for Azapo, and expects the organisation to poll not less than five percent of the white vote.

For Azapo, says Mabasa, the issues on which the election will be fought are repossession of the land by blacks, redistribution of wealth, and abandonment of racism and all forms of discrimination.

Mokaba Speaks His Mind

24 June 1993

On the question of who embodies the view of the Youth League in the ANC leadership

In looking at the gap left by Comrade Tambo, the Youth League and myself have taken a formal position that Comrade Thabo Mbeki is the man who should now become the deputy-president of the ANC, with an understanding that when the time comes for Comrade Mandela to rest, Comrade Thabo should become the president of the country. That is the decision of the Youth League, presented at the last NEC meeting of the ANC, where the slogan (issue) was also discussed.

On why the Youth League favours Thabo Mbeki

There is no other man who would want to oppose a man like Thabo: the Youth League will stick to that name. We are satisfied in our consultations with most of the regions, and structures such as MK, that Thabo is the choice, whether you go to conference or you do it today. We were not doing it against anybody. He is simply the best candidate suitable for the West and the East, he was also a leader of the youth in 1962, and has always showed boldness, for instance when they were opening up new fronts in order to infiltrate arms and ammunition inside the country.

He is also one of the most intelligent – in the very same class as Mandela, Tambo and Sisulu. He is also very humble. We have done our own research and we as the youth were hurt by distortions suggesting Thabo is a snob and never mixes with other people. The fact is that in the same way that Chris [Hani] used to work, when Thabo is in South Africa he is in Soweto discussing with our Youth League there, organising workshops. That aspect of his life is not known. I was myself surprised that the Youth League's decision was quite unanimous. It was not as if there was a number of names and then we chose him [Mbeki]. Everyone suggested him.

On whether the change in ANC leadership positions is imminent

We want this [election of Mbeki] to take place immediately and to be discussed at our meeting when the NEC next sits.

We need to go into an election campaign fully prepared and with young, energetic people.

When we decided this we also took into consideration the health of Walter Sisulu and discussed this issue. We think Comrade Sisulu should take the position of the late OR Tambo (the ANC national chairmanship), and Thabo should take the position of deputy president. It is the view of the youth that the constitution allows for this to happen before our next conference to give Thabo a very, very broad mandate – because the conference [would endorse our choice] – but we don't want to delay the strengthening of the movement, and therefore we have suggested that Thabo Mbeki should be moved to become deputy, or at least national chairperson if we don't have to change the deputy president now.

On how this affects Cyril Ramaphosa

We think Cyril is okay as a secretary-general. As I've said there was no other candidate. It is not as if we are choosing Thabo above any others. It's just that, in his class, there seems to be no other person. We would see Cyril as a secretary-general. At the [last ANC] conference the youth preferred Alfred Nzo, but once Cyril was elected we went to him and promised to work with him. He is a capable administrator.

On stopping the 'Kill the boer' slogan

The SABC and the National Party have succeeded in distorting the meaning of our songs. I understand the political reasons for which we [the ANC] have taken this decision [to stop the chant] – that farmers are being killed, and it is not our programme. We don't have to give people who are conducting these heinous acts a cover. That is not our programme, and we condemn it.

But I'm also worried that this might be extended to cover all our songs that refer to the boers. People fail to see that this is not racism – we are referring to white supremacy. I certainly do not like to be pushed around by the enemy – any threat they make against me makes me more adamant. If they had not said things like they are going to charge me, I would have looked at this matter differently. But then of course it became more and more difficult to continue defying the Government on that score. We decided we should also not aid the killers of the farmers. I agree with those reasons, but I also pointed out it needs to be recognised our people have always sung about the boers.

On the June 16 chanting incident

What is happening is that they are using the slogan 'Kill the boer, kill the farmer' to say we should not be toyi-toying. I specifically did not sing the chant, but at the end of my speech I toyi-toyied. That is what I have done since the ANC took the decision [to stop the chant].

On whether he supports a government of national unity (GNU)

I was deeply worried together with the Youth League on the question of a GNU. If we are unable to effect fundamental changes in the way things are done, we may end up with apartheid or neo-colonialism.

Those are not the kind of things I have spent my life fighting for. But we as the youth have always said that once the movement has taken a decision, all of us would be bound by it. The majority of the ANC has approved the GNU. Thabo Mbeki said we must ensure we win the election effectively so we can implement decisions. This situates the question of the GNU on our ability to organise, and no longer looks like the kind of compromise it looked like when it was first mooted.

On the possibility of a vice-presidency for F W de Klerk

The principle of majority rule should not be sacrificed. If De Klerk takes such a position, and the ANC is a majority party and he serves an ANC government, I have no problem. But if for any reason the president from the majority party is unable to continue [in office], then the deputy president from the majority party should become the new president.

On Chief Buthelezi in the GNU

As a person, I do not have problems with him. But when he allows the IFP to do the kind of things that it is doing he allows himself to become a puppet of De Klerk and I do not have compassion for him.

But even if [he] does not reach the [five percent] threshold, but commits himself to peace, reconstruction and unity and want to confound counter-revolution, I would approve (of his inclusion in government). I want a government in which the ANC has got the power and the magnanimity to take into our Cabinet people from other parties who are committed to peace, reconstruction and unity.

On his own future career

I intend to stay in politics to continue to serve my people. It is difficult to talk about oneself, because things will depend on other people. [But] I will make myself available for the ANC list for Parliament, if that is the desire of the people.

If the movement decided [I should be in a Cabinet], I would be available for that or for any kind of position. I would (prefer) something that brings me closer to the youth and rural people ... not something which would make me a bureaucrat. I am doing [tertiary] studies because if we South Africans are to be different from the rest of Africa we need to make sure that we are educated.

Big Money, Big Talk in Poll

22 June 1993

South Africa's first all-in election, tentatively scheduled for April 27, will be a mega-bucks affair.

And, judging by optimistic predictions – sometimes bordering on the incredible – the different political parties and organisations have been making, it seems that South Africans will have to cast multiple votes if the parties are to get what they each hope for.

Indications are that the historic election will be the dirtiest and most acrimonious. The ANC and the Pan Africanist Congress plan an all-out attack on the National Party's abysmal apartheid record and gross human rights violations.

Chief Mangosuthu Buthelezi's Inkatha Freedom Party will be portrayed as a puppet of the Government, and the 1991 'Inkathagate' scandal will not help matters. The ANC will be haunted by allegations of torture and widespread human rights violations in its camps in exile, despite its two commissions of inquiry into the claims.

The albatross around the PAC's neck will be the attacks by its armed wing on white civilians, even though this is not likely to cause much damage to the organisation since it is difficult to conceive of whites who will be queuing up to cast their votes for it. The election will be expensive, with most contestants planning to spend liberally.

Most ambitious is the PAC, which hopes to raise R190 million for the election, 60 percent of which will be used on the big day itself. Secretary-general Benny Alexander says the PAC will have more than 900 'precinct commanders' working in each township in the country, and will need an estimated 190 000 volunteers to do door-to-door canvassing.

Next in the big-money stakes is the ANC, which hopes to raise between R168 million and R200 million, and the IFP, which plans to amass between R160 million and R170 million, a third of which will be for head office expenses. As ANC election 'general' Popo Molefe explains, the ANC will recruit 180 000 election volunteers as 'foot soldiers', and will have one volunteer for every 100 voters.

The NP, which has superb election machinery and the advantage of being an incumbent in office, does not need as much money, according to chief information director Piet Coetzer. The party believes R100 million will be enough to launch a nationwide blitz. More modest is the Democratic Party, which believes R15 million will enable it to poll enough votes to remain a significant player in a government of national unity.

The Azanian People's Organisation, on the other hand, has no illusion that it can raise more than R1 million, and therefore plans to put pressure on the Government to fund it from the public purse and return to it R2 million confiscated from Black Consciousness organisations when they were banned in October 1977.

Some of the parties make bold predictions about their chances at the polls. The ANC expects to win the election convincingly, and has no doubt it will poll not less than 60 percent of the vote. The NP hopes to emerge from the election as 'the biggest single party', says Coetzer, and the PAC is convinced it will be the majority party after the election, according to Alexander.

ANC Youths Endorse Thabo Mbeki

24 June 1993

The ANC's powerful Youth League (AnCYL) has formally requested that international affairs director Thabo Mbeki be made deputy president of the ANC, and heir-apparent to Nelson Mandela.

The request, conveyed to the ANC executive by Youth League president Peter Mokaba, calls for the elevation of Mr Mbeki as soon as possible – and argues that the matter is too urgent to be held over for the next ANC conference.

Mokaba said the Youth League 'decision' was taken after consultation with ANC structures around the country and had received widespread support. If accepted by the parent body, the Youth League initiative could see ANC deputy president Walter Sisulu taking up the post of national chairman, previously held by the late Oliver Tambo.

Mokaba said the AnCYL felt that following the death of Tambo in mid-April, the next regular meeting of the ANC national executive committee should install Mbeki as deputy president. He made it clear that this would establish the ANC's line of succession: if anything were to happen to Mandela, Mbeki would lead the organisation.

The AnCYL said prominent ANC figure Cyril Ramaphosa should remain in his position as secretary-general. Mokaba said the promotion of Mbeki would strengthen the ANC considerably in the run-up to the country's first all-in election, scheduled for next year.

In a frank, wide-ranging interview with *The Star*, the controversy-dogged but influential Mokaba declared his loyalty to Mandela and said he accepted the ANC's decision that the 'kill the Boer, kill the farmer' chant should not be used.

He also said he would support the appointment of President De Klerk and Inkatha Freedom Party leader Chief Mangosuthu Buthelezi to a Cabinet in a government of national unity, provided they were prepared to serve under an ANC-dominated government. Buthelezi could be invited to serve in such a Cabinet even if his party did not poll the required votes, Mokaba said, as this would be in the interests of national reconciliation.

Neither would he be opposed to the vice-presidency of the country being given to De Klerk, as long as the National Party leader would not automatically ascend to the presidency if the majority party leader – Mandela – became indisposed.

Giving details of the surprise AnCYL endorsement of Mbeki as the ANC's 'crown prince', Mokaba said the international affairs director had been misrepresented.

He said Mbeki had in fact worked very closely with the youth and other members of the community, and had good relations with, and commanded the respect of, both the radical and moderate wings of the ANC. There was 'no other' candidate for the deputy presidency, he said.

In the exclusive interview Mokaba also:

- Categorically said the killing of white farmers – which he describes as 'a heinous act' – was not the AnCYL's programme and he condemned it unreservedly. He said the Government's 'threats' had encouraged him to be defiant regarding the use of the slogan; and
- came out in support of a multi-party government of national unity, but insisted that such a government would have to 'deliver' to the majority's satisfaction.

Who Will be Boss of Future ANC?

1 July 1993

The publication in *The Star* last week of ANC Youth League president Peter Mokaba's call that international affairs director Thabo Mbeki should become deputy president of the ANC sparked a lively debate within and outside the organisation.

Reflecting the AnCYL's view, Mokaba heaped praise on Mr Mbeki, and said his elevation to the ANC's deputy presidency would have to make him the logical successor to Mr Nelson Mandela as president of South Africa, if anything were to happen to the septuagenarian ANC leader.

Mokaba said there were at least two motivations for the AnCYL's decision. These were the death in mid-April of universally respected ANC stalwart Oliver Tambo, which left the position of national chairman vacant, and next year's impending elections.

He said the AnCYL's view was that the ANC had to approach the election 'fully prepared' with a young person as deputy president and that, in the league's view, Mbeki was the best qualified for the job. Not only was he well educated, but he had also distinguished himself in the armed struggle, and had good relations with the people in both the radical and the moderate wings of the ANC.

Mbeki's appointment as deputy president, said Mokaba, would considerably strengthen the ANC in the run-up to the country's first all-inclusive election.

'We are satisfied, in our consultation with most of the regions and structures such as MK, that Thabo is the choice, whether you go to conference or you do it today,' Mokaba said.

According to the AnCYL, octogenarian incumbent deputy president Walter Sisulu would move to the position left vacant by Tambo's death, and chief ANC negotiator Cyril Ramaphosa would remain secretary-general. There are those who have criticised the AnCYL leader for disclosing in an interview what they viewed as an internal debate, and some have questioned his motive.

That the AnCYL did present its proposal to the ANC's national executive committee (NEC) was not denied, and neither was the fact that as far as the AnCYL is concerned the issue has not been dispensed with. Some have taken issue with the AnCYL's description of Mbeki as the sole candidate for the job, and have pointed out that others would include – at the very least – Ramaphosa, his deputy Jacob Zuma, information head Dr Pallo Jordan, PWV regional chairman Tokyo Sexwale, and Western Cape secretary-general Tony Yengeni and his regional chairman Dr Allan Boesak.

But, according to Mokaba, Zuma would gladly stand aside for Mbeki. (Zuma himself has not publicly expressed himself on this issue.) It is important to point out that although Sisulu is greatly respected within the ANC, the view that the ANC should not go into the election with two elderly leaders – he and Mandela – is dominant in some circles within the organisation.

Also important is to remember that the debate at present going on within the ANC on this issue is not, as some of the organisation's detractors have been quick to claim, a power struggle. Instead, it is something which other organisations are likely to grapple with in their ranks as the election approaches.

When the ANC finally decides whether Sisulu needs to be replaced as deputy president, and who his successor will be, the different interest groups in the organisation will make their voices head. These are:

- AnCYL: This group has already cast its vote in favour of Mbeki. This is an important constituency, with the youth being the majority in the country's population. Mandela, Tambo and Sisulu were themselves founder-members of the AnCYL and, as Winnie Mandela recently said, they finally wrested the leadership of the organisation from the older generation.
- ANC Women's League: Yet another important constituency, which has begun to actively assert its influence in the organisation. Led by Gertrude Shope, the ANCWL has in the past three years remained loyal to the ANC leadership, and has not hesitated to flush Winnie Mandela out of its ranks when she fell out of favour with the parent body's leadership. As a block, it might go for Ramaphosa, Mbeki, Zuma (if he made himself available for the deputy presidency).
- Umkhonto weSizwe: Still a key constituency despite the suspension of the armed struggle as a result of the August 6 1990 Pretoria Minute, MK's views will also be important. This body's clear choice would no

doubt have been the popular Chris Hani.

- Former United Democratic Front/Mass Democratic Movement activists: The people who were at the forefront of the struggle inside the country, this group will also play an important role in deciding Mandela's deputy. Some of them have since been absorbed into senior positions in the organisation but others can be found among the rank and file, and even among civic structures.
- Returned exiles: They spent years outside the country waging a relentless war against Pretoria, and today happily rub shoulders with former UDF/MDM colleagues in the leadership. Others, however, are among the rank and file, and are struggling to get jobs.
- South African Communist Party: For years in a rock-solid alliance with the ANC before, during and after its banning, the SACP will most likely want as deputy president somebody with whom it has good relations. Mbeki, a former SACP politburo member, might get the nod from this group, but this is by no means guaranteed.
- Congress of South African Trade Unions: A third – but no less important – member of the tripartite alliance, Cosatu might prefer Ramaphosa, who was a respected trade unionist before beating then incumbent Alfred Nzo at the July 1991 congress in Durban to become ANC secretary-general.
- Civic structures such as Moses Mayekiso's South African National Civic Organisations (Sanco): Although ostensibly non-political and non-sectarian, Sanco has strong links with the ANC-SACP-Cosatu alliance, with some of its leaders holding senior positions in the tripartite alliance.

Sanco and the Civic Associations of Southern Africa – now led by Winnie Mandela – have maintained their independence from the ANC, and have at times embraced views that the ANC-led alliance's leadership has found embarrassing. Who their choice for the ANC's deputy presidency would be is hard to say.

Zambia Embraces Smiling F W

2 July 1993

Lusaka – President De Klerk scored a major political coup at the weekend when he was publicly embraced by the Zambian government and local citizens and hailed as a leader who had chosen the course of negotiations and peace for South Africa.

De Klerk was met at Lusaka International Airport by his Zambian counterpart and co-host, President Frederick Chiluba. His primary host was the Lusaka Agricultural and Commercial Show Society, which had invited him to open its 67th annual show.

Zambia rolled out the red carpet for De Klerk – whose regime was once regarded as a leper by African governments – with all the attendant pomp and ceremony usually reserved for heads of state. In the first visit to Zambia by a South African head of state, De Klerk – who clearly revelled in his new status as a regional statesman – laughed, joked and shook hands with the Zambians.

He called for greater economic co-operation among countries in southern Africa, joined Chiluba in a harsh denunciation of socialism as an economic system, and said a South Africa rehabilitated into the community of southern African countries would not seek to dominate its neighbours economically.

'We look forward to the day when South Africa, freed from the albatross of the past around its neck, will participate fully in a developing southern African region', he said.

De Klerk and Foreign Affairs Minister Pik Botha, who was one of three cabinet ministers accompanying him, visited Zambia as leader of the National Party in 1989 at the invitation of then president Kenneth Kaunda.

Kaunda, who was the leader of the Frontline states, had for years been one of the most vocal critics of Pretoria's apartheid policies and had close relations with the ANC, whose headquarters were in Lusaka.

That visit angered and precipitated the resignation of then President

P W Botha – he had relinquished his leadership of the NP after suffering a stroke early that year – who registered his strong disapproval of the two men.

Chiluba – whose country is facing serious economic hardships – invited foreign investment to Zambia 'from wherever', and told a press conference his country had become very investor-friendly since he came to power 18 months ago. He added that his country would never nationalise anyone's properties.

In a speech punctuated by applause and shown live on Zambian television at the weekend, De Klerk expressed confidence that the South African economy would begin to grow as soon as the country had solved what he called its constitutional problems.

This, he said, would benefit not only South Africa, but also the entire region. At a meeting at State House on Saturday evening, De Klerk briefed Chiluba about political and constitutional developments in South Africa.

He again expressed a fervent hope that the Inkatha Freedom Party could be wooed back into negotiations. All the 'bigger parties' he said, had to be part of a final solution to emerge from negotiations.

Petulant Pair's Childish Antics

12 July 1993

South Africa's two main leaders, President De Klerk and the man widely expected to succeed him, Nelson Mandela, owe the country an explanation. Their behaviour before a US president sympathetic to this country's cause, and before the watchful eye of the American public, during their recent visit to Washington left much to be desired, in spite of the fairly effective damage-control operation subsequently implemented.

Here were two men, both respected leaders in their respective rights, behaving like spoilt children vying for their parents' attention. Frankly, the whole saga was a performance South Africa could have done without.

We are told the once larger-than-life Mandela refused to be photographed with De Klerk and President Bill Clinton because he feared this might confer undeserved legitimacy on de Klerk. (This, incidentally, was the same reason why Mandela spent months equivocating after his release from jail before finally relenting to mounting pressure to meet IFP leader Chief Mangosuthu Buthelezi in 1991.)

We are told the two leaders – who once had such good chemistry between them – differed sharply on the lifting of sanctions, with Mandela calling De Klerk 'totally irrelevant' on the issue. A hurt De Klerk – whom Mandela once described as 'a man of integrity' – hit back with the riposte that the ANC was 'playing God' with sanctions.

Another man whose recent conduct is anything but impressive is the increasingly petulant Buthelezi, who appears bent on frustrating progress in negotiations so that the IFP can get its own *Boerestaat* in Natal-KwaZulu. That is not surprising, for a man can indeed be judged by the company he keeps.

Buthelezi, around whom there is a personality cut in IFP circles – the IFP central committee last week revealed that it had profound 'respect for Buthelezi, and [stands] in awe of how again and again he is proved right' – now wants negotiations halted and elections held late next year. Funny, is it not, that a man who has often portrayed himself as a champion of democracy should be so afraid of it?

The Government, which over the years sought to present Buthelezi as an alternative to the ANC – he was 'a leader of six million Zulus', remember? – is only now beginning to realise it created a Frankenstein monster. As they say, one reaps what one has sown.

Police 'Will Serve Any Government':

Interview with SAP Commissioner, General Johan van der Merwe

21 July 1993

On rumours of his impending retirement

The reports were unfounded. The situation is that I, in view of changes to come, told the [Law and Order Minister Hernus Kriel] at the beginning of this year that due to likely structural changes owing to a new dispensation, I was prepared to retire, when required. There is nothing at this stage that prevents me retiring before the completion of my tenure. I will be 57 in August, and can retire at any stage. It is still not possible for me to give any indication of constitutional changes.

On President de Klerk's political changes

It is well known that I fully supported the President. If not, then it would have been my obligation to resign. I am not the type of person to serve in any service if I do not agree with the principles on which the service is being run, as well as the policy, from a police point of view, of such a service.

His thoughts on South Africa's future

I think there is, irrespective of the present situation, enough goodwill. We have the resources and the leaders to make this a useful and prosperous country.

His views on Nelson Mandela and Chief Buthelezi

I think they are important leaders who play a very significant role in the developments in our country, and they can, through leadership, contribute tremendously to the well-being of the people of this country.

On whether he would serve under them

Let me put it to you this way: The police are there to serve the interests of the day, irrespective of who is in government. I am convinced that this view is held by a majority in the service.

On the high crime rate

If we compare our situation with that of other police forces in the world, which are in a far better position than we are – considering that at this stage we have constitutional developments, constitutional changes, uncertainty, violence and many other factors – it compares quite well. Nevertheless, I will immediately concede that the situation is not satisfactory.

We have over the past three years increased the number of crimes we have solved, and have succeeded in containing the increase in certain serious crimes. We have established mobile police stations [which we] would like to increase, because police visibility plays a very important role.

On people who want to leave the country because of soaring crime

I don't know where they will go because crime is soaring all over the world. The problem is that the man in the street does not understand the situation. He is not aware of the causes of crime. Playing a major role in our situation is unemployment, which I think is at its highest ever. Another matter is the uncertainty brought about by political changes.

On ANC and IFP accusations of police bias

The mere fact that we are being accused by both organisations in itself proves that as far as possible we try to be impartial. But, then, let's also be honest: there may be members in our ranks who are prejudiced. We are doing everything possible to deal with these prejudices. Unfortunately, we also have a certain history to consider. It's not an easy task, but we have addressed these problems and are doing everything possible to act impartially.

On the swoop on the PAC in April

Insofar as we could determine, we acted on reliable information and on sound legal grounds. We did not have any other objectives than to try to bring to justice the persons responsible for the killings of quite a large number of policemen.

On whether the swoop's timing was politically motivated

It was an investigation which we conducted over many months. After we had completed the investigation, I ordered my men to consult the respective Attorneys-General and to get their opinion with regard to the action we contemplated. That happened the week before our Budget [debate in Parliament], which was on Tuesday. We tried to arrange, through the Director-General of the Department of Justice, to get all the A-Gs in Pretoria, but due to circumstances it was not possible for them to come to Pretoria.

On the police's attitude to their jobs

I think the policemen who are doing active duty and have to face violent situations from time to time have a very difficult job to do, and to say they are happy with the present circumstances will obviously be incorrect. At this stage the work of an ordinary policeman in South Africa is most demanding. I think [the police] are still devoted to their task.

If it was not for the dedication of the SAP, the situation would have been much worse than it is now. They work long hours in very difficult circumstances, and stress is taking its toll. We have a special department to attend to their needs. With regard to the pay, I think it is common cause that the economic circumstances in our country are very difficult. Unemployment is soaring. I think they are quite happy with the pay.

On claims that police dealt effectively with the ANC as 'a terrorist organisation' but now fail to end the violence

For any police service to combat crime effectively it is important for [it] to have an effective intelligence network. In the case of the ANC (and other organisations at that time), the SAP had established a well-founded intelligence network over decades.

We had an organisation with a structure founded over many decades. It was therefore possible to penetrate the ranks of these organisations. In the case of the present violence, we are dealing with [people] who are not attached to any specific organisation by means of a structure. Obviously we are dealing with organisations, but according to our information the management structures of these organisations are not involved. In many of the instances, the perpetrators of violence act on their own or in very small groups, striking at random. Therefore, it is not possible to infiltrate the ranks of these perpetrators by means of informers.

[Also], in certain [cases] we don't get the co-operation of the community, which makes it very difficult for the police to track down the perpetrators.

On possible involvement in violence of SAP elements opposed to change

That's the one matter which has been investigated thoroughly by the Goldstone Commission and by many other judicial commissions. So far, no evidence could be found that the security forces as such are involved. In certain instances the allegations are also quite wilful and malicious.

Once these allegations are made, it is very difficult to change the perceptions created. I have appealed to political leaders and to the media to at least give the police a chance to explain our side of the story before they publish or make the allegations. But in many instances they still make these allegations without consulting the police or giving us a reasonable chance to tell our side.

On perceptions that police act more swiftly when violence victims are white

It is important to note that in the case of violence in certain black communities, we have established special investigating teams [working] on a full-time basis. We are deploying quite a large [part] of our Internal Stability Unit in these communities in an endeavour to contain the violence.

If one should give all the details of the number of men, man-hours and vehicles that we utilise to investigate the violence which occurs in certain black communities, I can say without any doubt that it is much more than we utilise for the same kind of investigation in white areas. The reason it appears that we devote more time, energy and men in the case of incidents in certain white communities is [that] we don't normally have these units there on a permanent basis. We have to utilise them for that specific reason.

In the case of certain black communities, [the police] are there on a permanent basis. We use our best men that we have at our disposal to investigate these matters. In many of these cases we indeed arrest some of the suspects, but unfortunately this information is not always published in such a manner that the man in the street can get the same perception as in the case of other incidents in the white areas.

Read My Lips: Words Can Kill

26 July 1993

Words can kill, and the sooner South Africa's political leaders realise that the better.

From the mouths of politicians respected by their often less sophisticated followers and supporters, words can be as lethal as an AK-47 or a 'cultural weapon' – and worse. In a violence-prone country such as ours, where tolerance is non-existent and tempers sometimes flare at the slightest provocation, ill-considered words can – and often do – leave a trail of destruction in their wake.

Some of the country's leaders are in the habit of using words recklessly, and do not care a hoot about the possible consequences. They, after all, are forever surrounded by bodyguards and are consequently, themselves, immune from the violence.

What South Africa now needs is strong leadership from all those in positions of political authority. Otherwise we might find ourselves staring at a civil war. With all the sabre-rattling and war-talk around, civil war might be just around the corner unless we *all* tread very, very carefully. There is a fine line between leadership and demagoguery and we can do without the latter.

Enough blood has flowed in this country, and it would be a pity if words carelessly tossed around in the form of threats further raised the political temperature and hastened our descent to civil war. One hopes that those with any claim to leadership will exercise restraint and not plunge us into a crisis from which we might never fully recover.

For the country's sake, for the sake of their own children and grandchildren, they should now allow their better judgement to prevail when next they feel tempted to make inciting and inflammatory statements.

But the responsibility to avoid a headlong rush to anarchy also rests with us in the journalistic profession. Those who see Zulus and Xhosas in every conflict do the truth a major disservice. They are also playing a very dangerous game. Headlines like 'The Zulus are coming' in 1991 and 'Gang executes seven Zulus' this week are terribly unfortunate.

They and the half-baked reports that accompany them incite people to engage in a Zulu/Xhosa witchhunt, and therefore to escalate the violence. In these times of intolerance, journalists have to be careful not to fan the flames of violence.

Meiring May Be the Stop-gap Man

11 August 1993

Although Defence Minister Kobie Coetsee's announcement that Army chief Lieutenant-General Georg Meiring will succeed retiring Chief of the Defence Force General Kat Liebenberg from November 1 was not entirely unexpected by military observers, it came as a bolt from the blue in some political circles, especially those on the left.

The 58-year-old Meiring, Chief of the Army since March 1990, gained the reputation of being the most political of the leaders of the three arms of the SADF, never missing an opportunity to take shots at the ANC, an organisation regarded by the security forces for decades as its 'enemy'.

Harmed

When Meiring clashed repeatedly with the ANC last year, it was thought that he had greatly harmed his chances of elevation to the top job in the defence force. But Coetsee – then not yet Defence Minister – knew better, it seems.

Making the announcement, he described Meiring as a soldier who is 'outstandingly equipped to develop peace and stability', and hailed him as the best man for the job of leading the SADF 'during the present circumstances in South Africa'.

Coetsee was effusive in his praise of Meiring, but also expressed concern about his controversial statements and political bent, about which they are unhappy. And Meiring's political gaffes – most of which took place last year – have been many. In September last year he alleged that armed members of the ANC's military wing, Umkhonto weSizwe (MK), and of self-defence units (SDUs) had been moved to Natal-KwaZulu as part of the ANC's plan to disrupt forcibly Shaka Day celebrations on September 27.

No disruptions of the celebration occurred. Later, Meiring alleged that MK members planned sabotage as part of the ANC-led tripartite alliance's 'rolling mass action'. The plan, he said, would target government installations and infrastructure in certain homelands and black residential areas to put the blame (for their actions) on the security forces.

He alleged that MK chief of staff Siphiwe Nyanda and SA Communist Party leader Ronnie Kasrils had given instructions to arm MK and SDU cadres. Again, he produced no evidence to substantiate the claim.

Some months later, *The Star* revealed details of Project Echoes, a clandestine SADF operation launched in April last year to discredit the ANC by gathering and feeding information to journalists about alleged links between MK and the Irish Republican Army, as well as the Palestinian Liberation Organisation.

Mr Justice Goldstone subsequently subpoenaed Meiring to testify before his Commission about the allegations, and Nyanda threatened to sue. However, Meiring defended his actions: he has to defend 'the safety and security of South Africa and all its people', he said.

Predictably, Liebenberg and the then Defence Minister, Gene Louw, jumped to Meiring's defence, denying that the statements were party-political. Meiring then adopted a low profile – until he was promoted.

The Conservative Party welcomed the appointment, the Democratic Party's retired General Bob Rogers let it be known he would have preferred Air Force chief Lieutenant-General James Kriel for the post, and the ANC said it would carefully monitor Meiring's performance with regard to the establishment of multi-party control of the security forces.

Theories abound regarding his promotion. Some have dismissed it as a stop-gap measure by President De Klerk, who wanted the conservative general to consolidate SADF support for the peace process during the transition and warm up the seat he would soon vacate for SADF Chief of Staff Lieutenant-General Pierre Steyn.

Unpopular

Steyn, described as more 'politically correct' and therefore acceptable to the ANC, is believed to be unpopular with the SADF old guard because he led the hunt for Military Intelligence dissidents undermining the ANC.

Military expert Dr Jakkie Celliers, co-director of the Institute for Defence Policy, said Meiring had been chosen 'because the Cabinet knows he can pull the army behind him. He was the officer commanding the South West Africa territorial forces at the time of Namibia's independence and knows what transition is about', Celliers was quoted as having said.

But Meiring might not be the proponent of military solutions that many think he is.

F W, Quit Stroking Buthelezi's Ego

23 August 1993

President De Klerk is playing a very dangerous game. Eager to pacify Chief Mangosuthu Buthelezi and in the process woo him back to the multi-party talks, De Klerk has been actively stroking the IFP leader's big ego these days.

He has consistently said the IFP is an important political player – surveys and opinion polls say otherwise – without whom no solution to South Africa's problems could be found. Until last week he has doggedly refused to countenance any progress in negotiations without the IFP's concurrence, and has repeatedly expressed optimism that the IFP would soon be returning to the talks.

Buthelezi has not shared De Klerk's optimism, and has become more intransigent by the day. It appears the more De Klerk and his Government bend over backwards to accommodate the IFP the more instransigent the chief and his lieutenants become. Unless he is careful, the State President will keep bending over backwards until he finds himself lying supine on the ground.

It is becoming increasingly difficult to fathom just exactly what Buthelezi wants. He keeps making demands and threats, refuses to compromise on anything himself, and stays away from negotiations while expecting others to meet him half-way. And now he has taken negotiators to court over the principle of 'sufficient consensus'.

De Klerk, whose unfortunate threat that elections will not be held until violence has been 'drastically reduced' has been rightly condemned, should now stop pandering to Buthelezi's whims. Buthelezi should not be allowed to hold negotiations and the transition process to ransom.

The time to cut him down to size is now: Pretoria should stop funding his KwaZulu government – which Buthelezi has used for the litigation – with the taxpayers' money. Maybe the chief and his fellow travellers on the right can then learn to appreciate the urgency of the situation.

The less said about De Klerk's threat regarding the elections the better. Apart from the fact that his government has failed to act against the violence, De Klerk simply has no authority to change the election date. The April 27 date was set not by his Government but by the Negotiating Council, and if it is to be changed that decision will be for the council to take. No matter how much he denies this, De Klerk is now a lameduck president. The number of issues on which he can still take unilateral action has dwindled.

The sophists who pay lip-service to democracy while adopting authoritarianism are a cause for grave concern.

Intimidation Must be Halted

26 August 1993

Four months ago, I interviewed Springs MP and then National Party Information Director Piet Coetzer, now a member of the Transvaal Executive Council, about his party's preparations for next year's election.

In the subsequent story, I mentioned Coetzer was accompanied by Itumeleng Mohlala, a young woman from KwaThema, in Springs. Mohlala had just joined the NP's publicity and information department. A week after the story appeared, I read in a Sunday paper that Mohlala's home – her elderly parents were also NP members – had been burnt by people unhappy about her political allegiance. I felt guilty. Was I right to have mentioned her name in the article? Was the burning of her home related to my story? Eventually, I concluded that I was justified in identifying her. She had not asked to remain anonymous and, indeed, seemed proud to be in the NP fold, in the same way ANC members are proud of their organisation.

A week before the interview, she and a few other black NP members had addressed a press conference in Cape Town to draw attention to the pervasive harassment to which they were subjected in the townships. Mohlala is not the only black NP member who has been harassed and intimidated. Many others, including Democratic Party (DP) members, have been given similar treatment.

Eight months before the watershed April 27 general election, the rivalry among the various political parties and organisations vying for votes is becoming intense. While negotiations continue at the World Trade Centre – albeit without the Inkatha Freedom Party (IFP) and the Conservative Party – electoral battle lines are being drawn.

Key political players on all sides are gradually bidding farewell to reason, adopting popular stances and assuming vote-catching postures. They engage in shameless point-scoring, wanting to 'out-radical' one another. And, as is often the case anywhere at election time, mudslinging will become the order of the day, and things will inevitably get worse as the big day approaches. Mudslinging is normal practice in democratic countries, but South Africa is straying from the acceptable with the widespread intimidation of people belonging to opposing parties and the disruption of their meetings.

The ANC and its allies have rightly complained about the lack of free political activity in certain homelands, notably Chief Mangosuthu Buthelezi's KwaZulu, Chief Lucas Mangope's Bophuthatswana and Brigadier Oupa Gqozo's Ciskei; and have vigorously campaigned for the right to mobilise in them.

Last year's ill-fated march on Bisho, which ended tragically when the Ciskei Defence Force opened fire on protesters, served a purpose by forcing Gqozo to allow the ANC and other parties to exercise their democratic right to canvass for support on his home turf. If the forthcoming election is to be free and fair, then all political parties and organisations must feel able to take their policies to every corner of the land and ask for support from all sections of the population. The disruption of DP and NP meetings in the townships must be a matter of grave concern to all South Africans, for it does not augur well for democracy.

If some parties intimidate and browbeat people to obtain votes, then one shudders to think of what they will do once they are in power. And the ANC leadership's deafening silence on this issue has been particularly disturbing. Where some people within the organisation have spoken out against this new authoritarianism, others have condoned and adduced justification for these aberrant and manifestly undemocratic tendencies.

The ANC is, of course, by no means the only organisation whose members have been guilty of breaking up other parties' meetings. Members of the Azanian People's Organisation and the Pan Africanist Congress have been just as culpable. Some of us still remember that the NP itself was not above disrupting the United Party's meetings in the run-up to the 1948 poll, and former State President P W Botha was a chief culprit in this regard.

We know how successive NP governments subsequently went on to silence dissent and imprison their opponents for merely daring to speak out against them. We know also that some within the ANC have been generally very intolerant of dissent – even within their own ranks – and have at times been involved in violent conflict with the Azanian People's Organisation, the Pan Africanist Congress and now the IFP.

Could it be that the ANC, which prides itself at every opportunity on a commitment to democracy, will not be different from the NP governments which have oppressed its members? Will it, too, be guilty of not practising the democracy it preaches? If that is the case, then we should be told now, well in advance of the election. ANC president Nelson Mandela has proved a marvellous leader in times of challenge, most notably following the murder of Chris Hani in April. That leadership is again sorely needed. Mandela needs to speak out strongly against the intimidation of people and the disruption of other parties' meetings.

He and his colleagues should take strong action against the misguided hotheads who drag their organisation's name through the mud. And unless the ANC leadership does this, it will be very difficult to take seriously its oft-repeated calls for political tolerance.

Jiyane – Nobody's Yes-man

30 August 1993

The Inkatha Freedom Party (IFP) will not be the same again now that academic and former high-ranking Pan Africanist Congress (PAC) official Dr Ziba Jiyane is in charge of its publicity department.

That is the unanimous verdict of those who know Jiyane (34) well, both inside and outside the country. Jiyane, who was described as 'very, very intelligent', 'brilliant' and 'nobody's yes-man', was appointed last week as IFP national spokesman and communications director, a position which might see influential IFP central committee member Walter Felgate's high public profile taking a dive.

A former head of the PAC's Radio Freedom in the Tanzanian capital Dar-es-Salaam, Jiyane has undertaken to 'put the IFP's case as convincingly as possible', change the party's tattered image to help it win more votes in next year's election, 'and to contribute to the democratisation of our country'.

Like many others before him who began as advisers to Buthelezi, Jiyane has been *appointed* to the IFP's elastic central committee. But, unlike Joe Matthews who came to the IFP from the ANC, Jiyane – reportedly with an impressive academic record – has a history of being fiercely Africanist. Some even say he harbours a deep mistrust of whites and believes in an African leadership.

This Jiyane freely admits, but insists he is not racist. 'The spirit of self-reliance in any community is, for me, the key to any community's improvement. I am not racist, but I still strongly believe in African leadership and the cultural pride of Africa', he says.

Political analyst Dr Seshi Chonco, who has known the new IFP spokesman since 1976 during their days in the Inkatha Youth Brigade, has great respect for Jiyane: 'He takes longer to get convinced because he looks at all sides of issues: your thorough academic. Once he has taken a position he gets fixated with it and can fight to the grave,' says Chonco.

PAC national executive council member and Natal leader Joe Mkhwanazi, who as PAC administrative secretary in exile worked with Jiyane in Dar-es-Salaam, says: 'I respect the young man. He is nobody's yes-man. He is very independent. Even when he is wrong he is wrong independently. I'm sure when you meet him you will confirm what I am saying.'

Jiyane's description of himself does not differ from the one given by the two men.

'Whatever I do, I do it with good intentions. I like people. When I believe in a cause it's very difficult for me to be swayed, but I respect others' right to say what they believe. I am a fair person and I like people to respect what I believe in and never to question my motives because they will never know them'.

Mkhwanazi says Jiyane, with whom he has always had a good relationship, told him about six months ago about his unhappiness with the PAC's continued armed struggle.

Jiyane, who had in the past supported the armed struggle but had never undergone military training himself, felt the armed struggle had had its day and had to be called off. But even during that discussion, Jiyane did not hint he was about to jump ship.

Jiyane himself gives as his reasons for disaffection with the PAC the organisation's initial egg-dance regarding negotiations following its unbanning in 1990, its lukewarm attitude towards fellow Africans who were homeland leaders, disillusionment with 'the socialist rhetoric and practice', and, of course, the continuation of the armed struggle.

However, he attributes his initial political re-think to a discussion he had with an Azanian People's Organisation (Azapo) member in the United States. He was criticising the ANC and the IFP as usual for the violence in Natal when the Azapo man told him 'the IFP was merely standing up to the ANC', which had a history of violent confrontations with organisations differing with it. He did some research and found the Azapo man's views 'to be true'.

Armed with an MA from the University of California in Los Angeles (UCLA) and a JD (Juris Doctor) – ANC northern Natal leader and University of Zululand political studies and public administration head Professor Aaron Ndlovu says it is equivalent to a local LLB – from Yale University, Jiyane returned home early last year. He is now putting the finishing touches to his doctoral thesis.

Still a PAC member, he took a low political profile at Chonco's suggestion, delivered lectures on democracy at forums organised by the

Institute for Multi-party Democracy, and taught in the same department as Ndlovu at the University of Zululand until this month. And then Buthelezi – whom he met during a brief visit here in 1991 – came knocking, and he obeyed.

Both Chonco and Mkhwanazi think Felgate's star in the IFP might begin to wane now that Jiyane, a lucid thinker with a strong personality, has joined the IFP fold. Mkhwanazi says Jiyane is unlikely to endorse moves 'which could delay the freedom of the African people', and Chonco believes the new IFP man will considerably strengthen the moderate faction led by Matthews in the party.

Says another source: 'Jiyane is in favour of negotiations. He is opposed to war-talk, he hates Felgate, whom he thinks gives the IFP a bad name, and he distrusts whites. He thinks it is possible to strike a deal with the ANC, and that the ANC is ready to strike a deal with the IFP.'

But if Jiyane hates Felgate, he will not talk about it. Instead, he parries the question, saying he hates nobody in the IFP leadership 'because I have had no reason to hate anybody; maybe as we go on we may differ democratically with some people.'

He will have it known, however, that he, too, is firmly convinced the IFP's return to negotiations would serve little purpose while the party's input 'is of little value' because of the 'sufficient consensus' decision-making principle.

'Why should we go there to bless a process in which we are taken as a non-factor? That must be resolved [first]. It hurts us to hear people saying our views do not count,' he says.

Sisulu's Bombshell

1 September 1993

Walter Sisulu stunned delegates at a crucial ANC executive meeting by proposing that Professor Kader Asmal replace the late Oliver Tambo as ANC national chairman.

The proposal by Sisulu, ANC deputy president, was defeated as the majority of the national executive committee (NEC) rallied around foreign affairs director Thabo Mbeki, whose elevation to the national chairmanship was announced on Monday.

Impeccable sources within the ANC's leadership told *The Star* that Sisulu stunned the NEC at its meeting on Sunday, outside Kempton Park, when he moved that Asmal – an NEC member and University of the Western Cape academic – should succeed Tambo as national chairman. According to the sources, Sisulu had apparently been asked by ANC president Nelson Mandela – who did not enter the debate himself – to broach the subject of Asmal's candidacy.

The sources believe the 'top five' at the apex of the organisation's hierarchy – Mandela, Sisulu, treasurer-general Thomas Nkobi, secretary-general Cyril Ramaphosa and his deputy Jacob Zuma – had discussed the issue in advance and wanted a non-Xhosa, and preferably someone other than a black African, for the position. It was hoped this would counter perceptions that the ANC was a black-dominated, Xhosa-dominated body, according to the sources.

Before there could be a debate on the proposal on Asmal, African National Congress Youth League president Peter Mokaba put paid to the plan. Opposing the proposal, Mokaba said the national chairmanship was an important position for which an election should be held by secret ballot in the NEC.

Mokaba's argument in favour of an election – instead of a unanimous, unopposed appointment – was backed by most NEC members. Mbeki was then elected by an overwhelming majority, defeating Asmal, the only other candidate. Sources said Asmal performed 'very badly'. Some delegates expressed surprise that Asmal had been proposed for the position.

'I don't know why they thought of Asmal', said one. 'Not even his region would have supported him'.

Another added: 'In terms of addressing racial imbalances in the organisation, I have no problem with whites, coloureds and Indians rising to senior positions. But they, like Africans, must also go through the ranks and prove themselves'.

The Mbeki-Asmal debate is believed to reflect the serious concern at the very top of the ANC that the organisation's leadership should become more racially representative before the election campaign begins in earnest.

Mandela, who has often expressed his concern publicly that the top leadership is not sufficiently representative of South Africa's population, was accused in 1991 of having intervened to ensure the election of Dr Allan Boesak to the Western Cape regional chairmanship.

In terms of the ANC's structure, the national chairmanship is the third rung on the ladder, following the presidency and deputy presidency. Now Mbeki's promotion means the national chairmanship – a position held by his father Govan before the banning of the ANC – changes to a powerful, non-ceremonial post.

Many observers believe it now outranks the deputy presidency in practical terms, making Mbeki number two to Mandela. There is no certainty as to when Sisulu will retire, and who would be in line for his post when he does. It is understood that Ramaphosa would make himself available for the position – but many insiders see the deputy presidency as Mbeki's next logical step as Mandela's heir-apparent.

Camps: Cast Not First Stone

3 September 1993

The release of the Motsuenyane Commission's findings has triggered off vociferous calls for all kinds of punitive measures – including expulsion and a ban from public office – to be taken against those implicated in the widespread and now well-documented human rights abuses in the ANC's camps in exile.

Even yesterday's autocrats whose hands are far bloodier than those of the ANC have piously beaten their chests and joined in the deafening chorus demanding punishment for the ANC 'torturers and killers'. Predictably, National Party spokesman Marthinus van Schalkwyk – seeing an opportunity to gain political capital for a party whose fortunes have been gradually declining in its traditionally white constituency – called for drastic action against the alleged abusers.

The revelation – the fourth in less than a year – indicated yet again that an ANC government would be bad news for South Africa, said Van Schalkwyk. And, equally predictably, Democratic Party justice spokesman Tony Leon joined the fray, calling for the offenders to be handed over for trial or independent judicial scrutiny in the countries where the crimes were committed.

But as Van Schalkwyk and Leon no doubt know, there are many within the National Party today – some still serving in Government – who, through acts of commission or omission, have far worse things to answer for. These people roam the streets of our towns and cities as free men and some even continue to draw salaries from the public purse.

To be sure, the crimes of which *some* people within the ANC stand accused – wholesale torture, detention without trial, solitary confinement and executions – are indeed hair-raising, especially when one considers the organisation's long-standing opposition to authoritarianism and the evils which go with it.

But it is important to remember that many others within the ANC – people like Zola Skweyiya, Thenjiwe Mtintso and former victim Dr

Pallo Jordan immediately come to mind – were against the human rights abuses catalogued by the various commissions – more than can be said for successive NP governments. Deaths in detention still take place even in present-day South Africa, and – as in the case of Black Consciousness leader Steve Biko whose death left former Justice Minister Jimmy Kruger 'cold' – those implicated in these deaths have been let off without so much as a slap, thanks to the pervasive pro-white bias of many magistrates and some judges.

And various Law and Order Ministers – ranging from the late Louis le Grange, Adriaan Vlok and now Hernus Kriel – have been sued for millions by people whose relatives had come to harm while in custody. The ministers, of course, were in a much better position than the hapless ANC because they could use *our* money as taxpayers to pay any compensation that was awarded.

The human rights abuses listed in the Amnesty International, Douglas, Skweyiya and Motsuenyane Commissions' reports are damning, and the ANC must be pressured to implement most of the commissions' reasonable recommendations. A public apology – such as the one issued this week – is in order, reparations to victims or their families are a must, and a strong censure of the individuals involved in the atrocities is a necessity.

But how far should the organisation go? Should it, as some of the commissions recommend, go as far as expelling the culprits from its ranks and barring them from public office for life? This seems particularly harsh considering that these aberrations were committed in the organisation's name and service. Which would explain the ANC leadership's wise decision to accept collective responsibility.

Admittedly, some within the ANC's intelligence and security establishment were over-zealous in the execution of their duties. However, the fact remains that the organisation was involved in a deadly war with Pretoria and that it was being infiltrated by agents whose actions cost the lives of many Umkhonto weSizwe cadres. That is the context within which the violations occurred.

And so while some gung-ho people within the ANC committed atrocities to supplant apartheid in this country, others within the NP have executed equally dastardly deeds – such as staging cross-border raids and in the process killing innocent people – in an effort to protect apartheid. Whatever the motives, neither of them has clean hands, and this goes for many other parties and organisations. The NP can cast the first stone only if its hands are cleaner.

A little perspective and balance are needed in assessing the way the ANC has dealt with the allegations which have dogged it since its unbanning in 1990. Thanks to Nelson Mandela's leadership – he appointed the first two commissions – the ANC has handled this embarrassing event quite well.

It has had the courage to appoint the commissions – albeit under considerable pressure from its detractors and the press – and to make their findings public. For that it has to be commended. The human rights violations will no doubt return to haunt the organisation in the electioneering that lies ahead, but so, too, will the apartheid past dog the NP.

The Humble Mbeki

3 September 1993

Newly elected ANC national chairman Thabo Mbeki has great difficulty talking about himself or the powerful position he now occupies in the organisation he joined at 14.

He prefers to talk about the ANC instead, and even then down-plays the role he has filled. Mbeki (51), it soon becomes clear, is a humble man not given to blowing his own trumpet. Elected national chairman at the end of the ANC's three-day national executive committee (NEC) meeting last weekend, Mbeki, who succeeds the late Oliver Tambo whom he once served loyally and with distinction in exile, has begun to gear himself for the challenges that lie ahead in the run-up to the country's first all-inclusive election next year.

Repay

He has no doubt he will be equal to the job and repay the confidence shown in him by the majority of NEC members when they installed him in the position ahead of the only other candidate, University of the Western Cape academic, Professor Kader Asmal, whom sources said fared 'very badly'.

As the new national chairman, Mbeki's constitutional responsibilities include presiding over national conferences, ensuring that conference resolutions are implemented and seeing to it that 'the organisation functions as it ought to function'. He sees his main responsibility within the next few months as overseeing the formulation of the ANC's election manifesto and ensuring that it falls strictly within the ANC's policy guidelines, and ascertaining the ANC's readiness to conduct – and win – an election campaign.

He will liaise very closely with the secretary-general, treasurer-general and president's offices, and will receive reports from the ANC's election commission. The top six people on the ANC hierarchy – referred to as 'officials' – meet regularly to discuss and co-ordinate the organisation's day-to-day work. At these meetings are the president, his deputy, the national chairman, the secretary-general and the treasurer-general.

Of the six, Mandela, Sisulu and treasurer-general Nkobi are all older than 70.

'The position [of national chairman] means maintaining contact with all the structures of the ANC, understanding their problems and helping them deal with them. In a sense, it is going to mean keeping an ear to the ground,' Mbeki says.

Although the ANC Youth League, which is solidly behind him, sees the national chairmanship as a transit position en route to the deputy presidency, and eventually the presidency, for Mbeki, he himself is noncommittal and even coy about it. He has no ambitions, he says, and merely sees the elevation as an opportunity to serve the ANC in another capacity.

'I have been in the ANC since 1956, and at no point did anyone of us in my generation approach the issue of participation in the struggle with an eye to positions of leadership. With the situation what it was then, what we knew was that we might die [fighting]. The idea that we could become professional politicians was never there. The idea of aspiring to a leadership position has not been part of our political upbringing,' he says.

Mbeki will not comment on speculation that his new position now makes him, as advocated by the AnCYL, heir-apparent to Mandela. That question, he says, does not arise because deputy president Sisulu – 'a man that all of us like and respect' – is doing 'a very good job'. Although many outside the ANC were surprised in June when the AnCYL publicly threw its weight behind Mbeki for the deputy presidency – the idea being that Sisulu would assume the then ceremonial chairmanship – Mbeki himself was not taken aback.

Unknown to the general public, he has worked closely with the youth and other structures of the ANC, often addressing small gatherings on negotiations, peace, problems facing the youth and many other issues. This he has done away from the glare of the media. The repeated criticism of him as a man aloof from the masses is incorrect, he says. But is he, as many believe, a moderate?

Mbeki hesitates. Then he spells out what he feels passionately about: violence should end, the much-awaited election should lead to a real democracy and the impoverished masses' concerns have to be addressed. If that makes him a moderate, then he is not much bothered.

'I think the leadership of the ANC has a very important responsibility to lead not just the ANC but also the whole country, and I think that job needs to be done in a very responsible manner. It would be wrong of me or anyone else to make promises just to get an ovation when we know the promises will never be fulfilled.'

Unprompted, Mbeki discusses the speculation that he and secretary-general Cyril Ramaphosa are competing for Sisulu's job. He categorically denies any competition or tension between them, and reveals that when Ramaphosa was elected secretary-general at the Durban congress in July 1991 he offered him his co-operation.

Resources

'I took him from the hall where the meeting took place to the hotel where I was staying and I had a drink with him. I said to him: "Chief, consider us as resources in your job." That has characterised our relationship ever since,' he says.

Mbeki remains international affairs director for the moment. This matter is receiving attention from the organisation, but someone would have to be found to succeed him, thereby enabling him to concentrate on his new job as national chairman.

Mbeki Now Well Placed for Top Job

4 September 1993

The elevation of the suave ANC international affairs director Thabo Mbeki to the organisation's national chairmanship earlier this week marked the culmination of intensive behind-the-scenes manoeuvres by Peter Mokaba's ANC Youth League (AnCYL) and others.

Mbeki, who has done very well as the man in charge of the ANC's international affairs – at its unbanning in 1990, the ANC had more offices abroad than Pretoria – will bring to his new position sound judgment and a sharp intellect. At 51, Mbeki now appears on the verge of bigger things, and his many admirers inside and outside the ANC believe the world is his to conquer.

He is number three in the ANC hierarchy, behind its president Nelson Mandela and his deputy Walter Sisulu. Both men, however, are cruising gently – some would say roughly, considering their often punishing schedules – towards retirement: Mandela is 75 and Sisulu 81.

Following the assassination of extremely popular ANC-South African Communist Party leader Chris Hani – Mbeki's opponent for the deputy presidency in the run-up to the July 1991 ANC national congress in Durban, before both men timeously withdrew from the race in favour of Sisulu – Mbeki's only serious competitor for Sisulu's job is the skilled secretary-general Cyril Ramaphosa.

Both men are capable and well respected in the movement. Both are good and quite effective in their respective jobs, but they, too, have their detractors in the ANC, an organisation Hani once privately described as 'an omnibus'. Unlike Ramaphosa, Mbeki has the solid backing of the influential AnCYL.

This organisation will not rest until he has stepped into Mandela's shoes when the hour comes. While Ramaphosa established himself as a trade unionist and activist inside the country, Mbeki made his mark as a consummate ANC diplomat in exile. Other names which have been bandied about for the deputy presidency when it finally becomes available are those of soldierly PWV regional chairman Tokyo Sexwale, who shot to national prominence and therefore some contention for the position after Hani's murder – and deputy secretary-general Jacob Zuma.

But according to Mokaba, Zuma – whose candidature must have been seriously damaged by allegations of human rights abuses in ANC camps in exile – is himself an Mbeki man and would gladly stand aside for the man who was apprenticed to the late Oliver Tambo.

Mbeki's advancement to the national chairmanship has been long in coming. In an exclusive interview with *The Star* in June, Mokaba revealed that the AnCYL had formally taken a position that the former SACP politburo member should become deputy president as soon as possible.

Sisulu, he said, would then assume what was at the time the largely ceremonial role of national chairman. Mokaba rattled off Mbeki's qualifications: he was intelligent and respected by all 'factions' in the ANC, was a key strategist who had worked with Tambo for years, had infiltrated South Africa on Umkhonto weSizwe missions, and had a good education from both the West and the East.

Mokaba, of the 'kill the boer, kill the farmer' chant controversy, was criticised by some in the ANC for making public what they saw as an internal matter. His harshest critic was Sexwale, who accused the AnCYL leader of 'engaging in pendulum politics' because of his suggestion that townships should be turned into tourist attractions. But Sexwale also attacked Mokaba's factual account of the meeting.

The matter, he said, had been raised by the AnCYL and was subsequently discussed 'briefly' before it was disposed with, never to be heard of again. But as things turned out, at the August 27–29 national executive committee (NEC) meeting, Sexwale was wrong. The matter did come up again – even though it was precipitated by Sisulu's unexpected nomination of academic and NEC member Professor Kader Asmal for the job – and Mbeki was voted national chairman by the overwhelming majority of NEC members.

Despite the AnCYL's belief that Mbeki is now well placed to succeed Mandela as ANC leader and president of South Africa when the time comes, the battle is by no means over. Admittedly, Mbeki is now in a formidable position, but anything could happen. As the general election approaches, the low-scale jockeying – first for inclusion in the ANC-led tripartite alliance's election lists and then for senior positions in government – will intensify.

Already the AnCYL has called for the formation of a 'shadow Cabinet' in readiness for governing after April 27, and observers' attention will inevitably centre on who between Ramaphosa and Mbeki will become prime minister.

F W in KwaZulu Quandary

20 September 1993

If Chief Mangosuthu Buthelezi approached his crucial meeting with President de Klerk on Thursday with any hope that some of his demands might be met, then he must have left Cape Town a disappointed man.

For Buthelezi must have known – he had said at the beginning of the meeting he did not think there was much the two leaders could talk about – that chances of De Klerk giving in to his comprehensive demands were slim if not non-existent. And not just because De Klerk is unwilling to make more concessions to the IFP leader whom he is now desperately trying to appease in an effort to woo him back into negotiations, but because he is simply unable to accommodate the KwaZulu Chief Minister more than he and the ANC have already done.

Buthelezi's 10-page 'preliminary remarks' – which he makes at the beginning of every important meeting he holds – to De Klerk on Thursday were very revealing. More than anything else, they indicated clearly what Buthelezi sees as his bottom line, and showed yet again that nothing anybody does will satisfy him.

In what can only be described as a terrible dressing down of De Klerk, Buthelezi demanded nothing less than the scrapping of the present multi-party negotiations and agreements reached in that process, notably the holding of South Africa's first all-inclusive elections on April 27. By so doing, he put De Klerk in a tight corner: while he is eager to accommodate Buthelezi and in the process keep his own National Party together, the concessions the chief now asks for are simply not his to give.

Vehicles

But back to the 'preliminary remarks'. Buthelezi sees these as vehicles for him to put his own concerns and priorities upfront, thereby ensuring the things he holds dear are discussed in the meetings.

His interlocutors, however, see them differently. ANC president Nelson Mandela, Archbishop Desmond Tutu, foreign leaders and ambassadors based here have often found themselves vehemently criticised and chided in Buthelezi's 'preliminary remarks' before meeting with him. Depending on the outcome of the meeting, such statements are sometimes not released to the press. And the fact that Buthelezi found it necessary to release his preliminary statement on Thursday, only about an hour before the end of the meeting, was the first signal that all had not gone well at Tuynhuys.

Clearly, Buthelezi is unhappy about what he sees as the Government's collusion with the ANC at the expense of his party, and he said so to De Klerk.

He is upset that negotiations have gone on without the IFP and KwaZulu while they were halted following the ANC's withdrawal from Codesa 2 last year, and he said so. He accused Government negotiators of not understanding 'black politics', accused the Government of having moved away from policies it once shared with the IFP, accused Pretoria of not taking seriously what he says, said the agreed-upon transitional executive council could take actions which 'could crash the financial operation and institutional autonomy of the KwaZulu government', and that his government would not implement agreements reached in the Negotiating Council.

He is also resentful about the international credit going to the Government and the ANC for progress in negotiations, and condemns 'the smiling, the receiving of [awards] and boastings that the talks were still within the time-frames that were agreed upon between the Government and the ANC/SACP alliance'.

Then he dropped the bombshell: negotiations must be halted and a national constitutional convention be called 'to review the negotiations mess we are in'. He told De Klerk and members of his Cabinet: 'We must now pause and reconsider what is happening in negotiations. This is probably the only reason for my being here today. If we cannot pause to do so, and if the South African government cannot even contemplate the putting off of the proposed election in April next year while we review things and find a way forward, then there is no need for me to be here.'

Blackmail

Increasingly isolated here and abroad, Buthelezi then resorted to emotional blackmail and the kind of threats he has recently been making: he would resign as IFP leader if the party's general conference decided against his wish to return to negotiations, and Pretoria would be responsible for 'the dramatic consequences' if it did not heed his calls.

But if Buthelezi is such a democrat, why would he resign and not abide by the decision of the majority of IFP members if they voted in favour of co-operation with other parties and organisations? His threats are hardly necessary.

Political observers know, and some of his top Cabinet Ministers privately agree, that he is *the* driving force behind the IFP and that the party's general conference and central committee often endorse whatever he wants. He need not fear that they might go against him. Buthelezi has now dared public opinion here and in the international community to do their damndest.

'No amount of pressure from within or from the international community will have any effect on me. I cannot be pressurised into persuading the people of this region (Natal-KwaZulu) to commit suicide,' he said.

From a man who used to be sensitive to gentle proddings from Washington DC, London and Bonn, this is very worrisome. South Africans should not be fooled by De Klerk's smiles at the end of the summit, the joint committees agreed upon and the undertaking to meet again. No progress was registered at what sources described as an acrimonious meeting.

It is now important for De Klerk to consider the options open to him to give legitimacy to agreements reached in negotiations, and calling a national and all-inclusive referendum might be the answer.

Volkstaat Might Avoid Unnecessary Conflict

30 September 1993

The four pieces of legislation agreed upon in multi-party negotiations at the World Trade Centre last month and passed by Parliament last week now usher in a new era in South African politics.

As commentators have rightly observed, the establishment of the Transitional Executive Council (TEC) – an issue which has touched raw nerves in black and white right-wing circles – means that for the first time in our chequered history blacks will have a role in the running of the country, albeit on a limited scale and in specifically defined areas.

It is an important stage in our transition since it clearly marks the interregnum: the end of the hideous past and the beginning of a new and hopefully democratic future. Given the importance of the phase, it was perhaps inevitable that the Government would seek to downplay the significance of the development in an attempt to allay the fears of its traditional support base, and that the ANC and its allies would read more into the agreement to give their followers the impression that a major victory has been won.

Neither side would be farther from the truth. For while the TEC will have considerable powers in those areas covered by its sub-councils, the National Party will remain the *de jure* Government of the country. Obviously, there will have to be a lot of give-and-take between the two.

Important though the four pieces of legislation may be – on the TEC, the Independent Media Commission, the Independent Electoral Commission and the Independent Broadcasting Authority – they have not been welcomed with glee by the Inkatha Freedom Party (IFP) and its fellow right-wing allies. These have reacted with the usual sabre-rattling and have threatened fire and brimstone, calling the proposed TEC a declaration of war.

In the same week the Conservative Party (CP) was making a spectacle of itself in what must now certainly be the last white Parliament – with one more short session scheduled for November – and it was revealed that the Afrikaner Volksfront (AVF), an umbrella organisation for a host of right-wing parties, had held a series of bilateral talks with the ANC.

In a subsequent joint statement, the ANC and the AVF committed themselves to a peaceful resolution of their differences, shared 'an overriding desire' to work for reconciliation between the 'two important sectors of citizens' represented by their organisations and disclosed that their talks had been characterised by 'frankness, mutual respect and sincerity'.

They revealed further that more discussions would take place and be intensified 'as a matter of urgency'.

'All participants were sincere in their desire to prevent further polarisation and possible war which would not be in the interest of anyone or the country as a whole,' said AVF leader General Constand Viljoen and ANC chairman Thabo Mbeki in the statement.

Predictably, Viljoen was criticised by other right-wing groups for holding talks with the ANC, with Herstigte Nasionale Party leader Jaap Marais accusing him of secret motives and political naivete. In an interview with this paper, Viljoen subsequently stressed that he wanted to eschew a civil war in this country as much as possible. He described himself as a politically non-aligned soldier, and expressed the hope that his people's aspirations would be accommodated.

Given the fact that surveys consistently show that the majority of South Africans have no sympathy for the coterie of black and white right-wingers, it would be easy to dismiss out of hand Viljoen's demands for provision to be made in the new dispensation for his people's self-determination. That, however, is a temptation we should not easily give in to because we might later rue that decision.

The right wing may be a menace, but it is a reality which cannot be wished away. No effort should be spared in accommodating those of its demands which are reasonable and separating those right-wing leaders who are amenable to reason from those whose racial prejudices blind them to reason. As Viljoen and Mbeki said in their joint statement, a civil war will not be in the interest of any group, least of all propertied white South Africans, who have much to lose from it.

If civil war finally does break out, we as a nation must be able to say all possibilities were considered to accommodate those who might one day resort to violence on a scale not yet seen. And what might be the right wing's 'reasonable' demands? Given their fear of wholesale change, it might not be a bad idea to let people like Viljoen and the

Afrikaner Volksfront have their 'volkstaat'.

They should have something to show for their involvement in negotiations, thus giving peace a chance. The proviso, however, would have to be that a 'volkstaat' remains part of a united, federal South Africa, that its laws do not contravene the Bill of Rights, and that non-Afrikaners living there will have the rights enjoyed by other South Africans.

The right wing would have to be told to come up with *practical* proposals about the location and size of such a 'volkstaat', and it would have to be made clear to them that forced removals of people would not be countenanced. Once established, the 'volkstaat' would then form one of the regions in the new South Africa.

Although this would be unacceptable to other right-wing groups, indications are that the AVF and Viljoen's followers could well embrace the idea. The same, of course, would have to apply to the IFP in KwaZulu-Natal. And what do we stand to lose by making this concession? Nothing, instead we would be doing our best to avoid unnecessary conflict. The alternative, as the saying goes, is 'too ghastly to contemplate'.

Black Takeover can Save DP

11 October 1993

About two months ago I attended a day-long Johannesburg conference on liberalism, where a motley of white liberals listened to speeches on the new threat facing liberal values both in present-day South Africa and in the future.

Also present, of course, were a few token black faces, with at least two of them – the DP's Stephen Ntsane from the Western Cape and Anglo American communications officer Jabu Maphalala – also addressing the august gathering.

Although not many were as explicit as the DP's Johannesburg councillor Jack Bloom – whose meeting on Orange Farm outside Johannesburg was violently disrupted two weeks before the conference – it was generally accepted that the biggest threat facing liberals and liberal values in South Africa today came from the ANC and others on the Left.

The Democratic Party and the Inkatha Freedom Party – at least *one* person in that distinguished audience challenged the IFP's inclusion in the list of angels – were the good guys who had to band together and jealously guard against the violation of that which they held dear.

Perhaps this was to be expected. After all, the conference had been organised by that once universally respected body, the South African Institute of Race Relations, whose reputation as a non-partisan institution now lies in tatters. To many, it has become a fiercely anti-ANC organisation, with the IFP and the DP being the only parties the institute tends to lean towards.

Misleading

It was the caveat which was sounded from the floor by the Institute for Multiparty Democracy's Reverend Richard Mkholo that caught my attention. It was misleading, Mkholo warned, to associate liberal values – as many were doing at the conference – with only the DP.

There were, he said, many black people in this country who warmly embraced liberal values – individual liberty, freedom of speech and expression, a free/social market economy – who would not be seen dead in DP circles. That, for me, was the most important contribution made at that conference but, unfortunately, one did not get the impression it was taken seriously.

For while 'liberal' (in the South African context the word conjures up images of well-meaning but often paternalistic whites) may or may not equal DP, 'liberal democrat' does not – and should not necessarily – equal DP. And that explains to some extent why the DP has not found it easy to sell itself to blacks.

The difference between the two may indeed turn out to be merely semantic, but the blacks who hold liberal values dear would feel much more comfortable with 'liberal democratic' than with the former label. The many black South Africans who embrace liberal values and share the DP's vision for the future would tend to be mostly politically sophisticated, well-educated and professional people realistic enough to know the country needs more than mere slogans if it is to develop and realise its full potential.

They may be sceptical of the ANC and its policies, and might feel it would not be good for democracy if any one party or organisation in the country obtained a landslide in the coming election and therefore did not feel obliged to be attentive to the electorate's wishes once it is comfortably ensconced in power.

However, these people are not about to rush helter-skelter to seek membership of the party which, to this day, they usually associate with wealth and big business. To many of them DP still equals white, liberal, hopelessly idealistic and often rich.

It is these perceptions which stand between the DP and the black middle class. And those who have now joined the DP – such as Ntsane, former University of the Western Cape rector Professor Dick van der Ross and former ANC activist Joe Marks – will continue to be pejoratively referred to as the party's 'big catches'.

Reports on the party's national congress in Cape Town more than a week ago monotonously pointed out that almost half the number of delegates were 'black or coloured', as though that were reason enough for the DP to be self-congratulatory and pat itself on the back.

The DP might find it easier to compete with the National Party for the votes of some 'ordinary' members of the black community who might be disillusioned with the ANC and the Inkatha Freedom Party –

which some strongly associate with the violence ripping the country apart – but it will be an uphill battle when it comes to getting the educated, black middle class's support.

That, ironically, would make them much more receptive to the DP's message. Were it not for the fact that the DP was seen as a party of mostly rich whites who often wanted to stay above the dust of party politics, and were it not for the fact that many blacks who embraced liberal values would generally hate to be called 'liberals' – an insult in certain political circles – the DP would do much better among blacks.

With things as they stand now, nothing short of a total 'takeover' of the party's leadership by blacks could save the DP as a viable alternative to the ANC and the NP.

And that means more than just having a certain acceptable number of coloured, Indian and African faces on the party's federal council. That, however, might be something for which the DP might not yet be ready. The current crop of DP leadership is no doubt a capable lot, but for as long as mention of the party's name evokes pictures of only Dr Zach de Beer, Tony Leon, Douglas Gibson, Ken Andrew *et al*, the DP will find it difficult to woo many quality black liberal democrats to its ranks.

No Justification for Mob-style Killing

18 October 1996

There is a name for the horrendous murder of five children at an Umtata, Transkei, house during a South African Defence Force (SADF) raid in the early hours of the morning slightly more than a week ago: State terrorism.

It was, as the independent violence-monitoring organisation Peace Action said last week, 'an act of terrorism as unwarranted as the St James massacre' in Cape Town in July.

The cold-blooded killing of children aged between 12 and 19 by the SADF is as shocking and barbaric as the murder of people in that attack on a church in Cape Town, or the murder of American exchange student Amy Biehl in a township in the Western Cape for no reason other than that she was white.

But for a government to authorise a Mafia-style execution of its citizens, such as Pretoria has implicitly admitted to having done, is much, much more shocking – especially at this sensitive time in our history.

As usual, the Government says it has 'conclusive evidence' that the Sgqibo Pendulo household in Umtata was a training house for the PAC's Azanian People's Liberation Army (Apla), blamed for many racist attacks on whites in the country.

None of the documents allegedly seized by the SADF during the raid, now in possession of this newspaper, remotely confirms this 'conclusive evidence'. But even if the assassinated children were indeed Apla cadres – this the family has vehemently denied – and even if there was any evidence directly linking them to any attacks on whites in the country, Pretoria's bully-boy display of power would still have deserved the strongest censure possible.

State terrorism and Mafia-style execution of suspects have no place in present-day South Africa – or in any civilised country, for that matter. The thing to do would have been for the police to round up the alleged

Apla members together with the entire chain in command through which the orders to kill came.

At the very least, ever-bungling Defence Minister Kobie Coetsee should also be given the boot. Immediately. Then the Transitional Executive Council's sub-council on defence should have complete joint control of the security forces.

We should not allow the Government and the security forces to dispense jungle justice to those we dislike, because tomorrow we could be the ones on the receiving end of similarly diabolic actions.

Today the PAC's Apla, tomorrow it could be – who knows? – the newly formed Freedom Alliance or the Afrikaner Volksfront. It's a very chilling thought, indeed.

Repent, F W, Before Receiving the Nobel

1 November 1993

The furore which greeted the announcement two weeks ago that President de Klerk and Nelson Mandela had been awarded this year's Nobel Peace Prize was predictable.

It was to be expected that some would seek to make political capital from what should have served as a unifying moment of triumph for South Africa. Not many, however, took issue with the Nobel committee for giving the prize to Mandela. It was De Klerk they tore apart, arguing that extending the award to Mandela and him was like equating the jailer with the prisoner, the oppressor with the victim, Beelzebub with Lucifer.

Neither man is an angel, but they are indeed deserving of the award: Mandela for his courageous and principled fight against apartheid over the years, and De Klerk for the moves he took on February 2 1990 to normalise politics in this country.

That is not to say they are equally deserving of the award: the ANC leader is without doubt more deserving of it. It is, instead, recognition of the fact that South Africa would not be where it is now had De Klerk not taken the actions he did.

He has split the once monolithic Afrikanerdom down the middle and some of his own *volk* call him a traitor. He had the vision to take the course of action he embarked upon and consequently took timeous action to steer our beloved country away from the precipice on which it was delicately poised. For that he deserves recognition.

De Klerk has at times also made breathtaking errors of judgement, the most notorious being his authorisation of the Umtata raid in which children were recently butchered. That was an incredible lapse reminiscent of the *kragdadigheid* of old.

Before the President travels to Norway to receive the Nobel Peace Prize with Mandela on December 10, he needs to make an unconditional apology for both the ill-advised raid and apartheid. He has so far defended both things, and has said the architects of apartheid were well-meaning and well-intentioned individuals whose social experimentation did not work out.

His two half-hearted attempts at an apology for the inequities of apartheid have so far been carefully hedged and conditional. He will have to do better than that, for if he does not do so he will be reminded a hundred times in the next six months. Fortunately for him, he need look no further than Leon Wessels for a lesson on an unconditional *mea culpa*.

Accountability from people holding public office is important in a democracy, and some of De Klerk's Cabinet colleagues and some homeland leaders score very low in this regard.

In recent weeks Justice and Defence Minister Kobie Coetsee and Lebowa Chief Minister Nelson Ramodike wanted to send civil servants to programmes such as *Agenda* and *Newsline* to defend their various actions. Somehow they seem to think they do either the interviewers or the public a favour by availing themselves for interviews.

Squatter Debacle Hurts ANC

10 November 1993

Whoever had the brainwave to get black squatters to move into unoccupied houses designated for coloureds and Indians in Tafelsig and Cato Manor was either a genius or an absolute dunce.

If the intention was to strain race relations further and do incalculable harm to the African National Congress's non-racial image in the run-up to the election, then getting frustrated blacks, who had spent years on housing waiting lists, to move into houses designated for others was the right move.

If not, then it is safe to say the ANC won't easily forgive them. Already, Nelson Mandela has distanced his organisation from the illegal occupations, strongly implying that the National Party was behind the contretemps in an attempt to discredit the ANC in the eyes of coloured and Indian voters, most of whom are already quite sceptical about his organisation.

If those behind the occupations genuinely believed they could successfully take over houses set aside for coloureds and Indians, the strategy may prove incredibly short-sighted. Whatever the reasons, the occupations have done the ANC tremendous harm in the communities.

This observation is backed up by the recently published results of an important survey commissioned by the Washington-based International Republican Institute (IRI). The survey shows that coloureds and Indians – especially coloureds – are apprehensive about the country's political future, and, in general, find themselves closer to the attitudes of whites on many issues.

All three communities – Indians, coloureds and Africans – have been oppressed and disadvantaged under apartheid to varying degrees, and the once better-off Indians and coloureds are worried that a future black-dominated government will turn the tables, putting the interests of Africans first at their expense.

Palpable tensions

Already, some charge that affirmative action is just an excuse to advance Africans ahead of them and whites in the workplace. These tensions are palpable in the Western Cape, where coloureds, who have for years been beneficiaries of a coloured preferential employment policy, now fear seeing the same policy being applied in favour of Africans.

At the root of the tensions is fierce competition for scarce resources, and perceptions that one group will be favoured at the expense of others do not help matters. But if the findings of the important IRI survey are anything to go by, there is not much the ANC can do to change the attitudes of coloureds or win their confidence between now and next year's election.

Perhaps more disturbing for the organisation, the majority of coloureds interviewed for the survey were quite conservative, sharing with whites important concerns and reservations about the country's future. The startling findings of the survey, which was intended to establish 'a benchmark of attitudes among potential voters in South Africa in order for workers in the political field to understand the political environment in which election preparations are being conducted', included, among others, are the revelations that:

- Most whites (60 percent) and coloureds (43 percent) want the present flag and national anthem to stay the same after the elections, while the majority of Africans (71 percent) and Indians (49 percent) want them to change.
- Although most whites (67 percent) and Africans (78 percent) think Africans will control the government next year, most coloureds (52 percent) think otherwise: they see whites continuing to control government after the election, and largely agree with whites that Africans would 'make a mess of this country'.
- Most South Africans (aggregate 51 percent) say they are 'extremely likely' to vote in next year's elections, with the percentage of whites (67 percent) and Africans (63 percent) much higher than for coloureds (35 percent) and Indians (18 percent).

The implications of the survey are clear for the ANC: although most of the coloureds interviewed across the country favoured political change, they nevertheless did not want the present status quo altered beyond recognition. Even more surprisingly, most of them would be happier with a white-led government in Pretoria.

Election machine

This makes them much more vulnerable to NP propaganda as President de Klerk's redoubtable and well-oiled election machine moves into top gear within the next few weeks. It will be relatively easy to convince them that their interests as a group will be better protected by the NP.

Although equally apprehensive about the future, most Indians are fairly open-minded about next year's regional and national elections. Their ideological/political preferences do not readily come through from the findings of the survey, and the majority seems to be undecided.

Issues like violence are a great concern, but it seems they can be persuaded to give a fairly sympathetic hearing to most of the big parties which will contest the elections.

The IRI survey also shows that most Africans have dangerously high expectations of a new government and consequently see the April 27 elections and undoubted ANC victory as a panacea for all their social, economic and political problems. This, too, has serious implications for an ANC-led government of national unity: while coloureds and Indians will also expect to benefit from the new dispensation, Africans – on the lowest rung of the economic ladder – will consider it their right to receive preferential treatment from a Mandela-led government.

Balancing Africans' high expectations and aspirations against the fears and concerns of whites, coloureds and Indians will require a skilful, trapeze-like performance from the elderly ANC leader and his government.

But as ANC PWV regional secretary Paul Mashatile said last week, it may well be that *realpolitik* will dictate a simpler electoral strategy for the ANC – that in these elections the organisation might be best served by expending most of its energies and resources on the African vote, with only token efforts in the white, coloured and Indian communities.

SA Moves Closer to Joint Rule

27 November 1993

South Africa yesterday moved closer to its first phase of joint rule, with the installation of the multi-party Transitional Executive Council now only days away.

The TEC, whose establishment some right wing groups have described as a declaration of war, has its first meeting scheduled for December 8. President de Klerk yesterday signed a proclamation calling on the parties and organisations which have participated in multi-party talks since they resumed on April 1 this year to nominate people to serve on the TEC and its seven sub-councils, a well-placed government source confirmed last night.

This was done at the request of multi-party negotiators at the World Trade Centre, and a notice proclaiming the TEC was to have appeared in a special *Government Gazette* yesterday. Although the TEC's establishment will effectively mean the beginning of joint rule or power-sharing, the Government will continue to run the country, with the TEC having authority only over defined areas related to the April 27 election.

Agreement on observers

In terms of the agreements reached, all 29 parties that were part of the multi-party talks which resumed on April 1 this year – including the Freedom Alliance (FA) which subsequently walked out – qualify to nominate people to serve on the TEC and its sub-councils. So far, no FA member has indicated a willingness to serve on the TEC.

According to sources, each party has until midnight on Monday to submit the name of its representative on the council. De Klerk is expected to announce, in a *Government Gazette*, the names of people who will be on the TEC on December 6 – two days before the council's first meeting.

On a day when the Democratic Party failed to get discussion reopened on the number of ballot papers to be used in next year's national and regional elections, negotiators also agreed to formally request international bodies such as the United Nations and the European Community to send observers to monitor next year's election and to take part in the Independent Electoral Commission, which will run the election.

The DP, which last week reluctantly agreed to a single ballot in the election in return for a deal removing political intervention in the appointment of judges for the still-to-be-established Constitutional Court, submitted a resolution to the Negotiating Council asking that the debate be reopened 'to attempt to achieve a solution which has the support of as abroad a consensus of parties as possible.'

Supported only by the Pan Africanist Congress, the DP lost the fight to reopen the debate, with the ANC and the Government warning against revisiting of any issue already agreed to. They said the transitional constitutional package adopted by the November 17 plenary session of leaders was based on compromise, and that reopening debate on any one issue could lead to similar demands from other parties on other matters.

The council was emptier than usual, with the Afrikaner Volksunie conspicuous by its absence.

South African Communist Party chairman Joe Slovo accused the DP of 'a dishonourable attempt' to renege on the earlier agreement, but he later admitted in a statement to Sapa that the single ballot agreement was not ideal.

'We know that their [the DP's] word is not their bond. To put it at its lowest, if accepted, it [the DP's demand] will bring great discredit to the very culture of negotiations,' Slovo said.

Disappointed DP negotiator Ken Andrew told *Saturday Star* his party now doubted the ANC-led alliance's commitment to strong regional/federal government. His scepticism, he said, was strengthened by the fact that the alliance was insisting on having people who did not necessarily live in a region to be in its election list for that region.

Negotiators yesterday also agreed to be involved in a R250 000 election-monitoring conference to take place from December 8–10. Funding for the multi-party conference will come from both the EC and the Government. The Electoral Bill, to be passed by Parliament together with the Interim Constitution, will be distributed in the Negotiating Council on Tuesday, and discussion on some aspects of the document is expected to be finalised on Wednesday.

By then, the reincorporation of TBVC states into South Africa as well as the transfer of Walvis Bay and the off-shore island to Namibia will have been debated.

Only the Beginning

29 November 1993

Four important field-levelling pieces of legislation concluded at the World Trade Centre (WTC) were passed by Parliament during its short session in September. Two months later, Parliament has again convened to pass another set of agreements: this time the Interim Constitution and the Electoral Act.

Also to bite the dust during this session is a host of discriminatory laws and those impeding free political activity in some homelands, and these products of apartheid are themselves set to bid us a farewell. We as South Africans are, therefore, making history, and we should be proud of what has been achieved so far. We have sailed through stormy seas – remember the assassination of Chris Hani and the countrywide police swoop on PAC members and leaders early this year? – and the delicate negotiations process has survived. The road ahead is sure to be even tougher.

Impressive though it is, the constitutional package which emerged from the WTC is not perfect. Insofar as it is an important breakthrough which paves the way for a better – and hopefully democratic – future, it is to be welcomed, but we should also acknowledge some of its glaring shortcomings.

Since the ANC and the Government finally bowed to public pressure and desisted from an agreement which would have bestowed upon us a politically loaded constitutional court, the most important thing which now needs to be revisited urgently is the question of a single ballot paper in next year's elections.

This is a terrible smirch on the Electoral Act. It, more than anything, will severely disadvantage small, regional parties in the coming elections. Like most of the pre-concluded agreements foisted on negotiators by the ANC and the Government, this is a deal struck between two parties which believe themselves to be in the running for power.

It shows clearly that the ANC and the Government will not be happy with power at the centre only, but want all the power that can possibly be obtained. They want absolute power – and we know what absolute power does to politicians.

This is inimical to democracy, notwithstanding the many checks and balances built into the Interim Constitution. This deal deprives South Africans of the opportunity to vote for one party in the national election and for another one in their regions, as sometimes happens in other countries.

If the elections will be for the national assembly and regional legislatures, then South Africans should be allowed to cast two votes. The ANC and the Government would do well to allow themselves to be persuaded against this illiberal and undemocratic deal of theirs.

So Azapo has finally decided to take part in next year's elections without contesting them. If you find this confusing, then you are not alone. And we should not hesitate to pay compliments where they are due: at least the organisation now masters that special art of doublespeak long perfected by the National Party.

Patience, they say, is a virtue: we will wait to see just what form that participation in the elections will take, and whether it will in the end translate into contesting the elections if the ANC and the PAC should be agreeable to an election front.

Who's Who and What's What of the TEC

8 December 1993

The inaugural meeting of the Transitional Executive Council (TEC) in the old President's Council building in Cape Town yesterday marked the first time in South Africa that blacks have been involved at the highest level of national decision-making.

The TEC is intended to level the political playing field and ensure that no party, organisation or government has an unfair advantage in the coming election. It will have seven multi-party sub-councils. In terms of agreements reached at the World Trade Centre, all the 26 parties which participated in multi-party talks since their resumption on April 1 this year are eligible to nominate a representative and his/her alternate on the TEC.

This includes those members of the Freedom Alliance which were once in the process and have since walked out, such as the Inkatha Freedom Party, the KwaZulu government, the Conservative Party and the governments of Bophuthatswana and Ciskei. The Afrikaner Volksunie, which was in the process until the November 17 plenary session which formally adopted the package of World Trade Centre agreements, has decided against taking its seat.

For now, the Pan Africanist Congress is also out of the TEC, even though indications are that the organisation is gearing itself for participation once its president, Clarence Makwetu, has held talks with President de Klerk some time next week. This leaves 19 parties. Three groups representing traditional leaders were understood yesterday to have opted for observer status.

Those represented on the TEC yesterday were KaNgwane's Inyandza National Movement, KwaNdebele's Intando Yesizwe Party, QwaQwa's Dikwankwetla Party, the Democratic Party, the National People's Party, the Natal/Transvaal Indian Congress, Solidarity Party, the South African Communist Party, the Transkei government, Lebowa's United People's Front, the Venda government and Gazankulu's Ximoko Progressive Party.

'Big Brother' ANC in 1994

13 December 1993

The ANC has planned massive infiltration of its opponents' organisations and a nationwide surveillance of its own members – including people sitting on its national executive committee (NEC) – in an efforts to contain any possible threat to the transitional process, according to top-secret documents in *The Star's* possession.

The documents, drawn up by the organisation's department of intelligence and security (DIS) – commonly known as NAT or Mbokodo – at a secret meeting in Broederstroom from August 23 to 25, also reveal the ANC's grave concern about violence and the threat posed by the right wing to the democratisation process, and detail DIS's stragegy to deal with them.

Among groups targeted for infiltration are the SAP, the public service, the SADF and hostels. But both ANC and DIS sources yesterday vigorously denied they were planning 'a Broederbond-style bid to take control of key organs of the State after the April elections', as reported in a Sunday newspaper. The ANC, said the sources, was concerned more about protecting the transitional process than about power for itself.

Part of the strategy involves strengthening the hands of Government and National Party negotiators so that they could take conservatives within the Cabinet and the NP caucus along with them in the transitional process. The strategy, mapped out following ANC President Nelson Mandela's concerns about threats to the process and the ANC itself, encompasses efforts to strengthen the moderate faction within the NP and State security forces.

It also includes winning over rightwingers – including the Inkatha Freedom Party – to the process and infiltrating all hostels. 'Our commitment to defend the transition must be total,' said a DIS source. He said it was important to strengthen NP leaders so that they could 'contain the dissidents among them and prevail over them on matters regarding the democratisation process.'

Other decisions include:

- The 'democratic centre' – comprising the ANC and the Government – should be strengthened during the transitional process. 'It must be strong and we must not allow it to breal because, if it brakes, the process collapses,' said a DIS source.
- Some statements by various ANC leaders, including personal attacks on De Klerk, were 'incompatible witht he process of democratisation'. It was decided that the ANC, according to the DIS source, had to realise that there were 'fears among whites and blacks about the dominance of the ANC in government.'
- While De Klerk should not 'be spared' in the run-up to the election, he should also not 'be bashed irresponsibly'.
- 'We said these fears cannot be separated from the anxieties and fears of our own people about the (possible) failure of the process. The process must not fail because if that should happen, then the country goes into an abyss,' said the source.
- DIS should infiltrate every hostel and be present in every room in every hostel to prevent anyone establishing attacks which could be planned in the run-up to the election. The Goldstone Commission would have to be used as much as possible to expose plans to foment violence, even though a DIS delegate charged that it was difficult to work with the commission 'as it appeared to be against the ANC'.

The organisation's old policy of 'blanket nationalisation' was no longer acceptable, although a formula would have to be found to effect redistribution, address the economic imbalances among whites and blacks, and create political and economic stability.

A national security council made up of Mandela, secretary-general Cyril Ramaphosa, DIS head Joe Nhlanhla and his deputy Alfred Nzo was established.

How We Got into this Mess in the First Place

23 December 1993

Now that the long wait for news from Cape Town has finally ended with a tentative agreement between the Government-ANC and the Freedom Alliance, it is worth reflecting on what it was that brought us to this mess in the first place.

A combination of pride, political shortsightedness and tantrums led to withdrawal from negotiations first by the Conservative Party, the Inkatha Freedom Party (IFP) and the KwaZulu government, and then by the other FA members. Although this strategy may have paid off to an extent, allowing the IFP in particular to extract more concessions from the Government and the ANC than it would have if it had stayed in the process, it has also had its severe limitations. It is doubtful whether, if the FA members knew then what they know now, they would have embarked on the same strategy.

IFP leader and KwaZulu Chief Minister Mangosuthu Buthelezi, who has never forgiven the ANC and its allies for the collapse – which he attributes to the ANC-led alliance – of talks in Codesa 2 last year, had clearly hoped the IFP's withdrawal from the multi-party talks would similarly cripple the process. Believing then that the IFP was one of the three major players in the country – the others being the Government and the ANC – he had no doubt his party's withdrawal from the talks would have an effect similar to that caused by the Codesa 2 deadlock. And here he miscalculated badly.

Not only has the process continued, but the ANC and the Government were also able to get the Negotiating Council (NC) to adopt things FA members – backed on some issues by the Democratic Party (DP), the Pan Africanist Congress (PAC) and the miniscule Afrikaner Volksunie (AVU) – would have been able to overturn.

Object

Once FA members were out of the multi-party talks, only the PAC, the

DP and the AVU objected to agreements that members of regional legislatures need no longer be 'ordinarily resident' in those regions and that only one and not two votes be allowed in the national and regional elections, among other things. These and a few other agreements to which, as NC records will show, the PAC in particular objected, are issues dear to the FA's heart.

Had the FA been there to join forces with the DP, the AVU and the PAC, these agreements would not have been reached on 'sufficient consensus', as was the case. But because of political myopia on the FA's part, the ANC and the Government were able to get NC endorsement for agreements and deals struck in their bilateral meetings.

Buthelezi has never hidden his disappointment with the fact that the process has gone on without the IFP and KwaZulu in particular and the FA in general. He is angered by the fact that this proves to many people here and abroad that although his IFP is essential to the process, it does not enjoy a status equal to that of the big two, the ANC and the Government. Simply put, unlike the ANC and the Government, the IFP has no veto in the process.

This, of course, was his demand when he argued that 'sufficient consensus' should be defined to mean that for anything to be approved by the NC, it must have the approval of 'the big three': the Government, the ANC and the IFP/KwaZulu government. Be that as it may, the FA does have very genuine concerns which ought to be taken seriously and addressed.

The IFP has now quietly dropped its opposition to the two-phased process – which makes allowance for a constituent assembly to write the final constitution – and has now dropped its demands to a bare minimum.

These include the following: that two votes should be allowed in the elections, that members of regional parliaments should be 'ordinarily resident' in the regions, that exclusive – as opposed to concurrent – powers should be given to regional governments, that these governments should be able to write their own constitutions subject to the approval of the Constitutional Court, and the easiest one, that KwaZulu/Natal – and not just Natal – be the name of that region.

Enhance

Most of these, to use ANC secretary-general Cyril Ramaphosa's words, are 'eminently reasonable' demands which enhance, rather than detract from, democracy. Once the FA leaders have given the unequivocal commitment to the transitional process demanded by the Government and the ANC, efforts should be made to accommodate the FA's demands.

Some of these things are so minor that they are definitely not worth going to war for. Nobody would lose anything if the region in which Buthelezi lives were to be called KwaZulu/Natal. Indeed, it might also appease Zulu King Zwelithini, himself an important player in the politics of that province.

As I have argued in the past, restricting voters to a single ballot when the elections will be for the National Assembly and the provincial legislatures is undemocratic. It disadvantages small, regional parties and favours the ANC and the National Party. The argument that uneducated blacks are so stupid that they will be confused by two ballots is both patronising and offensive.

And allowing people to be members of provincial legislatures without living in those provinces is absurd. In theory, at least, we can get a situation where a person lives in Johannesburg but is a member of the regional parliament in, say, the Eastern Cape. This, too, must be changed.

Given the nature of negotiations, obviously the FA cannot get everything it wants – compromises have to be made on both sides. However, everything possible should be done to avert a possible civil war. When agreements can be reached, the unnecessary alienation of some political players should be avoided.

F W Roadshow Drops In On an Eastern Transvaal King

28 January 1994

Rietvlei – President de Klerk started off his three-day election trail to the Eastern Transvaal with a visit to KwaNdebele's King Makhosonke II of the Manala tribe, where he tried to sell the NP to about 200 people, mostly children and members of the Zion Christian Church.

De Klerk, who arrived to a muted welcome at Makhosonke's royal kraal, told his audience that the April 27 election – made possible by his government since he took office – would not be about the past, but the future. In a speech aimed at winning the support of Makhosonke, who said he made his kraal available to leaders of all political parties, De Klerk said his government and the NP had always stood for traditional leaders' rights and had made certain that these rights were entrenched in the Interim Constitution.

De Klerk, who was met at the gate to the kraal by a handful of placard-waving ANC supporters, acknowledged that the NP Government had in the past given KwaNdebele residents reason to be angry with it, but it had also done 'many good things'. He said that although he would not want to abuse the opportunity given to him by Makhosonke, he nevertheless wanted to caution that some of the parties contesting the April election were 'dangerous'.

Turning to the ANC members who had protested on his arrival, De Klerk said: 'I did not feel offended by the people with placards, who might be my opponents. I have no doubt that if they gave me an opportunity to talk to them they would also vote for me'.

Makhosonke, who described De Klerk's visit as a courtesy call on him, said there was great ignorance among his people about the forthcoming election. He appealed to De Klerk to help enable tribal authorities to impart voter education themselves. The king congratulated De Klerk and president Nelson Mandela on being named winners of the 1993 Nobel Peace Prize and expressed the hope that they would 'continue planting the seeds of friendship'.

F W Disarms and Charms Crowds

31 January 1994

The task facing National Party leader President de Klerk on his three-day election trail in the Eastern Transvaal was enormous. Some have even likened his efforts to win black votes to that of an ant trying to move a hill.

And yet it has not all been in vain. Take Friday, for instance. On the second day of his roadshow, De Klerk had to try to ignore a small group of vociferous ANC supporters who toyi-toyied outside a KwaGuqa, Witbank, flat inside which he was taking tea with his host.

When he came out of the flat, a number of people spontaneously broke away from the chanting crowd to shake his hand – much to the chagrin of those who had organised the protest. The daughter of De Klerk's host, 21-year-old Rebecca Skhobela, who made tea for the president, wore an ANC T-shirt. She said that she was a member of neither the ANC nor the NP, and that the T-shirt belonged to her boyfriend.

This week Skhobela will be travelling to Hammanskraal Police College to begin her police training.

Good Friends

And some black NP supporters had some fascinating reasons for joining the party, ranging from its economic policies to the fact that it 'took care' of them.

Asked why she would vote for the NP, one woman said: 'Well, ANC, NP – same thing'. Pressed further, she responded, '[FW] de Klerk, [Nelson] Mandela – good friends!!'

In what must be the highlight of the roadshow, members of a formerly hostile 500-strong group of ANC supporters at Driekoppies Dam applauded politely – and with some newly found respect for him – when de Klerk stood up and told them about his contribution to the new dispensation and answered questions.

Then, of course, there were the farmworkers who were forced by their employers to accompany them to some of De Klerk's meetings. At a Lilliefontein farm outside Belfast, farmworkers sat passively during the president's Afrikaans speech.

The workers clapped their hands only when told by the black NP organiser to do so. When De Klerk finished speaking, most told *The Star* they did not understand a word of what he had said. When told that one farmer had advised the president to speak in Afrikaans because all the workers understood it, one journalist said: 'Maybe that farmer was a member of the Conservative Party. Maybe that's what the right wing means by sabotage.'

F W Winning Grudging Black Respect

1 February 1994

For the second time in two weeks, National Party leader F W de Klerk took to the road last week to campaign for votes for his party ahead of the April election. The destination, this time, was Eastern Transvaal, one of nine regions agreed upon in the multi-party talks last year.

Geographically the region is a vast area. It begins a few kilometres outside Pretoria in KwaNdebele, takes in the entire highveld and lowveld areas and ends with the homeland of KaNgwane which borders Swaziland. A question mark still hangs over the future of some part of the region, which Swazi King Mswati II has again claimed to be part of his kingdom.

People in what presently constitutes KaNgwane have greeted Mswati's latest claim with a sense of *déjà vu*: they have been through it all before. In as polite a language as he could muster, KaNgwane Chief Minister Mangisi Zitha has in fact told the young king to get lost, gently reminding him that South African-born Swazis regarded themselves as South Africans first and Swazis second.

This is a region where chiefs, kings and farmers have some influence, and De Klerk meant to use them all. Although he kissed no children, he did shake quite a number of hands, address farmers and their employees and confer with chiefs.

And for his labour he was rewarded with being dubbed an 'honorary Ndebele' by King Makhosonke Mabhena of the Manala tribe in KwaNdebele and an 'honorary Swazi' by Chief C M Dlamini of Badplaas.

Considering that the trip had been dubbed a roadshow with De Klerk, one's first and main disappointment was immediate. Although the NP had laid on a bus for the journalists on the trip, De Klerk was not on it – and neither was his entourage. They were driving ahead of the bus.

The journalists simply did not see them until they got to one of the stops. The reason given – and it was a very sound one – was that chances could not be taken with his security.

And there is a delicious irony about this campaign. Whereas in the past NP leaders have not hesitated to use the trusted *swart gevaar* strategy to win elections, this time an NP leader was actually out to court blacks and to persuade them to vote for his party in the election. Even farm labourers were no longer just labourers, but important citizens who could make a difference.

De Klerk himself did not appear bothered by the contradiction. He had permanently reconciled himself to the reality of what he had started, and everywhere he went he said again and again: the NP was wrong to have embarked on apartheid, and now stood for all South Africans, black and white. But it is when he addressed farmworkers that he did not appear to make much headway. In a company-owned compound called Kanhym just outside Middleburg, De Klerk – wearing a suit and a jacket – spoke to farmworkers who were still wearing overalls.

They had been ordered by their employers to attend the meeting, and were not told De Klerk would be there. At Lilliefontein farm outside Belfast, he spoke exclusively in Afrikaans, and NP organiser Simon Vilakazi gave a two-minute summary at the end of his speech.

In KwaNdebele he spoke to about 200 members of the Zion Christian Church, some of whom said they had been invited to a Thursday afternoon service without being informed about his visit. It was when he addressed meetings to which his audience had not gone voluntarily that his campaign failed most disastrously. Most of the workers at the two meetings said they had been ordered to attend.

Most of these people just sat passively throughout De Klerk's speech, patiently waiting for him to finish so that they could go about their lives. They would, they said, vote for the ANC because their employers – who now wanted them to vote for the NP – treated them badly on the farms.

But when the President ventured into the black residential areas, such as when he went to Hlalani Kahle squatter camp and KwaGuqa township outside Witbank and Mzinoni outside Bethal, he proved a big hit – despite the fact that it was here that he encountered his most serious challenge from angry ANC supporters.

The goodwill towards him was still there, and one often overheard frightened people saying some complimentary things about him as a person, and even inquiring about where and how they could join the NP. In KwaGuqa one woman told someone who raised eyebrows when she asked about joining the NP, that she, like everyone else, had 'a democratic right' to choose.

And black NP members and supporters were encouraged by his visit to their townships. This, they said, indicated concretely that he cared and would not allow himself to be intimidated by ANC supporters. The distinct impression one got was that although not many would now be so daring as to openly flaunt their membership of the NP, they had nevertheless been emboldened by De Klerk's visit and had consequently gained a new resolve.

Driekoppies Dam must have been the cherry on top for De Klerk. He had gone there for a private chat with a local chief, and found about 500 demonstrating ANC supporters. Something in him snapped, and he decided to stand up to the crowd.

He told them about his own contribution to the new political dispensation about to dawn in the country, and reminded them it was he who had released ANC leader Nelson Mandela, unbanned political organisations and repealed discriminatory legislation. Then he took questions. After a long response to one of the questions, he concluded: 'Don't believe everything you hear about the NP. We are not the devil.'

And, much to his own surprise, the formerly hostile crowd politely applauded him, with some newly found respect.

DP Razzmatazz Takes Off

7 February 1994

Be careful. You are entering Tony Leon country.

That may have been the large inscription just in front of the elevators on the second floor of Johannesburg's Carlton Hotel yesterday, and well it would have fitted.

But no, there was no such prior warning to those who may have wandered by accident on to the floor. Instead, there was fervour characteristic of this party's campaign workers and members.

The occasion is the launch of the DP's PWV provincial election campaign and Leon, with a razor-sharp mind and a penchant for that ringing phrase, is king. It is an American affair replete with the razzmatazz typical of party conventions in the land of Uncle Sam.

Proceedings are liberally interspersed with American music, including the popular *We will, we will rock you,* when the party's PWV regional elections candidates are introduced. There is order and discipline here. No foot-thumping, toyi-toying or occasional 'Vivas!'

This, after all, is the party of discipline, order and decorum. Delegates have come from branches throughout the PWV, and the hall is choc-a-bloc. And if the Conservative Party, the Afrikaner Volksfront and the Afrikaner Weerstaandsbeweging think they stand for Afrikaner interest, Benoni-based senior court interpreter and DP PWV vice-chairman William Mnisi has a surprise for them.

Speaking in Afrikaans, Mnisi tells his audience only the DP – which he contends is not 'a white party' – will protect Afrikaners' interests in the new dispensation.

Phama: 'Parallels with Hani'

11 February 1994

Sabelo Victor Phama was sitting on the bed in his hotel room when I walked in. He stood up to shake my hand firmly before sitting down again and motioning me to do the same. He and his bodyguards had been expecting me.

He looked every bit a soldier. It was around 10.00 pm, and he was a little tired after a long day during which he and others had participated in day-long – and at times heated – deliberations in a consultative conference to decide his organisation's response to the Government's invitation to exploratory talks. The place was Harare, Zimbabwe, and the time was September 1990, seven months after the Pan Africanist Congress (PAC), the ANC and their respective military wings had been unbanned in South Africa. This was our first meeting, and Phama's first interview with a South African journalist.

This was no Chris Hani. Indeed, in many circles in South Africa he was an unknown man. And yet he, sitting in that hotel room in Zimbabwe, had the same effect on me that Hani, the Umkhonto weSizwe chief of staff, had had in our first meeting in Johannesburg – in his first interview with a local journalist on South African soil – about three months earlier.

Like Hani, Phama was an affable person. He could have just met you but could talk to you as though he had known you all this time. In the months and years that were to follow, Phama was to become a household name in some circles in the townships, and public enemy number one to many white South Africans as his Azanian People's Liberation Army (Apla) staged repeated attacks first on policemen and then, over the past year, on whites. The PAC defence secretary had finally emerged from obscurity and the shadow of Hani, and South Africa had taken notice.

But the parallels between the two leaders did not end there. Although in the eyes of white South Africa both were demonised at various stages of their lives and were hated with a passion for leading their respective guerilla armies, towards the end of their lives they were among the most articulate of missionaries for peace. In our interview in that hotel room about four years ago as well as in all subsequent interviews, Phama emphasised that the PAC's armed struggle was not war for war's sake and a time would come when arms would have to be laid down to give peace a chance. And once the PAC leadership had taken the decision to suspend the organisation's armed struggle early last month, Phama was one of the strongest of the decision's backers.

He and his colleagues on the Apla high command immediately instructed Apla cadres in various parts of the country to observe the ceasefire, and categorically distanced the guerilla army from statements from individuals claiming to be dissident Apla members unhappy with the decision.

The next – and last – time I saw Phama alive was in Umtata, Transkei, early last year. He had flown secretly to Umtata for a meeting of the PAC's national executive council, of which he was a member. I had been promised an exclusive interview with him just a stone's throw away from South Africa.

I arrived in Umtata on Saturday morning, and Phama was brought to the local hotel to meet me amid tight security. He arrived with a train of Apla and Transkei security, and these men stood guard outside both the hotel and the room wherein we sat. Again, he was warm and friendly, and looked forward to the interview. He recalled our last face-to-face encounter in Zimbabwe. However, the interview, unfortunately, was not to be concluded.

Although Phama was keen to proceed with it, his advisers were edgy about the security risk, and did not want it known the Apla leader had been in Transkei. We reached a compromise: the interview would continue as arranged, but I would publish it only two weeks later, once Phama was out of Transkei and safely back in Harare or in Dar-es-Salaam.

Once this deal had been struck, some of Phama's advisers called him out for a briefing just before the interview began. They said he would be back soon. I waited for a long time, but Phama had been whisked away to his hideout in the homeland. I returned to Johannesburg without the interview.

Born in Umtata, Phama joined the PAC at the age of 13 in 1962. He matriculated from Ngangelizwe High School in 1967, and three years later worked and studied part-time at the University of the Witwatersrand. In 1972 he moved to the University of Fort Hare, where he was expelled during a strike the following year.

Between 1974 and 1975 he was involved in PAC underground activities while assisting his brother in a building business. It was during these years that the young Phama first met the then PAC president and founder member Robert Mangaliso Sobukwe, the late Zephania Mothopeng and Clarence Makwetu.

Phama left the country in 1975, and a year later received military training in China. On his return to Dar-es-Salaam he assisted in the PAC's publicity department, specialising in ideological training for Apla. He and a group of more than 20 Apla cadres sneaked into the country in 1978 and were later arrested in Transkei, where they were detained for over two years before being released on bail and later skipping the country.

He was first elected to the PAC's central committee in 1982, before being appointed the organisation's defence secretary in the same year.

Think of Your People

21 February 1994

Last week we came very close to a possible all-inclusive deal which could have helped steer this country away from unnecessary confrontation. Very, very close indeed.

If right-wing terrorism should become a reality over the weeks and months that lie ahead and violence in Natal flare up on a scale never before seen in this country, as most believe it will if the IFP continues to refuse to contest the April election, we will at least be able to look back and recall just how close we would once have been to a deal which would have set this country on a course of reconciliation and stability.

If an all-inclusive settlement should continue to elude us, as seems to be the case now, then it will not have been for lack of trying on the part of the ANC and the Government to avert a looming showdown. With the ANC Government concessions announced last week, everything that could reasonably have been done to satisfy the Freedom Alliance (FA) has now been done.

Hardly 12 hours after ANC president Nelson Mandela publicly unveiled the concessions many had hoped would meet the FA's demands, IFP leader Chief Mangosuthu Buthelezi threw cold water on them, reiterating that his party would not fight the election.

Buthelezi, who worked within the apartheid system to oppose NP machinations, now doggedly refuses to work within a much more democratic system to oppose it from within. The Interim Constitution, he avers, is 'fatally flawed' – as if the white Parliament which gave us bantustans had been a shining beacon of democracy.

This time he did not even pretend he was going to first consult his central committee before responding to the concessions. He and his key adviser, Walter Felgate, rejected the concessions out of hand as insufficient, notwithstanding the fact that IFP central committee member Hennie Bekker had given the impression on a TV programme that the compromise would possibly lead to the IFP's rethink of its position on the election.

As Bosnians, Somalis, Angolans will tell you, there are no winners in a civil war. We all stand to be losers, Shenge, you and your people included. Would you, Sokwalisa, want future generations to remember you as the black leader who entered into a pact with the white right to oppose democracy – however flawed it may be – and blacks' freedom?

You now have the opportunity to lead your party into the election without losing face. Most of your demands have been met, and surely that should provide you with a potent platform in the election. For the sake of this country, for the sake of your people and future generations, please do not allow yourself to be party to the destruction of this country, Shenge.

Former ANC Youth League leader Peter Mokaba has strongly denied having put pressure on the organisers and sponsors of the Miss South Africa pageant, and that should be welcomed. The thought of the ANC seeking to be involved in all aspects of our lives, including such mundane things as beauty contests, is a very worrying one, indeed. Hence Mokaba's denial must come as huge relief to many worried about how an ANC-led government might interfere in their lives.

Doing the DP Boogie-Woogie Across Alex

24 February 1994

Democratic Party PWV leader Tony Leon and his formidable election team went a-wooing yesterday in the sprawling township of Alexandra, where they tried to sell the party to sceptical residents.

Boasting the added attraction of former Miss South Africa Michelle Bruce, Leon's election roadshow aboard the 'Battle Bus' draped in DP colours saw him crisscrossing Alexandra. 'Not left, not right, AHEAD', read the back of the bus.

From the slummy parts of the township to the beautiful and middle-class East Bank area – where the houses could easily have been in any Johannesburg suburb – the message, blurted across the public address system in Zulu and Sotho, was singularly the same: the DP is a party of peace-loving individuals whose only blemish was killing apartheid and not people.

'Vote DP for peace, economic growth and the protection of your human rights,' the message, liberally interspersed with music, boomed out. Although Leon is the star – his smiling face stares at you from pictures on the sides of the bus – in Alexandra it is SABC archivist Sibongile Mahlangu and multilingual former Labour Party northern Transvaal MP Solly Kerveen, now a Democrat, who do the vernacular hard-sell. Helen Suzman is mentioned a few hundred times, and her virtues as lone liberal parliamentarian for years extolled. Other members of the team are MPs Douglas Gibson, Brian Goodall and Lester Fuchs.

The locals are incredibly nice and restrained, some waving benignly at the 'Battle Bus'. But then, Alex is very heavily policed. As the bus snakes around, a yellow SAP Husky combi trails it, followed by a police Casspir.

Other stops on Leon's campaign trail were relatively easier: an old age home in Highlands North, the Highlands North Boy's High School and a furniture factory in Wynberg. If the campaign is without drama, at least something positive can be said for Leon's team – it has good taste in music.

Few Tears Shed for this Megalomaniac

28 February 1994

How low the mighty have fallen!

Erstwhile Bophuthatswana dictator, His Excellency Kgosi Lucas Mangope, today finds himself without a job. And not a moment too soon.

Of the four leaders of the nominally independent homelands, Mangope has shown the most breathtaking shortsightedness and an amazing disregard for the will of the people.

Now, of course, he is gone and, except for his family and close friends who may have benefited from his iron-fisted rule in Bophuthatswana, not many will shed a tear for this megalomaniac.

Despots often have these delusions of grandeur which tend to blind them to reality, and Mangope was no exception. Not only did he preside over a one-party dictatorship, often cocking a snoot at the unfolding democratisation process in greater South Africa and even vowing never to allow his territory to be reincorporated into the Republic, but he also brooked no opposition in his banana republic.

He silenced opposition, prohibited other parties from operating freely in the homeland and, like his friend Chief Mangosuthu Buthelezi, ended up in an alliance with rabid racists in the Freedom Alliance. But such a marriage of convenience was doomed from the beginning, and it was only a question of time before it would fall apart.

While Mangope looked upon the TerreBlanches of this world as allies within the FA, his right-wing friends continued to see blacks as objects of racial degradation and dehumanisation and heaped insult after insult upon them. Even when they got to Mmabatho, ostensibly seeing themselves as saviours, they continued to show little respect for the locals.

So deep-seated was the resentment on the ground that at least two of Mangope's own security forces brutally turned their guns on the men who had rushed to their leader's rescue last week.

And, if the truth be told, the black masses both inside and outside Bophuthatswana rejoiced at these most shocking murders. At last, they said, the AWB had got its come-uppance.

We must be prepared to draw the line and, like one caller to Radio Metro's evening talkshow, pledge our willingness to defend our fledgling democracy from those still hankering after the past.

Zulu King Goodwill Zwelithini has now fully entered the political arena on the side of his uncle's IFP, and suddenly suffers from a serious bout of nostalgia for a pre-1834 KwaZulu kingdom he has only heard about. He will have us believe he speaks for all Zulus.

The Afrikaner Volksfront, on the other hand, demands a volkstaat in the name of all Afrikaners, thus giving the impression all Afrikaners are racists who are afraid of democracy. Together, we are often told, the two groups are potent allies against the new South Africa we are heading for.

But there are many Zulus and Afrikaners who love their country, South Africa, and do not want to live in some God-forsaken Zulu or Afrikaner homeland. They are fully behind the democratisation process.

Why are they so quiet as Zwelithini and the AVF continue to make these claims on their behalf?

The time is now ripe for these people to stand up and tell Zwelithini and the AVF to refrain from claiming to speak on their behalf unless mandated to do so. Otherwise, they stand the risk of being thought to be going along with these anti-democratic forces which were ever so quiet during the apartheid era.

Time to Draw Bottom Line for Politicians

14 March 1994

The ANC and the Government have taken a lot of hammering in the media in recent weeks because of the lack of progress in their talks with the misnamed Freedom Alliance (FA).

There was a growing body of opinion then that although the FA was intransigent and – in the words of ANC secretary-general Cyril Ramaphosa – 'a difficult customer to negotiate with', the ANC and the Government had not done enough to address the alliance's concerns.

This view was justified. Not only had the two parties pushed through the multi-party Negotiating Council at the World Trade Centre a deal which best suited them while leaving others disadvantaged, they sometimes even showed amazingly undemocratic inclinations.

One has only to recall their misguided deal which would have bequeathed on us a politically loaded Constitutional Court, and their steadfast commitment to a single-ballot system in what will be simultaneous elections for a National Assembly and regional legislatures.

Thanks to enormous pressure from the press, the public and some political parties the two parties withdrew their proposals.

As the main contenders for power, the ANC and the National Party had a responsibility to do everything possible to avoid strife and civil war.

With the six-point package of concessions adopted by the Negotiating Council last week and to come before Parliament today, the ANC and the Government have now done more than enough to address the conservative alliance's demands. Calls for them to keep giving without the FA ever reciprocating can no longer be justified.

The latest concessions go to the core of the FA's demands and the ANC cannot keep giving without ultimately alienating its own constituency. The right-wing alliance should no longer be allowed to keep prevaricating and moving goalposts. It should be told in no uncertain terms that while South Africans yearn for an all-inclusive dispensation, they will not be forever patient with organisations which want to hold the country and the democratisation process to ransom.

The right-wing threats of violence are not just the ANC's and the Government's problem; they are our problem, every one of us. It is now time we the people – at least that segment of the population that wants peace, stability and a democratic dispensation – made it plain to all politicians we have no desire to see this beautiful country go the way of Angola, Bosnia and Somalia.

Now that the political dinosaur that is Mangope has effectively been consigned to the dustbin of history where he belongs, the people of Bophuthatswana can savour the restoration of their full South African citizenship and get ready to cast their votes in next month's first truly national general election.

The lesson is clear for Mangope's friends in Ulundi and others who may be tempted to allow power to go to their heads: the will of the people cannot be recklessly trampled upon. Any leader who does so does so at his peril. The people in KwaZulu/Natal will no doubt have followed developments in Mmabatho with keen interest over the past few days.

Verbum satis sapienti, Chief Buthelezi.

The ANC has recently issued commendable statements denouncing those louts within its midst who make a habit of disrupting other parties' meetings. To these social misfits, who shamelessly harass and intimidate those who belong to other parties, democracy has no meaning.

ANC leader Nelson Mandela, in particular, has in recent weeks made strong calls for political tolerance but, as usual, these calls have gone unheeded.

As I have said before, the ANC should now do more than just condemn this disturbing and manifestly undemocratic practice. It should take action against the perpetrators.

Commendable though they may be, statements from Mandela, Popo Molefe *et al* merely denouncing this scourge of our times are not enough. Tough action – including suspension or even expulsion from the ANC – should be taken.

The ANC may not be aware of it, but this may even cost the organisation votes in next month's election. After all, some of us hate bossy Goliaths who go around harassing little Davids.

'Breakthrough' Must be Balanced with Caution

17 March 1994

At last, a ray of hope on the horizon.

Just when it looked like the IFP and its Freedom Alliance (FA) partners were set to boycott the April election, IFP leader Chief Mangosuthu Buthelezi announced his party would consider registering provisionally for the poll.

For a country badly in need of good news, that was as good news as it possible to get in these troubled times of ever-present threats of civil war. Anything that can be constructive to the transitional process and at least to a reasonably peaceful election must no doubt be welcomed.

Buthelezi's announcement, made at the end of a crucial meeting with Nelson Mandela, was swiftly endorsed by his party's central committee – and rumblings of discontent within FA ranks were soon heard.

Reports of a major breakthrough and a possible split in the FA were subsequently splashed throughout the country, and the nation's spirit collectively soared. It would be advisable to apply the brakes to whatever excitement was occasioned by the news and instead to exercise caution.

Granted, Buthelezi's decision to have the IFP register provisionally for the election is a significant development which ought to be roundly applauded, but in the resulting excitement we should not lose sight of two equally important riders.

The IFP's registration is provisional subject to the involvement of international mediators in continued negotiation between the IFP, the ANC and the Government. Secondly, this means that the party's registration cannot be regarded as final until the mediation has run its full course and yielded results acceptable to Buthelezi.

A tall order indeed to whoever will have the misfortune of sitting on that mediation panel.

The question must be asked: what can international mediation achieve that the FA, the ANC and the Government could not attain in their protracted trilateral talks which began last year? What magic wand – exclusive only to them – will the international mediators wave in their search for a solution to what is essentially a South African problem?

As a concept international mediation is fine, but it presupposes a willingness on the part of those involved in a conflict to resolve their differences through dialogue. It further presupposes a willingness from all sides to compromise. Otherwise it, too, is bound to fail.

Unless there is a change of heart from the FA parties – and right now there is no reason to believe there is – then the mediation will go the way of all talks involving the three interlocutors. It will all be an expensive exercise which will not leave us any closer to an all-inclusive settlement.

Although preconditions are by their nature not helpful in talks of this nature, it would not be too much to ask that those involved in the talks should commit themselves upfront to a peaceful resolution of their differences.

There is a more pressing form of international involvement that we need in this country right now, an that is an UNTAG-type of international peacekeeping force. The National Peacekeeping Force (NPKF) being trained outside Bloemfontein is too small for the task ahead and has numerous problems of its own.

It simply makes no sense for the ANC and the Government to continue pouring cold water on the idea of an international peacekeeping force during what will be an historical but emotion-charged election, and to pretend the fledging NPKF will be equal to the task at hand.

Mandela has gone flat out to reach out to the FA and his recent statements – including that he would go on his knees to beg FA leaders to come aboard the transition train – are those of a statesman concerned for his country. During this time of uncertainty, South Africa needs more leaders like you, Madiba.

Let's Put the Shoulder to the Wheel for our New Country

4 April 1994

After all the wrangling and mudslinging, a new reality will dawn at the end of this month.

Slightly more than a month from today, South Africa's new and representative two-chamber Parliament will convene in Cape Town and a few days later the country's new president – widely expected to be septuagenarian ANC leader Nelson Mandela – will be sworn in.

It will be a momentous occasion that will mark the beginning of a new era. Gone will be the oppressive and suffocating stranglehold of apartheid.

The challenge facing all 'new' South Africans then will be to cast our numerous and legendary differences aside and collectively put the shoulder to the wheel in an effort to rebuild the country and fashion out a common identity for ourselves.

It will behove us all, regardless of our race and background, to do our best to make this a better country.

The politicians may wield a lot of power and influence, but we, the ordinary citizens, are not at all impotent.

Indeed, collectively we have more power and influence than all the politicians put together.

We will have to do what little we can to make this a country we can all be proud to live in – and this we can do by doing the best we can in whatever we do.

Only when we all do something to improve our lot and our beloved country, instead of forever expecting handouts, can we hope for a reasonably better future.

That is a month from now. At the moment, however, we have an election campaign in full swing and, predictably, politicians cannot quite resist taking swipes at one another from time to time.

That is to be expected: elections do often bring out the worst in them. After April 28, however, we can expect these selfsame politicians to shake hands and work together.

It would be a great pity, therefore, if politicians were so preoccupied with winning votes that they further polarised our already heavily divided society in the process.

We do not expect them to treat their opponents with kid gloves, but we have every right to demand that they remain mindful of the potentially harmful consequences of some of their actions and strategies.

Take the National Party, for instance. In its understandable overeagerness to capture the Western Cape and get Hernus Kriel to be premier of the region, it has resorted to its oft-used *swart gevaar* tactics.

It has stooped so low that it has now taken to driving a wedge between Africans and coloureds in the only part of the country where Africans are in a minority.

So much has the NP whipped up racial emotions that many coloureds in the Western Cape – some of whom have always considered themselves closer to whites and therefore 'superior' to Africans – are made to find refuge in old racism.

This is most deplorable and regrettable, especially coming as it does from a party that now claims to be above racism. It is amazing that President de Klerk conveniently turns a blind eye to something that will make racial reconciliation in the region even harder.

Now that the long political interregnum is only three weeks away from being over, surely it would be right and proper to ask how much things have changed.

Politically, the change has been phenomenal. However, the average black person has not seen any changes in his or her personal circumstances. Real economic power still resides in white hands, and will continue to do so for a few years to come. The Mshenguvilles of this country are still with us, and will be with us a little longer.

These people, often described as 'the poorest of the poor', will be hoping the new South Africa will be kinder to them.

Happy Easter, everyone.

Larger-than-life Hani did not Depart this World in Vain

11 April 1994

A year ago yesterday, an assassin's bullet robbed this country of its second most popular political leader, Thembisile Chris Hani.

A man with a huge following in townships across the country, Hani was mowed down in cold blood outside his Dawn Park, Boksburg home on the morning of April 10 by Polish-born Janus Walusz – now sitting in jail with former Conservative Party President's Council member Clive Derby-Lewis.

South Africa was shocked, for never before had so serious a threat been posed to the transitional process then already under way.

Although a few on the right rejoiced, gleefully citing Hani's leadership of the SA Communist Party as justification for this vilest of deeds, the overwhelming majority of South Africans of all races were horrified. The townships seethed with anger and parts of the country went up in flames.

With the assassination making international headlines, this was one murder the authorities would not be able to sweep under the carpet, like many others before. And so international investigators were called in to assist the SAP, and the result was the conviction of the culprits.

A year later, this country stands on the threshold of a new future. Our historic, first all-race election is only a few days away.

Indeed, the election date was agreed upon shortly after Hani's murder – a fitting tribute to a man who did so much to fight apartheid.

He was a larger-than-life figure. To his legion of followers he was a hero second only to Nelson Mandela, and to his mostly white enemies he was a dangerous communist whose every word was suspect. To his family and those who knew him well, he was a warm, passionate man.

May his soul rest in peace.

General elections are important in any functioning democracy, providing as they do an opportunity to the electorate to choose governments.

However, they also have the unintended effect of turning most politicians into shrewd schemers who will do anything to get elected or get more votes for their parties.

Not that at any other moment this species does not get involved in scheming, arm-twisting and bending the truth, but elections do often bring out the worst in them, as this column pointed out last week.

Take the PAC, for instance. This organisation is now turning political opportunism into an art form. Indeed, it can be relied upon to rail against anything the ANC supports, such as the state of emergency in KwaZulu/Natal.

The PAC, which made similar noises about negotiations before finally entering them, has not lost an opportunity to criticise the emergency. As usual, the organisation has not proposed an alternative.

Has it no interest in ending the carnage in Natal?

Like the Democratic Party, the PAC can now claim – with an eye on the election, of course – that its hands are clean. After all, it is not in the Transitional Executive Council and was therefore not party to the decision.

But that may just be the problem with these two parties: they shun responsibility and anything unpopular. They need to accept their share of responsibility and get their hands dirty.

A shock wave swept through the country early last week when a committee convened by the Independent Electoral Commission pronounced that free and fair elections would not be possible in KwaZulu/Natal 'in the current political climate'.

Quite rightly, the ANC and the Government put their foot down firmly and said the election would not be postponed.

To do so would amount to giving *carte blanche* to forces bent on making sure the poll never takes place. It is dangerous politics.

Interestingly, the PAC – which considers itself the vanguard of 'the African people' – said it would welcome a postponement of the poll.

No Surprise the Wise Men made their Journey in Vain

18 April 1994

The international mediation which was supposed to have got off the ground last week is off – and only those who are incurable optimists will have been surprised.

Those of us who have followed closely the political drama in the country over the past four years are not surprised.

As this column pointed out about two months ago, mediation – like any other kind of negotiations – presupposes a willingness from all parties concerned to be flexible and to comprise.

Now flexibility has never been the hallmark of Chief Mangosuthu Buthelezi's IFP. Indeed, that party has been wont to make one demand after another and expect others to meet its demands without making any real compromises itself.

It is a terrible thing to say, but the mediation was doomed right from the beginning. Through it the IFP sought to achieve, among other things, the postponement of this month's election – clearly something to which most South Africans are opposed.

Although some suspected the international mediation would fail, not many would have expected it to fail before it even began. Now that was a surprise.

Although the chances of the mediation succeeding were as slim as those of someone trying to find a needle in a haystack, the fact that men of the stature of former US secretary of state Henry Kissinger, former British foreign secretary Lord Carrington and Indian Chief Justice HK Bhagwati came to this country for something which never even got off the ground is embarrassing.

It is embarrassing not only for the IFP, at whose instigation the seven men agreed to put everything aside to come to these shores. The embarrassment must be shared by the ANC and the Government, both party to the aborted mediation, and by all South Africans.

There was a lot of international interest in the mediation. Footage of the seven men being welcomed at the Carlton Hotel on their arrival by leaders of the three parties was relayed around the world, and only two days later the same international community saw news footage of a press conference at which the mediators announced they were returning home. I can only echo the University of Cape Town's Professor Robert Schrire on this issue: the IFP was wrong to suggest international mediation, the ANC was foolish to agree to it, and the Government miscalculated when it allowed itself to be drawn belatedly into the process. We must hope they've all learnt a lesson.

Our first all-inclusive election has caught the interest of the international media, and many foreign journalists have flocked to the country to cover what must certainly rank – perhaps along with Nelson Mandela's release from prison – as one of the most important news stories of the decade.

They are welcome here. Foreign journalists have always played a very important role in exposing to the world the ills of apartheid over the years. Even when PW Botha's states of emergency in the mid-'80s made it difficult for the local press to document certain things, the foreign journalists stationed here were able – often at great personal risk – to get the story out to the their respective countries.

It is with a sense of great sadness, therefore, that I must comment on the way some among them seem to perceive developments in this country. The conclusion is inescapable that some among them might be secretly hoping that our country becomes another Yugoslavia or Bosnia-Herzegovina so that it would look good on their CVs.

At a press conference in Johannesburg on Thursday, after the failure of international mediation, a few of them tried very hard to put words into Chief Buthelezi's mouth. Repeatedly they asked leading questions, trying to get him to say he would now take up the armed struggle.

Will you now lead 'your people' in armed insurrection? No? But what if 'your people' want you to go underground and fight? Will it, as you have recently warned, now be a fight to the finish between your party and the ANC? On and on they badgered him.

Fortunately, Buthelezi, who will make threats of civil war without any prompting, did not fall into their trap. Relaxed and dignified, he said he had no intention of doing what they were trying to get him to say he would do.

Those of us who are South Africans will be hoping the Chief Minister meant it.

Now is His Hour:

Interview with ANC Leader, Nelson Mandela, on the Eve of the Country's First All-inclusive Election

25 April 1994

On prospects for a peaceful election

I have assurances from the SAP and SADF that they are going to be ruthless against anybody who tries to interfere with the elections.

They have briefed me on detailed plans which they are adopting. That does not mean that there will not be areas where it will be difficult to [have a free and fair vote], because the country is very big. The SADF and SAP may not be strong enough to deploy men throughout the country, to cover every area. There may be isolated cases where it will not be possible for people to vote at all, but generally speaking I am convinced from the plans I have seen that we have taken all the precautions that are necessary.

On FW de Klerk

In spite of all the quarrels we've had with Mr de Klerk, he remains quite an interesting chap. He is big. Some of our most unpleasant quarrels have been on a one-on-one basis – we've said very cruel things to each other.

One of the things that [angered] me was the fact that he did not use his capacity to stop the violence, when he could do so. This was the major cause of conflict between us but he has the capacity of quarrelling with you, and the next moment shaking hands and sitting down to coffee. I don't think we're going to have trouble from Mr de Klerk. I think we're going to work with him very smoothly.

On the mood of the country

The people have high expectations and though we have warned them repeatedly that to address their basic needs is going to take years, nevertheless there are those expectations, it is something we must warn against. But the encouraging thing is that we are entering a very exciting period and we are approaching that with real enthusiasm – spirits are high. There's been a shift in the country's mood from fear to excitement. My impression is of a feeling of hope.

On fears of post-election anarchy

There have been prophets of doom suggesting that after April 29 our people are going to run riot attacking property and individuals and that there is going to be chaos. I don't think so. I've been warning against that. People must not concentrate very much on what happened in Bophuthatswana. I condemned that in the strongest terms. I said if we find any member of the ANC to be involved in such activities, we will expel him because we don't want criminals in our organisation. So now we are taking precautions to ensure that our people are properly informed as to how to behave if we manage to be victorious in this election. Our people have written to all the regional executive committees indicating programmes in which our people should be involved, so they should not think in terms of looting and other forms of lawlessness.

On the future of whites

We attach a great deal of importance to whites. In spite of all the criticism we have made about apartheid, the reality is that whites have had opportunities we have not had. They have had education, they have got knowledge, skills and expertise. We want that knowledge and expertise now that we are building our country.

That is why I have appealed to them repeatedly not to leave the country at this particular moment, and even to ask those who have left to come back. Because we are going to need them, we're going to rely on them.

On the Government of National Unity

We bring different approaches. De Klerk is bringing the approach of an Afrikaner whose community has been dominant, especially since 1948. I bring into the GNU the tradition of a freedom fighter who has struggled against apartheid.

I think we will be able to resolve the gap between the two of us. Especially because we will not be alone. We have a very good team from the ANC and from the NP. There are men in the NP who are prepared to serve South Africa, very sincerely. So we must not concentrate on two people.

Organisations are not run by individuals, they are run by a team of men and women. We've got highly talented people like Thabo Mbeki and Cyril Ramaphosa. And strangely enough, in spite of the perceptions, a chap like Kobie Coetsee, people like Roelf Meyer, whatever their record has been in the past. I don't think there are going to be such sharp differences as to paralyse government.

On the toughest challenges ahead

We are faced with two problems. We are committed to form a Government of National Unity which brings in those people who for 46 years applied apartheid. We are bringing their conservatism in the GNU. That is one problem.

We have another coming from the liberation movement – our people who have been brought up against the legacy of resistance and who, at a time when they should now be upfront in addressing the problems of the country [and be] preparing to govern, still think in terms of resistance, and oppose everything that comes from the other side. They are not yet attuned to addressing problems.

On national reconciliation

The leadership should not now be engaged in fighting talk. We have made the breakthrough [with the IFP] and it is hoped that leaders... will have a better chance of uniting the country. What is encouraging is the emergence of men and women from all racial groups who are bound in their common loyalty and common love for their fatherland. That is what we should be emphasising. Healing the wounds of the past, not opening wounds at this critical moment. I have been saying [to my followers] throughout this election: do not disrupt the meetings of other political organisations. Remember that these men, although we are fighting an election, we are going to work with them in the GNU.

On his acceptance speech

It is of course difficult to know what form the [acceptance] speech would take, but the question of lawlessness is one that should be uppermost in our minds. Because what has concerned me throughout are the concerns of the minorities. Whenever there is a transformation in any country, the minorities are worried about their positions, what is going to happen to them and their families. It is worse in this country, and it is the duty of the leadership to address those fears and to make sure that the minorities feel they are involved in the transformation, that we build the new South Africa. There's not going to be any discrimination against any groups. It's our task to make sure of that.

On criticism of ANC/SACP links

It is of course difficult to convince people of the reality of our alliance with the Communist Party. The alliance between the ANC and the SACP is based on mutual respect and some of the most important contributions have actually been made by members of the SACP, people like Joe Slovo and the late Chris Hani. They have been so productive in addressing problems that the whole question of an alliance between the ANC and SACP is a non-issue to us.

On amnesty for security force members

This is a very sensitive question. A form of indemnity is unavoidable. At the moment there is a great deal of insecurity in the SADF, SAP and the civil service. Now we cannot even have free and fair elections if we do not get the support of the SAP and SADF. It is absolutely necessary for us to remove this state of insecurity.

I am discussing with [SAP commissioner General Johan van der Merwe] this question of indemnity and the question of making sure that we have the support of the police, because the people who have committed crimes before October 8, 1990 are really worried that a new government is going to put them on trial. We have gone further to say Parliament will have a discretion to grant an indemnity to people who have committed crimes between October 8, 1990 and December 6, 1993. We are saying let's forget the past, let's think in terms of the present and the future. [But] what we cannot do is give indemnity to people who after December 1993 have been killing people. We are working out details. In Chile, for example, people were able to come forward and say we did so an so, without publishing their names. We [could] then look at what they have done and decide whether we should give indemnity.

On amnesty for Chris Hani's killers

We have made a statement that we will abolish the death sentence, but this is a matter that has to be considered very, very carefully. I, as an individual, am against the death sentence, but the feelings among the people are very strong. This is a highly sensitive matter. Our people are very angry, especially because of the arrogant statements that were made by the wife of [Clive] Derby-Lewis and his attitude in court – that of gloating.

On Chief Buthelezi

We have been able to get him to take decisions which he never thought he would take. He has [now] made statements in which he said he will respect the result of an election. It is a very good statement.

On the ANC's election prospects

I have said to our people that our greatest enemy is no the NP, it is the ANC itself. Because for us to proceed as if we are going to have a landslide victory is more dangerous than the opposition from the NP. And we have many problems. A surprising number of our people do not have IDs.

On his possible successor

We have a lot of talent in the ANC. People like Thabo Mbeki, Cyril Ramaphosa, Valli Moosa, Joe Slovo and Mac Maharaj. These are very capable people who stand head and shoulders above everybody else. Leaders will come and go but the policy of the Freedom Charter will remain. It is not individuals that are crucial, it is the organisation that will continue.

On the ANC deputy presidency

This is a question I have to decide. I have to set up the Cabinet and from that angle, I am not going to consult anybody. If I am elected, if my party emerges with a majority, I will decide who should fill what position. We have a wide choice. I can't go into the matter now, but I have an idea of who should be the first deputy president, if the ANC wins. It is not an easy thing to decide because we have people who have so many talents, who deserve that position. My problem is the talent that we have. I like all our people.

On a possible volkstaat

We have said we will not accept a volkstaat. But we have made a concession that, after the election, there can be a referendum on the question because we would like to hear the views of the community on behalf of whom these people say they are speaking. We are convinced that they are in a minority but we would like that to be demonstrated by democratic means.

On General Viljoen for Cabinet

Oh yes. General Viljoen is a very honest man, and I would welcome him in a Government of National Unity. It would strengthen the Government. He may not be so astute politically – he is a soldier – but he is a man of integrity and in all the meetings I have had with him I have come out feeling that this is a man with whom we can work and solve problems. And that fact that he has broken away from the Afrikaner Volksfront indicates what a strong personality he is. I have a lot of confidence in him.

On his finger-pointing habit

Well. I've got this habit of finger-pointing. I was warned very strictly that I should avoid that in the television debate. But a habit that you've had for 75 years is not easy to get rid of! And I hope people will accept it in the way in which I mean it. I use it not to make a threat, but to emphasise a point. When I use a finger, I use it innocently. I regret that I reminded people of PW Botha

Yanked Back from the Precipice – Just in Time

25 April 1994

Last week South Africa got the best news in recent months when, after a long period of wrangling, point-scoring and finger-pointing, Chief Mangosuthu Buthelezi's Inkatha Freedom Party (IFP) agreed to take part in this weeks's historic elections.

It was the kind of news for which South Africa was starving. Bad news we have had aplenty, including the failure of both the four-way Skukuza summit and the aborted international mediation.

Just when some political commentators here and abroad were beginning to prognosticate for us all kinds of doomsday scenarios, we were yanked back from the dangerous precipice on which we were hanging precariously. Once again there was hope on the horizon.

For all this we ought to be grateful to Kenyan political scientist Professor Washington Okumu who brokered the historic accord by prevailing upon Buthelezi to compromise on a number of issues, including on his then inflexible opposition to the elections proceeding this week.

And by finally agreeing to contest the elections just a week before they were to begin, Buthelezi – whose party is now significantly disadvantaged – displayed the kind of statesmanship we have not seen from him in recent years. He put the country's interest first, and in that process rose in stature and endeared himself to many peace-loving people here and abroad.

Deserve praise

Also deserving of praise are ANC leader Nelson Mandela and President F W de Klerk, who made it possible for Buthelezi to come aboard the proverbial train without losing face.

But none of these leaders' three parties can claim any victory, tempted though they might be to do so. Instead, it is our country, South Africa, which has emerged the victor, and we all ought to be thankful for that.

It is great pity, however, that so many people had to die before this agreement could be reached.

With the IFP in the elections, we now have a much more inclusive political settlement, with only Azapo and the extreme right out of the elections. As we approach this week's elections, we need to consider carefully the kind of future we want for ourselves and our country.

We should ask ourselves what future we want to bequeath our children. Is it going to be a fully functional democracy or a skewed one where the governing party has absolute power, with the combined opposition so negligibly small that our new rulers will be able to ride roughshod over it?

It is in the country's interest that no single party should emerge from the elections with a crushing victory. Indeed, the soon-to-be ruling party should have to be forever on its toes, knowing that it could easily be ousted if it did not deliver the goods.

Also in the country's interest is that the IFP should do reasonably well in the elections, obtaining at the very least the required five percent so that Buthelezi can be in the new multi-party cabinet.

This would send a powerful message to his traditional supporters in KwaZulu and the PWV that he has not been sidelined. After all, the enemy within is not as dangerous as the enemy without.

Cruising

The ANC is cruising to victory in these elections, and we should not begrudge it. Its victory will be well deserved. However, we must all hope that the National Party and the IFP – both of which need to be supported – will do reasonably well in the polls.

We must hope these two will emerge as the second and third biggest parties respectively, so that both President F W de Klerk – who looks set to be our new second deputy president – and Buthelezi can be in that new Cabinet.

Others, like the PAC and the DP, must also have a respectable showing.

Since we now have two votes in these elections, we can – and should – vote for two different parties – for the National Assembly and for our regional legislatures to balance power.

The best possible scenario for the country is one where the ANC wins the national election, with at least the NP and the IFP having a good showing. We, the people, have the opportunity this week to give South Africa that kind of result.

PAC: We Always Mean What We Say

26 April 1994

Even at the best of times, Pan Africanist Congress (PAC) leader Clarence Makwetu is not the most expressive of men.

His friendly smile is engaging, yes, but his answers are usually short. He is not exactly an interviewer's dream.

On this occasion, however, just days before South Africa's first all-race election, he is more than willing to talk. In fact, he even seems to be enjoying it.

But as all politicians at this phase of the campaign will tell you, time is not a commodity he has in abundance these days. As we speak he keeps looking at his watch. Within the next half hour he has to be on the plane on his way to Durban to continue drumming up support for his organisation.

Uphill battle

It has been an uphill battle all the way, and the odds stacked against his organisation are quite considerable – but he is not about to throw in the towel and concede defeat even before polling begins.

He fancies his organisation's chances, pronounces that 'on the whole' the PAC's campaign has been successful, and confidently predicts that the organisation will win 'the majority of the nine provinces'.

His office is small and sparsely furnished, and the formal reception at the organisation's new headquarters – it had to change offices early this month – tells of a party barely surviving.

Not for the first time, poverty has come knocking at the door, but love and dedication have not gone out through the window. The men and women milling around the reception area, all praying for a miraculous PAC victory in the election, have given freely of their time. Theirs is a labour of love.

Makwetu, sitting in his office, is a man from whose chest – as he often likes to say – hope springs eternal. He pays little attention to opinion polls whose findings have not been very encouraging.

What percentage does he think the PAC will get in the election?

'I will not be able to put a percentage, really. Normally you judge your success or failure by the enthusiasm of the crowds, the number of people flocking to the rallies. However, it is not wise for one to assume that simply because people attended rallies they will vote for you. That is not a wise assumption.

'But the key players of the organisation do their work, and that is why we are confident. Even on voting day they are the people who will see to it that voters get to the polls,' he says.

Makwetu is confident that the fact that the PAC's name is the first on the ballot box is an advantage for the organisation. However, he will not say whether he would accept a position in the multi-party Cabinet of national unity if the PAC made the required 5 percent cut-off point.

After all the PAC, he says, is opposed to the concept of power-sharing, which he finds to be the same thing as the envisaged government of national unity.

'We will have to consider that position [whether or not to accept a Cabinet seat], but we do not aspire to that,' he says.

In the event of a PAC victory, he has already compiled his Cabinet. And if the PAC wins the election, at least two aspects of the Interim Constitution would be changed: the power-sharing arrangement and the entrenchment of property rights.

Makwetu hastens to add, however, that his organisation is not opposed to coalitions and alliances.

With the election now just around the corner, what have been his main problems at the hustings? His rejoinder is swift: 'Biased coverage' by the media – especially the SABC – and lack of funds.

'Our main problem has been, and continues to be, resources. We have found it difficult to implement our schemes. We are tied down and this has hampered our work. We feel that right up to now the playing field has not been levelled,' he says.

Makwetu welcomes the Inkatha Freedom Party's last-minute entry into the election race, and insists it will not affect his organisation's fortunes.

He confirms that the PAC's military wing, the Azanian People's Liberation Army, will be part of the new South African National Defence Force, and says he can work well with any party after the election as long as that is not the incumbent 'racist regime'.

He is also critical of politicians who promise the electorate heaven and earth now in order to get more votes, and says promising people things politicians know cannot be fulfilled 'is tantamount to saying the people you are addressing are not intelligent enough'.

'Ready to die'

Asked why anyone should vote for the PAC, Makwetu concludes: 'They should consider that the PAC has been the most consistent of all the parties, throughout the struggle and right up to now, and we have at no stage ever doubted the intelligence of our followers.

'For instance, when we had problems of finances, I think we were the only party that came out to tell our people that this is the problem. We were never shy about it.

'Even our past record shows that we always mean what we say. Therefore if anyone is wise, they should vote for a party that is principled, that is consistent, that is prepared to die for the African people.'

Making the Best of a Bad Situation

29 April 1994

As South Africa today begins a few days' wait for the results of its first truly national election, one thing can be said with absolute certainty: it was not the smoothest of elections.

There are many things for which people will remember this poll, apart from the fact that for the vast majority of the country's citizens this was their first time to vote. Among lingering memories are likely to be the images of long queues on the first day of voting, and of whites and blacks – for years 'masters' and 'servants', 'madams' and 'maids' – standing in the same lines, waiting to exercise the same right to vote.

Problems began to surface as soon as the voting commenced and some people, therefore, will find it difficult to square their experiences on the three historic days with confidence shown by the Independent Electoral Commission (IEC) in the run-up to the watershed event.

They will also recall the IEC's advertisements exhorting people to vote. 'We are ready. You are ready. Let's do it', the advertisements said.

They will also recall the IEC's grand performance at a televised press conference at Midrand's Gallagher Estates on the eve of the election on Monday. Exuding confidence, IEC chairman Mr Justice Johann Kriegler – who has reminded the electorate throughout that the election was theirs and not the IEC's – said the commission was ready for the tough task ahead.

'In all, I'm pleased and proud to say that the IEC has just pulled off the impossible. We will be ready for you, the voter, tomorrow,' he said. Equally upbeat was his deputy, advocate Dikgang Moseneke.

'We are going to do our damnedest to make sure that we deliver the election. What we ask of our people is calm and patience. We are not going to war, we are going into an election,' Moseneke said.

Indeed, there was no reason then for anybody to doubt the IEC's preparedness. The commision's Gallagher Estates operations were impressive, and the media centre constructed there – big enough to accommodate a huge contingent of local and foreign journalists – reinforced one's confidence in the commission.

Then the election began on Tuesday morning, and the problems started.

Disturbing reports of voting stations which had not opened when they should have, of IEC officials not turning up at some polling stations and of a shortage of Inkatha Freedom Party (IFP) stickers for the ballot papers began coming through.

Senior citizens, pregnant women, the handicapped and the physically infirm waited in lines for hours to cast their votes, sometimes at polling stations which opened late or did not open at all. The public's fickle mood began to swing against the IEC, and question marks began to be placed on the IEC's preparedness, and the election's possible freeness and fairness.

Politicians ever eager to criticise took full advantage of the situation.

Havoc

Democratic Party PWV leader Tony Leon accused the IEC of 'gross incompetence' and said the first day of voting had been 'absolutely shambolic'. Pan Africanist Congress Western Cape premier nominee Patricia de Lille made unsubstantiated allegations of voting irregularities, and the IFP leader Chief Mangosuthu Buthelezi held a dagger over the heads of South Africans, threatening to pull out of the election and demanding that voting be extended to today.

The by-now-embattled IEC had a lot of explaining to do. The IFP's late entry into the election a week before polling was to begin, the IEC explained, had played havoc with the commission's planning. More than 90 000 IFP ballot stickers had been hastily produced, but there had been a delay in getting them to some polling stations on time.

The printing had been done in Johannesburg where the IEC has its headquarters, and so the commission had supplied these to far-flung, far-away places first. The PWV, which was the province from which the printing had taken place, had had it stickers delivered late Monday evening.

The IEC explained further that many more people – some of whom did not qualify to cast special votes – had turned up on the first day, and this had resulted in a shortage of voting materials. And, so the IEC said, some voters had turned up at polling stations which had not been designated for special votes, hence the absence of IEC officials.

The IEC had, in Moseneke's words, done its 'damnedest'. Kriegler said the situation had been far from perfect, but also very, very much farther from disaster.

Wednesday, the real start to the general election, saw even longer queues of voters. Wanting to take advantage of the fact that the day was a public holiday, many more people turned up than the IEC had expected, and – although the situation was much better than the previous day – voting materials again ran out at some polling stations.

The IEC again went into top gear, voting material – ballot papers, IFP stickers, marking ink – were delivered at a number of polling stations, and in places such as Katlehong voting began late in the afternoon.

Another problem became apparent: although the IEC had ordered 80 million ballot papers, there was now a shortage even at the commission's headquarters. Another set of close to 9 million ballot papers – now including the IFP's name and logo – was printed, this time inside the country.

More ballot boxes and marking pens were ordered, and these were flown to areas of need throughout the night and early yesterday morning. And so when polling began yesterday – which, at the IEC's request, had also been declared a public holiday to enable more voters to cast their ballots – there were much shorter queues and most polling stations were functional.

By lunch-time yesterday the IEC was confident that by the time polls closed last night all those who wanted to vote would have had the opportunity to do so. It is fair to say, therefore, that although problems were experienced over the past three days, they were not of the IEC's making. Instead, the commission, which was clearly out of its depth, worked very hard to make the best of what would otherwise have been a very bad situation.

Our Uncool Politicians

2 May 1994

The past week has shown clearly which politicians easily lose their heads when things do not go well.

In the past week alone, I have lost respect for quite a number of politicians given to shooting their mouths off before even thinking about the possible consequences of their careless and ill-timed words.

At a time when they should have put the national interest first, they have proved yet again just how incapable they often are of separating their own parties' narrow interests from those of the country.

I was particularly dissappointed in people like the PAC's Patricia de Lille and the Democratic Party's Tony Leon, who had more complaints to make about the Independent Electoral Commission's bungling than they had any suggestions on how its shortcomings could be addressed to salvage a process which could not be allowed to fail: South Africa's first truly democratic election.

And then there were Nelson Mandela's equally ill-timed comments that the election – going reasonably well despite the numerous hiccups – had been 'massively sabotaged'.

South Africa has reason to expect better of its leaders, especially those who have pretensions to high national office.

We need men and women who can maintain their cool at all times, and who will be more concerned about rescuing a dithering process than about scoring cheap political points.

Interestingly, IFP leader Chief Mangosuthu Buthelezi scored higher than the others last week.

Once he had been assured that voting in KwaZulu-Natal would be extended to Friday, he made no further noises.

That is not to say that the IEC's performance last week was beyond reproach. Far from it. But to accuse it of 'gross incompetence' and describe the day for special votes as having been 'absolutely shambolic' – as Leon did – was to take liberties with the truth. The IEC's bungling at times notwithstanding, it was the Commission that turned things around and ensured that the election proceeded reasonably smoothly.

It got Thursday declared a public holiday and got the powers-that-be to extend voting in six homelands to Friday.

A disaster was averted and the election ended positively.

For this the IEC was also subtly criticised. At Gallagher Estate, where I was based for the rest of the week, I witnessed the most amazing small-mindedness. How much had it cost the taxpayers to have the election extended to Friday in the six homelands, IEC officials were asked.

To most of us, the cost did not matter. It was important that the election succeeded.

Indeed, the cost to the country, in both financial and human terms, would have been far greater had the elections failed.

Two things are worth recording about last week. One is that thousands of people – ranging from wellknown heroes like Robert Sobukwe, Oliver Tambo, Steve Biko *et al*, through to unknown people like my mother, Maria (nee Nkambule), – did not live long enough to share in our moment of triumph last week.

A Brave New Beginning of Peace and Harmony

11 May 1994

Anyone unfamiliar with recent developments in South African politics who turned up at the Union Buildings yesterday would have concluded – wrongly – that ours has always been a country of peace and harmony.

Barely four hours had passed since the sun had risen when the country's top political figures, some of whom were not even on speaking terms a mere three years ago, started arriving.

There were the country's nine new regional premiers and their wives, some of South Africa's former Cabinet Ministers and our new parliamentarians.

And then there was Inkatha Freedom Party leader Chief Mangosuthu Buthelezi, who only a month ago appeared to be heading for the political wilderness, blessing the auspicious gathering with his presence.

Zulu King Goodwill Zwelithini, who only a month ago was calling on his subjects to boycott the election, was there too, in honour of the man he had dressed down at the summit of leaders at Skukuza two months ago.

But the most noteworthy presence was that of Freedom Front leader General Constand Viljoen, whose erstwhile colleague in the Afrikaner Volksfront, Dr Ferdi Hartzenberg, still clamours for a whites-only Afrikaner volkstaat.

Harmony was everywhere in this former city of apartheid yesterday.

The security forces, former ruthless enforcers of 'the system', were out in full force and had taken over every street corner in and around Pretoria.

Now, in the service of the new South Africa, they were friendlier and more helpful than usual. They, too, had fully embraced the spirit of the times.

And so had the thousands of whites who had joined the huge crowd on the lawn in front of the Union Buildings. It was a new, brave beginning.

Country of Lost Youth

23 May 1994

The sweeping political changes which have taken place here over the past four years – but especially in recent weeks and months – have come very close to making us an ordinary society like any other anywhere in the world.

In most countries with established democracies people are not as preoccupied with politics as we have been over the years in the country.

While black youths here grew up fully aware of – and even involved in – the greater political issues which have shaped our daily lives, in the US, the UK and most countries in continental Europe children have had other pastimes.

Politics, which did not hold as much fascination for them as it did for their counterparts here, has not been something in which they have taken great interest. It was not, as it was here, a question of life and death.

We have been closer to societies in other war-torn and conflict-ridden countries such as Northern Ireland, Beirut and Israel, where children have routinely lost their innocence at a very early age.

President Mandela alluded to this phenomenon when he addressed the crowd which had gathered at the Union Buildings in Pretoria to witness his inauguration two weeks ago. He described First Deputy President Thabo Mbeki as someone 'who had never known his youth'.

Mbeki has not been an exception. Many others had their youth violently raped by apartheid, and were left embittered and with gaping wounds which will never heal in their hearts. Others – Hector Petersen, Sicelo Dhlomo *et al* come to mind – were not as lucky: they did not survive the brutality of apartheid to celebrate our hard-won freedom.

With the long-awaited demise of apartheid now a reality, we must hope our children and younger siblings will grow up in a much less violent society, content to leave the dangerous game of politics to adults.

The end of apartheid has other benefits, both material and psychological, for South Africa. It has restored our citizenship of the international community and its bodies. They all want our fledgling democracy to succeed, and are keenly aware of the dangers posed to our settlement if the new Government should fail to satisfy the dangerously high expectations of the country's majority.

The UN, the Commonwealth, the OAU, the International Monetary Fund and the World Bank have all been winking seductively at us.

All this, of course, comes at a price. For a country not used to being the centre of positive international attention, our newly found status as the most favoured country of the moment might very easily go to our heads as a nation. We might begin to believe, wrongly, that the international community will always be at our beck and call, and that all we need to do in future is just to say what it is we want and it shall be granted.

That is as dangerous a belief as one can get and we should vigilantly guard against it.

The other danger, of course, is that, in our desire to be seen as the regional superpower the world says we are, we could fall into the trap of taking on to our already heavily burdened shoulders the problems of the entire sub-region. We could allow ourselves to be pushed into boots much bigger than ourselves by agreeing to send our soldiers to Rwanda as part of a UN peacekeeping force.

Pure Poetry from Poignant Mandela

25 May 1994

The late Afrikaans poet Ingrid Jonker, who committed suicide about three decades ago following a serious bout of depression, came to life again in Parliament yesterday, and the man who resurrected her briefly was President Mandela.

In his speech as he opened Parliament, Mandela came close to canonising Jonker, to whom he referred repeatedly in the most glowing of terms in his state-of-the-nation address.

'She was both a poet and a South African. She was both Afrikaner and African. She was both an artist and a human being.

'In the midst of despair, she celebrated hope.

'Confronted by death, she asserted the beauty of life. In the dark days when all seemed hopeless in our country, when many refused to hear her resonant voice, she took her own life.

'To her and others like her, we owe a debt to life itself. To her and others like her, we owe a commitment to the poor, the oppressed, the wretched and the despised,' Mandela said.

He then proceeded to quote in full her moving poem 'The Child', originally written in Afrikaans in March 1960.

According to Jonker, it had been inspired by the shooting of a mother and her child in Nyanga.

Parliament was dead quiet as Mandela read the poem, and a few heads from the ranks of the predominantly white and Afrikaner opposition benches kept nodding. But when he said immediately afterwards that freedom could not be fully attained until women had been freed from all forms of oppression, only the women in the ANC benches clapped hands loudly.

The daughter of a former MP, Jonker threw herself into the sea in Cape Town and drowned herself five years after she wrote the poem.

Jonker took her life on July 19 1965, a day after Mandela's 47th birthday.

The President, whose prepared speech had mentioned 'comrades' along with the usual other parliamentary honorifics, omitted that reference and proceeded straight to the more acceptable 'ladies and gentlemen'.

But not everybody was captivated by his speech. At least one of his Ministers from the ANC was seen leisurely looking at photographs inside his diary as Mandela spoke.

Mandela Travels Bushy Road

27 May 1994

South Africa's President, Nelson Mandela, does not have much in common with former US President George Bush, who, for years, regarded the ANC as a 'terrorist organisation'.

But in the next few months and years he may find himself increasingly likened to Bush. One of the things for which many Americans never forgave the former Republic president was his ill-advised 'Watch my lips: No new taxes' pledge in the run-up to the 1988 presidential election. Later, he was forced to raise taxes.

There are things Mandela said in the run-up to our first all-race election that he has reason to regret now. Apart from a tax increase being in the offing to help fund the Reconstruction and Development Programme, despite the ANC's spirited denials in the run-up to the election, there were his repeated personal attacks on then President F W de Klerk.

De Klerk, Mandela used to tell his supporters, was going to be 'a forgotten man' who would not have a role to play after the election. This he said while knowing that, according to the Interim Constitution his organisation had helped fashion, the NP leader was assured of the second deputy presidency.

And now, two weeks into his Government's term, he seems to be bending over backwards to accommodate De Klerk and the NP in a manner that has already antagonised many within the ANC in Parliament.

He is so firmly committed to allaying the fears – perceived and real – of whites and the business community that he is in danger of soon finding himself a captive of white South Africa.

Since he took over as President, Mandela has, some times rightly, had a lot to say about reconciliation. In particular, he has urged blacks to reach out to whites, to learn and sing their anthem 'Die Stem', and generally make them feel they have no reason to be apprehensive.

Predictably, the loudest applause has come from the white community, which praises him for his statesmanship.

Hailed

His state-of-the-nation address when he opened Parliament this week was positive overall, and had something for everyone. Overwhelmingly, however, it was a speech aimed at the white and business communities which, predictably, again hailed him for, in the words of the *Cape Times* on Wednesday, a 'refreshing absence of ideological cant'.

Bluntly, this was a conservative speech which went down better in areas like Constantia and Houghton than in Guguletu and Soweto. As one journalist remarked, it was a dour speech which unveiled remarkably moderate plans for a former 'liberation movement'.

And that is why it is very unfortunate that Azapo stayed out of the election and the PAC fared as badly in it as it did. A voice to the left of the ANC is sorely needed in Parliament to remind the new ANC-led government of its responsibility to the black masses as well.

We must now hope that some within the ANC itself will see the need to play this watchdog role themselves. There is now a danger that unless the too-eager-to please attitude of Mandela's Government of National Unity alters, change will be felt only at the political level, where black leaders are in control – or appear to be in control – of the reins of power and not where it matters most, at the socio-economic level.

Should this remain the case, then only the black political and professional elite will benefit from the new dispensation, while the majority of blacks will remain at the lowest rung of the economic ladder.

And unless the ANC fully asserts itself as soon as possible in the coalition Government, where it has a considerable majority, and begins to redirect the Government's priorities, unprecedented disillusionment will set in in the months ahead.

Some within the organisation do not even seem to have the will to govern, with an NP which got 20 percent of the national vote retaining power far beyond its numerical strength.

In order to pacify De Klerk, Mandela agreed to relinquish the presidency of the Senate to the NP's Kobie Coetsee, a man to whom he feels indebted for historical reasons, in exchange for the ANC's retention of the security ministries, Defence and Public Safety and Security.

As though this were not enough, Mandela effectively vetoed this week a decision taken democratically by the ANC's parliamentary caucus and agreed to the deputy chairmanship of the Constitutional Assembly (CA) being given to the NP's Leon Wessels.

Conferred

But the issue here is not who holds the position, but rather the fact that the ANC caucus had elected lawyer Bridgitte Mabandla to be secretary-general Cyril Ramaphosa's deputy as chairman of the CA.

This decision having been taken and made public, Mandela conferred with De Klerk and agreed that Wessels, and not Mabandla, would be deputy chairman. All, of course, in the name of reconciliation and, according to some ANC sources, without Mabandla even being informed about it.

To preserve the appearance of unity, horrified ANC MPs bit their lips but remained on their seats when the NP nominated Wessels for the position, with none being willing to stand up and nominate Mabandla. There is no better way of describing this disturbing new pattern other than to say it is deplorable.

And apart from Housing Minister Joe Slovo, who has already appointed his own director-general, all the other Cabinet Ministers have so far retained directors-general and media spokesmen inherited from their predecessors. With only a few exceptions these ministries continue to be white, excepting the cabinet ministers.

If Ministers cannot effect changes in the racial composition of their ministries, it will be too much to expect of them to do this in their departments and other spheres.

For Mandela's own sake, for the ANC's and indeed the whole country's, we must hope our leaders will be able to combine reconciliatory moves with concrete steps, to send a message that the lot of blacks will not stay the same, and that some sacrifices by those who have been beneficiaries of apartheid in the past will have to be made.

That requires more than the announcement of a token feeding scheme for poor school children and free medical treatment at state hospitals for children and pregnant women. The alternative, to borrow former President Botha's phrase, will be 'too ghastly to contemplate'.

No Fracture Likely Before '96

16 August 1994

South Africa may not be world-beaters in sport or trading, but when it comes to purveying pessimism and gloom we are not far behind. In recent weeks, some people have worked themselves into quite a panic over the perceived state of affairs in the Government of National Unity (GNU), with all kinds of apocalyptic predictions being made.

There are those who, citing recent developments, have argued that all is not well within the coalition Government, and have gone so far as to suggest that the GNU may even be on the verge of collapse.

On the other hand, others have deliberately sought to paper over the apparent cracks in the GNU, and have tried to suggest, without much success, that everything is still hunky-dory in the coalition.

The truth lies somewhere in the middle. It is that the honeymoon – which had begun to lull some into a false belief that our country was now some fairyland in which everybody would live happily ever after – is finally over. It came to an end even before the GNU's first 100 days in office ended, and not a moment too soon.

Instead of worrying about tensions in the GNU or the increasingly strident tone of debates in Parliament, we should welcome this new development. Not only were these developments to be expected, but they are also healthy for the country.

But let us retrace our steps to the time in July when reports of trouble within the GNU first became public knowledge. Some, including people within the National Party (NP), had expressed concern that NP leader and Second Deputy President F W De Klerk had been very quiet in the first two months of the GNU.

He did not keep a low profile after the May 10 inauguration, he simply had no profile at all, wrote one journalist. He had lost interest in politics, some 'experts' opined sagaciously.

Interest reaffirmed

And then came that bombshell: some NP MPs wanted De Klerk and their party to quit the GNU.

Now under pressure to increase his profile, De Klerk returned from an overseas visit to reaffirm his interest in politics. In his defence, he said he had deliberately stayed out of the limelight to allow the ANC to come to grips with its new responsibilities and in order not to be seen to be upstaging President Mandela.

He also observed that the local press was not used to coalition governments in general, and the GNU in particular, and expected the traditional politics of the past, which saw opposition parties routinely criticising the Government for the sake of criticising, to continue.

Sadly, he was right. It would indeed appear that some had grown used to the ding-dong politics of the past, characterised by conflict and disagreements, which produced countless newspaper headlines. And as long as there was no open dissent in the GNU, politics was now boring. So De Klerk had to be goaded into rocking the boat.

De Klerk's reasons for his post-inauguration low profile, as given above, are entirely plausible. Not only would he have failed to upstage Mandela had he tried to do so, but he would also have been accused of failing to come to terms with the fact that he was no longer running the country. The man is now one of two deputy presidents, neither of whom has any clearly spelt out constitutional responsibilities.

It stands to reason, therefore, that he no longer commands the kind of public interest that he once did.

Clearly, the NP will now be much more critical of the ANC-led Government than it has been in the first two months of the GNU, and we can expect the Inkatha Freedom Party (IFP), whose leader, Chief Mangosuthu Buthelezi, cannot be accused of ever having taken a low profile, to do the same. We can also expect the language used in parliamentary debates to be more robust from now on, and that is as it should be.

'Nothing alarming'

It is healthy for our democracy, especially in view of the fact that, because of the constitutionally enforced coalition, we have a weak parliamentary opposition. Nobody should be alarmed about this trend.

There is also no reason to believe that the NP might pull out of the GNU between now and the end of 1996.

The NP had been in power for 45 years, had become used to the taste. It is unlikely to relinquish its share.

Likelier to happen, however, is that tensions within the GNU will intensify as we move closer to the 1999 election. It is reasonable to expect that once the country's new constitution has been finalised, and the Constitutional Assembly has until May 1996 to finish it, a lot of inter-party posturing will begin to take place in the GNU as the three parties cast their eyes on the next election.

It is quite conceivable, therefore, as Buthelezi has often said, that the next general election may be held well before 1999. Until at least the end of 1996, however, the GNU is safe and news of its impending demise has been greatly exaggerated.

That is not to say there are no lessons to be learnt by the three parties in the GNU. There are growing pains, to be sure, but these are nothing more than that at this stage.

Indications are that the NP has more learning to do than the ANC and the IFP. Although De Klerk says he does not need to be reminded that he is no longer running the country, it would seem that some within his party do need a constant reminder. It is their actions, which at times show a lack of understanding of how democracy functions, that will increase tensions in the coalition.

Their insistence on some form of a veto power for the NP in government, including their demand that NP MPs *must* be given – without a vote – the chairmanships of some of the 26 parliamentary standing committees is one example.

They need to accept that – with its 62 percent of the popular vote to the NP's 20 percent and the IFP's 10 percent – the ANC is the party with the ultimate responsibility to govern. The NP's views matter, but should not amount to vetoes.

F W Fulfilled in his Co-pilot's Role

23 August 1994

On his low post-election profile

I have specifically kept a low profile and concentrated within the GNU on being helpful in establishing a good and sound working relationship.

On being no longer in charge of Government

Not being in charge is the result of the election. It did not come as a shock to me, and I am finding it difficult to adapt because the whole process affords me many opportunities to play a very constructive role. I feel that is my duty at the moment. I am not in the job for the glamour and the honour and the powers. I am doing what I am doing because I believe South Africa has a one-off chance to really break through to a new and prosperous future for all.

On the honeymoon

In the sense of everybody being extra-cautious, yes, the honeymoon is over. That does not mean the NP is now taking the gloves half-off and [will] in three months' time become very rough and aggressive. However, as I said recently on the issue of parliamentary chairpersonships, we will not allow ourselves to be pushed around. Opposition is a role which we will play, but we'll do so with responsibility and in a very constructive spirit. We don't have a strategy to walk out of the GNU at a specific moment.

On the GNU's first 100 days

I think we couldn't have done much more in the first 100 days. Taking into account that the biggest percentage of the members of the Cabinet have no experience of governing, [that they] had to get to know departments, establish themselves freshly in office, build relationships with senior advisers – and all of us are on a learning curve in this sort of coalition – we could not have done much more.

On progress made by the GNU

Behind the scenes good progress has been made, not all of it visible. The White Paper on the RDP, which is fundamental, has made very good progress.

On problems encountered

There were a few problems, especially during July. [I am] critical of the fact that a few individual ministers jumped the gun and made statements which do not reflect agreed-upon policy, such as statements on the Truth Commission. I am also concerned about the decision on the allocation of chairpersonships of parliamentary standing committees. I am particularly worried about the implications of this in terms of the role being played by elements within the ANC caucus. [However], I do not think any harm has been done that cannot be repaired.

On the masses' expectations

I can understand the feeling of expectancy in certain quarters. They want to see results. I would support the statements of the president and my colleague, deputy president Mbeki, that people must [temper] their expectations and realise that, looking at the magnitude of the task, things cannot be done in a month or two. Within the GNU there is a deep understanding that we have to deliver progress sooner rather than later.

On whether he has been under pressure from the NP to quit

No, I have not been under pressure from my caucus at all. I am firing on all my cylinders and pistons and I am enjoying what I am doing. There were even stories that I am due to resign. Somewhere, somehow, someone is being very malicious in this regard. I have never considered it.

On dissension in the GNU

I see basically three scenarios with regard to decisions and statements within the GNU. Firstly, if we have agreed on an issue then we will constructively and loyally support such policies that we have agreed upon. Secondly, there is the possibility that we cannot reach consensus but are not dealing with a matter of fundamental importance.

The way to handle that would be to say publicly that I am against it. What we must avoid is the third category, where on matters of fundamental importance we do not reach consensus. Where fundamental principles come into play, where it might become a matter [on which] a majority party tries to force through an issue: that we must avoid.

On lessons of negotiations

It is not as if we are without experience – we have come through the whole negotiations process with regard to the new constitution and we reached, on real fundamental issues from time to time, such moments and we were able to build bridges and to reach compromise.

On possible future threats to the GNU

I could identify a number of risks lying ahead. One would be that all parties, the leaders present in the GNU, must continue to carry their constituencies with them. Serious divisions – specifically within the ANC – would pose a serious threat to the GNU.

Deviation from what has already been agreed upon would pose a very serious threat and, let's pray to God it will not happen, but a revival of violence on a wide scale will pose a very serious threat.

On finance minister Derek Keys's shock resignation

I tried to the very last moment [to prevent it]; it was an evolutionary situation with regard to Minister Keys. I tried right to the last moment to prevent him from taking the final decision.

He felt – and I agreed with him – that it was the decent thing to do. The moment that his decision became final [it was important] to announce it so that his successor could be chosen as soon as possible and could become party already to the budget-making process.

On the new Cabinet position now available to the NP

We are still in negotiations with the president. It is not just appointing somebody, it is deciding what the responsibility of such a minister will be and, in terms of the constitution, that has to be negotiated. I have had preliminary discussions with the president. I am consulting the leaders of the NP at the moment and there is no hurry.

His assessment of the new Cabinet's competence

I think the Cabinet can be described as a group of people who can develop into a good team, and they have good talent (on the whole).

On the IFP's role in the GNU

I think the IFP is adapting well. It is being constructive in the GNU and

I have no criticism. I praise the way in which Mr Buthelezi and his colleagues are co-operative in the GNU.

On the NP's post-election state of preparedness

The NP is not a defeated party in the sense that it is down in the dumps. There was an element of disappointment [with the outcome of the election]; there is a firm belief that we have done much better than the actual results reflect. But there is striving, and the NP is already gearing itself towards growth.

Our plans are ready, our budget is ready; we are not in the red. We are not a rich party but we are not in the red and we are raring to go. You will be hearing more and more and seeing more of us.

We have regrouped, and we are organised for what lies ahead, and it is our goal to become the biggest party in South Africa at the next election.

On whether he believes the election result was rigged

I do not think the election result was rigged, but I think many people were issued with voting cards [when they] were below age or did not qualify. I think there were many irregularities, and it is on that basis that we say had that been totally avoided successfully, our percentage would have been substantially higher.

On continuing white dominance of the NP

Nothing is further from the truth. The NP would regard it as an insult to appoint people on the basis of their colour merely to reflect a picture. I have within the party black people in leading positions.

On the possibility of realignment before the next election

I think not at this particular point in time. I think that maybe a moment [might come] when it might become [possible] – when we have finalised negotiation on the new constitution – after about two years. It is not NP strategy to play petty politics with regard to potential divisions in other parties.

On possible changes in the Interim Constitution

I think our transitional constitution is basically a good one. I would like to see the main principles continued and taken up in the final constitution.

One area which will obviously have to be addressed is the question of the executive. As for the rest, I don't think we need to deviate much, and I predict that the final constitution will not look all that much different. I would like to [see] a greater distance between the executive and the legislature.

On what he misses by no longer being president

The capacity to, after I have become convinced that the decision is the right one, take it and implement it. [That is] the essence because apart from that, my life has not really changed that much in a sense. Status as such has never been really important to me.

On the recent wave of strikes

I feel very strongly about the question of labour stability and stability in the workplace. [The present problems] can or should be solved by all role players.

They should not waste any time, get together and work for an economic [pact] which can offer to the workers the certainty that their interest will be catered for in an orderly manner, even if they are asked to initially make sacrifices in order to ensure that the economy gets the necessary kick-start. [It should be] an agreement, likewise, which will offer to the employers and private sector the certainty that there would be stability in the workplace, and they can plan on that basis.

On the high crime rate

I think the successful implementation of the RDP – which, to my mind, must address the question of the so called 'lost generation' – can make a significant contribution. Simultaneously, I think the de-politicising of the police force will hopefully result in much closer co-operation between the police and the community, and that can make a significant contribution.

Therefore, I think the criminals must be on their guards. I regard the fighting of crime as one of the top priorities because crime is having a terrible effect on our country at the moment. I perceive the same attitude among our partners in the GNU and, therefore, I have high hopes that we will develop strategies which will successfully cut the crime rate down.

ANC Takes Long Look at Itself in the Mirror

2 September 1994

For more than 80 years the ANC waged a long and sometimes bloody war against white minority rule in South Africa.

Now comfortably ensconced in Government, the ANC finds that it has yet another battle to fight, this time against a less identifiable but nevertheless far more potent adversary.

The new challenges are listed in a 37-page discussion document presented to the ANC's national executive committee early this week, and which is in the possession of *The Star*. It was written by Deputy President Thabo Mbeki, the ANC national chairman.

The document, 'From resistance to reconstruction: Task of the ANC in the new epoch of democratic transformation', is the first known attempt within the ANC to look at the organisation's strengths and weaknesses since the election.

It also shows a growing concern – bordering on paranoia – about differences inside the ANC itself, and between it and its allies in the 'mass democratic movement' – Cosatu, the SA Communist Party and civic organisations.

Although the document, marked 'unmandated reflections', will now be discussed by the ANC's regions and branches before the organisation's national congress in Bloemfontein in December, sources said it had received a fairly warm reception in the NEC.

The document says the ANC emerged from the election 'as the party of the African masses (which is) consistent with the historic objective of the democratic revolution of securing the emancipation of the most oppressed and exploited section of our population'.

According to the document, the next test of the ANC's strength will be next year's local elections: 'Obtaining a decisive victory in the forthcoming local government elections is one of the most important and urgent tasks facing the movement.'

To achieve this, says the document, four things will have to be done.

Firstly, the ANC will have to hold on to its 'proven African support' by delivering real change to the masses and maintaining intra-organisational unity.

'This approach ensures that we move away from the dangerous concept that the movement has split into various factions – the extra-parliamentary, the parliamentary and the executive – and ensures that all members of the organisation act together in pursuit of common goals, regardless of where they are deployed,' says the document.

Secondly, the ANC will have 'to win back the traditional ANC constituency that we lost to the IFP'. To this end, action will have to be taken to end violence in KwaZulu/Natal and on the East Rand.

The Zulu royal house and traditional leaders in the province will have to be 'persuaded that they should not be involved in supporting any of the parties and organisations that will participate in the local government elections.'

'It is imperative that we deal firmly and decisively with violence originating from within our own ranks, whether directed against competing political parties or other members and supporters of the movement.'

Thirdly, work would have to be done to counter National Party propaganda aimed at coloureds and Indians, and to actively woo these minority groups.

Says the document: 'Common sense should tell us that one of the principal issues of the next five years will be the national question, in whatever way it expresses itself. This will put great pressure on the democratic movement to address the interests of all national and ethnic groups in a manner that uplifts the most disadvantaged, the Africans, while not being seen as threatening by the rest of the population.'

Finally, the organisation will seek to 'retain and increase our support among the coloured, Indian and white middle strata' by involving these groups in the planning and implementation of programmes for reconstruction and development at local and national levels.

It is when the document turns to possible actions the opposition might take to discredit both the ANC and the Government of National Unity that paranoia becomes over-arching. It is feared that the opposition – which includes other political parties, 'liberal establishments', the press and 'counter-revolutionary forces' – would intensify its efforts to discredit the ANC.

The opposition, says the document, will take advantage of 'the critical posture' of the white-owned and controlled mass media to broadcast its message far and wide.

'It is necessary to bear in mind that this media is itself driven by fear of a truly non-racial order, because of its concern to preserve its own racial status quo with regard to various matters, including ownership, editorial control and policy and staffing,' says the document.

The document also anticipates the power struggle that will intensify in the run-up to the December congress as elections for the NEC loom, and says the opposition will set up ANC leaders against one another 'on the basis that they represent different tendencies'.

It warns that the SACP, Cosatu and ANC parliamentarians could be 'used', 'encouraged' and 'incited' to project themselves as watchdogs of the ANC in government.

To counter this perceived threat, it would be necessary to foster unity among ANC leaders and within the organisation generally, to deliver change and to be wary of the 'dangerous drift towards "federalism"'.

The document strongly urges that the Government and relevant ANC structures must take measures to ensure that structures originally established for counter-revolutionary purposes are dismantled.

But the document adds a caveat: 'The movement must also get ready to deal with the challenge of the exposure of some of its members as having been informers and agents of the apartheid secret service.'

A Typical Day in the Life of Mandela

12 September 1994

Of all black South Africans, President Nelson Mandela has the most reason to be angry and bitter.

After all, successive National Party governments locked him up for almost three decades and thanks to them he ascended to power too late, and will most certainly be unable to serve more than one term in office. But hear Mandela talking about the things he used to do in prison, things for which he no longer has time, and you would think he was missing those years behind bars.

'These days I have time to read only the newspaper headings in the mornings, and may read one in-depth article as well, and I get briefings from my staff.

'I used to have a lot of time in prison, to think and read books and newspapers. I used to read the papers from front page through to the sports pages.'

As even a few minutes with Mandela will reveal, he is a charming and most remarkable man. He is warm, humble and self effacing, has a lively sense of humour and an incredibly sharp mind.

He is, as some in the ANC have often pointed out, a hard task master. Meetings with him are not a mere formality. He asks questions, makes suggestions and issues instructions, whether dealing with one of his cabinet ministers, advisers or members of his immediate staff.

I had been told to be at the Waterkloof Air Force Base in Pretoria at 6 am on Thursday, and that we would leave for Cape Town aboard the president's Falcon 900.

By 5.30 I was already waiting at the air force base's VIP Lounge, where I found presidential spokesman Joel Netshitenzhe. Next to arrive shortly thereafter was Mandela's private secretary, Mary Mxadana. Formerly with the South African Council of Churches, Mxadana is a powerful but friendly woman.

She it is who runs Mandela's diary, and ensures at all times that he has time to rest and is not unduly troubled by matters which could be handled by others.

Mandela himself arrives at 5.55, clad in a navy-blue suit. He reveals later that none of his suits has been purchased. Instead, they have all been given to him as presents. Once comfortably seated inside the luxurious presidential plane he takes his shoes off.

There is a frank conversation with me and the *New York Times's* Bill Keller, the only other journalist spending a day with him, that remains indelible in my mind. It is a revealing conversation that tells more about Mandela the man, whether he is talking about the media or about Deputy President Thabo Mbeki and ANC Secretary-General Cyril Ramaphosa, for whom he professes to have equal respect.

Even in this relaxed atmosphere, he will not be coaxed into disclosing his favourite between the two men, one of whom is bound to be his successor.

All he is prepared to say, both on and off the record, is that both men are eminently qualified to jump into his shoes.

At Ysterplaat Air Force Base in Cape Town, the president is whisked away by his security personnel, and we follow behind in an old Citi Golf. By the time we get to his spacious office at Tuynhuys, it is 8.30.

The proverbial flies on the wall, Mxadana keeps explaining to those who have appointments with the president, we sit through all but one meeting – with deputy presidents Mbeki and F W de Klerk – in that office, and observe at close range how Mandela spends his day.

It is in that office, he soon points out to us, that he first met then President P W Botha in July 1989, following a letter he had written to Botha four months earlier. He talks about the preparations that were made for the historic meeting, and describes how the 'extraordinary steps' that were taken by the authorities – security was tighter than usual and samples of his blood had been taken 'just in case something happened to me' – made him feel 'very tense'.

As things turned out, the meeting went well, with an amiable Botha even personally serving tea to his prisoner.

But there are no traces of Botha in that office now.

There is an African ambience, and on the walls hang numerous pictures: of the house in which Mandela was born in Qumbu in the Transkei, of Mandela shadow-boxing with Jerry Moloi (who died while the president was still in prison), and, on a picture stand next to the president's big table, of Mandela with Pieter-Dirk Uys, alias Evita Bezuidenhout. Two big new South African flags stand on either side.

Around 8.45 Mxadana – who keeps going in and out of the office – comes in to discuss the day's diary. Mandela, who calls her 'one of my many bosses', asks her to phone Mbeki and De Klerk.

When they arrive and Mandela informs them about our shadowing him all day, De Klerk remarks: 'When you become a president, you lose control of your life.'

Unfortunately, we cannot be present in the one meeting we would most have wanted to sit in on. First to emerge is De Klerk at 1.15, followed by Mbeki five minutes later.

But back to the morning. Mandela's first engagement for the day begins at 9.30 when he has to receive five new ambassadors in a row.

Before that, an unscheduled briefing on the situation in Lesotho takes place at 9 am, and this is the other meeting we are not allowed to attend. But before presentation of credentials starts, a Japanese business delegation, led by the Japanese ambassador, 'gatecrashes' the office for a few minutes. They have no appointment, but Mandela does not refuse them.

Other phone callers are Pick 'n Pay's Raymond Ackerman on his private line and SABC chief executive and former newspaper editor Zwelakhe Sisulu, who phoned to confirm his attendance at a private dinner.

'Hello,' 'Lakhe. How is the new crown that you are wearing? Has it got thorns? I know you can do it,' Mandela said to Sisulu on the phone.

Now it's lunchtime, and we enjoy chicken, rice, carrots and mushrooms. Mandela passes the bread around and later stands up to serve us natural orange juice. By the time he pours for himself, there is little juice left.

While we are eating, Mxadana reports that a child who came with her parents, five-year-old Ntokozo, refuses to leave until she has seen Mandela. The president excuses himself and goes to her at the reception area, where he carries her up.

After lunch there are more appointments, scheduled and some unscheduled, and documents to read and be signed.

One is from the Black Sash protesting against the amendment of the Interim Constitution to allow for banker Chris Liebenberg's appointment as next Finance Minister.

Mandela quips: 'I had thought the Black Sash would agree with everything we did.'

The last appointment of the day, which starts at 4.05 pm, is an interview with the *Christian Science Monitor*. By this time, we have been up for no less than 12 hours, and Keller and I are dead tired, even drowsy.

Not Mandela, who emerges from the interview looking as fresh as he did in the morning. He then leaves for Pretoria, where the only other official engagement awaiting him is a hastily arranged meeting with a delegation from Lesotho's King Letsie III.

Zulu King Fears for Life as Bitter Dispute Deepens

22 September 1994

Ulundi – The dispute between Zulu King Goodwill Zwelithini and IFP leader Chief Mangosuthu Buthelezi showed no signs of abating last night, with the king expressing fears for his own safety.

Delivering a pre-recorded message on SABC-TV last night, Zwelithini made it clear he now feared for his life and asked pointedly: 'What is being planned about my life and the Zulu monarchy?'

Speaking in Zulu, he said he found it strange that some indunas in the PWV had come out on Buthelezi's side in the bitter dispute.

When *The Star* yesterday visited Nongoma – where the monarch normally lives – residents spoke openly about the danger facing the king and they said they felt his life could be at risk if he went against Buthelezi.

Although earlier reports this week said Zwelithini had fled Nongoma to a farm about 200 km away, *The Star* was told this morning that he was back at his Enyokeni residence in Nongoma yesterday, where KwaZulu Police Force members were seen guarding the entrance.

Some SA National Defence Force personnel were on guard at the residence and at the Dlamahlahla palace.

Meanwhile, IFP leaders, including Buthelezi, national chairman and KwaZulu/Natal Premier Dr Frank Mdlalose, and IFP secretary-general Dr Ziba Jiyane have insisted that Saturday's Shaka Day celebrations in Stanger will go ahead as scheduled, in spite of Zwelithini's announcement that the event has been cancelled.

'He [Zwelithini] does not exercise direct power over his subjects. He is a ceremonial figurehead,' said Jiyane.

'The celebrations are so deeply imbedded in the psyche of the KwaZulu people, and it can only take the Zulus to stop the function.'

The monarch has been roundly condemned for 'acting unilaterally' in calling off celebrations for a day that means so much to Zulus, and IFP members here have made it clear they will not only attend the celebrations but also ensure others attend.

A snap survey conducted by *The Star* in Ulundi and Nongoma yesterday revealed that the overwhelming majority of Zulus were solidly behind Buthelezi and are angry with the king.

Investigations in Ulundi this morning showed that the trucks and buses in which IFP members were transported to Dlamahlahla palace when the king met President Nelson Mandela and Buthelezi on Monday are owned by the former KwaZulu Government. Sources here said the buses were provided free of charge by officials in Ulundi who now work for the new KwaZulu/Natal government.

Zwelithini told his subjects on Radio Zulu yesterday that his move to cancel Shaka Day festivities and sever ties with Buthelezi was sparked by the violent protests and damaging of property at the palace by people transported in buses bearing ZG registration numbers.

King Evacuated From his Palace

23 September 1994

Ulundi – The South African National Defence Force (SANDF) yesterday flew Zulu King Goodwill Zwelithini out of Nongoma to get him away from the tension-filled areas of rural KwaZulu/Natal on the eve of tomorrow's Shaka Day celebrations.

The Star was one of only two newspapers (the other is based in Durban) present when Zwelithini and six members of his family – two women and four men – were flown out of Enyokeni Palace by officers of the Durban-based Fifteen Squadron late yesterday afternoon.

An SANDF helicopter arrived at the palace at 3.50 pm.

The commanding officer for Northern Natal said he had been in a meeting in Eshowe when he had received instructions at 1.00 pm to take a Fifteen Squadron pilot to the king's palace.

'We have been told to fly him to Richard's Bay, but I don't know where he will be proceeding to from there,' one officer said.

As the monarch's bags were transported from the palace to be loaded on to the helicopter amid tight security, excited school children surrounded the military plane to look at it.

Smartly dressed, gun-carrying men stood sentry at the main gate to the palace as others stayed in the car, bringing the luggage to the plane.

An impeccably dressed but visibly worried Zwelithini, who tried to look relaxed, came out of Enyokeni Palace at 4.40 pm and stood at the gate for about five minutes talking to his advisers and members of his family. He refused to be photographed as he got on to the plane.

The helicopter took off at 4.45 pm after the pilot had told him and his family what to do in case of an emergency and informed them that the flight to Richard's Bay would take 30 minutes.

Before that, *The Star's* news team had driven first to Zwelithini's Khangela Palace on the road towards Pongola and then to Dlamahlahla Palace outside Nongoma in an attempt to establish Zwelithini's whereabouts.

A Khangela Palace member said the monarch had arrived there with a huge contingent at 4.00 am and had left around noon.

At Dlamahlahla Palace it was reported that the king had arrived shortly after lunch and had left soon afterwards.

KwaZulu Police (ZP) members at the Enyokeni Palace said Zwelithini arrived there at 3.00 pm.

Contrary to widespread reports that the SANDF had been deployed to protect the king at his palaces, apart from the officers who came on the helicopter, there was no sign of SANDF presence at any of the palaces.

Instead, ZP members manned all the entrances and said no SANDF troops had been sent to the respective palaces.

ANC Adopts Mbeki Strategy Document

2 December 1994

Deputy President Thabo Mbeki's strategic document committing the ANC to 'the advancement of the struggle towards the completion of the current phase of the democratic revolution' was adopted by the ANC's decision-making structures last weekend, *The Star* can now reveal.

Entitled 'Discussion Document: ANC Strategy and Tactics', the paper outlines a clear strategy shift for the ANC in government, with the organisation's core black constituency now earmarked for more attention that it has received so far.

First reported on in *The Star* last week, the document was presented to the national executive committees of the ANC, the ANC Women's League and the ANC Youth League last weekend, and some suggestions were made before its adoption.

Now amended, it has increased from its original 13-page length to 18 pages, and will be presented to the ANC's national congress in Bloemfontein this month. The amended document is not much different from its forerunner, but does add a few more issues to receive special attention at the December 17–21 congress.

The triennial congress will draw heavily from Mbeki's discussion paper, with the 11 commissions planned for the conference all taking their themes directly from the document.

At a news conference in Johannesburg this week, ANC secretary-general Cyril Ramaphosa said: 'The central thrust of the conference will revolve around strategy and tactics to be adopted by the ANC. We will receive a presentation from our national chairman [Mbeki] on this issue.'

Ramaphosa also acknowledged that concerns that the ANC had spent its first six months in office allaying the fears of whites at thc expense of blacks would come under discussion.

'The conference will look at everything. Delegates will not be censored. The issue you raise will indeed be discussed,' Ramaphosa said in response to a question.

The document spells a clear shift in emphasis from the reconciliation rhetoric of the past six months to elevation of ANC constituents' concerns to the national agenda.

It says the April election did not mark 'a complete transfer of political power', and adds that the struggle to transform South Africa into a united, democratic, non-racial, non-sexist and prosperous society is far from over.

Emancipation

'The democratic majority has won only some of the important elements of that political power necessary for the advancement of the struggle towards the completion of the current phase of the democratic revolution,' says the document.

It commits the ANC to 'the all-round political, economic and social emancipation and upliftment of the black majority'.

It regards the black working class, the black rural poor and 'the significant section of the black middle strata' as 'the main motive forces of this democratic transformation'.

The document adds: 'The act of restructuring and transforming organs of State power constitutes one of the most important tasks in the process of broadening and consolidating the national democratic settlement.

'It is with the completion of this process that the revolution can truly be said to set firm foundations for its permanent defence.'

Mandela's ANC Leadership Plan

8 December 1994

In an unprecedented move, President Nelson Mandela has embarked on an ambitious plan aimed at ensuring that the new ANC leadership to be elected at the organisation's Bloemfontein congress next week is 'representative of all ethnic and racial groups in the country, as well as both sexes'.

The plan, known in ANC circles as the 'Mandela Initiative', will effectively override the nomination process presently under way in the different sections of the ANC and the organisation's 14 regions.

Reliable and well-placed ANC sources have told *The Star* that Mandela has appointed a four-man committee to draw up a list of recommended candidates for the ANC's national executive committee (NEC).

Made up of ANC deputy president Walter Sisulu, SACP general secretary Charles Nqakula, Cosatu secretary-general Sam Shilowa and South African National Civic Organisations president Lechesa Tsenoli, the committee will receive nominations for the NEC from the ANC Women's League, the ANC Youth League, the organisation's 14 regions and the ANC's allies.

It will then produce one composite and representative list of candidates, which will be debated and finally endorsed.

The sources said the same procedure will also apply to the 'top six officials' – the president and his deputy, the secretary-general and his deputy, the national chairman and the treasurer-general – although it would not affect Mandela's election as president and deputy president respectively.

The four-man committee will try to achieve consensus on the 'top six' by ensuring all 14 regions agree to the suggested candidates. Should there be no agreement on some position then some names will be voted upon.

Mandela, who has long expressed his concern that the ANC

leadership was dominated by Africans, has already held talks with the various regions and components of the ANC and its allies to sell his idea.

A meeting with the Free State leadership yesterday was cancelled at the last minute because the provincial delegation was late.

The sources also said Mandela wanted to ensure the new ANC was 'a truly mass-based organisation and that it remains strong'. He is understood to be keen to ensure that the new NEC was made up of 'people from all over the country and who represent true constituencies'.

To this end, Mandela has suggested that each region should have at least six representatives on the NEC – as opposed to the present two ex officio members – and that the new leadership 'represents all sections in the ANC'.

According to the sources, the 'Mandela Initiative' has been widely canvassed within the ANC and among its allies and has won the support of the majority.

'The idea is that we have a truly balanced and representative leadership so that we don't have people getting elected because they shout more than others at the congress or because they have appeared many times on TV.

'This has generally been accepted by everybody. At first there was resistance in the NEC to the idea because some comrades felt that this would somehow short-circuit the democratic process. It has now been accepted that the list will be tabled at the conference and people will debate it and vote on it.

'The idea is to ensure that the first pool of candidates is representative,' said one source.

What's in Store for Cyril

15 December 1994

Cyril Ramaphosa chooses his words carefully – very carefully. Certainly, he is quite genial and relaxed, but he is too good a politician to allow himself to get carried away in his pronouncements.

And so, like a skilled artist trying hard not to give away too much, he culls his words most adroitly while also managing to remain warm and engaging.

The place is his ninth-floor office at ANC headquarters in Johannesburg. The time is shortly after 8.00 am. He looks like he has not had much sleep, and is dressed informally.

For hours on end the previous day and well into the night he worked on the report he will deliver at the ANC's 49th national congress in Bloemfontein this weekend.

Now, Ramaphosa has been the subject of intense speculation of late. The questions have been the same: Has Ramaphosa finally accepted defeat and decided against contesting the ANC deputy presidency to be vacated by Walter Sisulu and most likely to be filled by Thabo Mbeki?

Will he, in light of reports that he was seriously thinking of not standing for re-election as secretary-general, make himself available?

And, after his meteoric rise to the top, are knives out for Ramaphosa?

If Ramaphosa is worried about all these things, he does not show it.

Admittedly, there is in the course of the interview the odd moment when he does not sound too confident of his future, such as when he repeatedly states that it is the delegates at the Bloemfontein congress who will decide his position.

And so, will the man who is widely acknowledged – even by his detractors – to have led the ANC negotiating team at the World Trade Centre with distinction stand, at the very least, for re-election to his present job?

Ramaphosa is non-committal. He talks about ongoing internal ANC discussions, expected to be settled at the congress, about whelther or not the position of secretary-general should be filled full-time.

Neither will the 43-year-old chairman of the Constitutional Assembly (CA) say why he will not be contesting the deputy presidency, a position for which he and Mbeki have always been accepted as the *only* candidates.

'If I run for any position, it will be the position of secretary-general. In the end, obviously, whether I run or not will be decided by conference.

'We need to see how best all of us can make a contribution to the ANC, and I think the contribution that I can make will be in the position that I am in now,' he says.

The record will show, however, that until President Nelson Mandela announced that he had chosen Mbeki as South Africa's first deputy president, Ramaphosa was a major contender for the job.

It will show further that Ramaphosa subsequently declined a Cabinet position as foreign affairs minister, choosing instead – or so he said and still says – to remain outside of government to concentrate on rebuilding the ANC.

Re-election

The record will show even further that it was not until Mandela gave him a talking to about a fortnight ago that Ramaphosa finally changed his mind and decided to make himself available for re-election as secretary-general, a position he is tipped to retain.

But it was not long into Parliament's first sitting that Ramaphosa accepted an appointment as chairman of the CA, the body charged with the responsibility of writing South Africa's final constitution.

The man who had wanted to devote his energies to re-building the ANC ended up spending a lot of time on his work as CA chairman.

In the process, the ANC suffered. It is common cause in political circles that the ANC's structures at branch, regional and national levels are now a shadow of their former selves.

However, to heap the blame for the state of affairs on Ramaphosa's shoulders, as some are wont to do, would be unfair.

The former National Union of Mineworkers secretary-general will be the first to concede that he has not spent as much time as he would have liked on ANC work.

But the fact is that most of the ANC's bright leaders were swallowed into Government at national and provincial level, as well as into the civil service.

It is this, more than Ramaphosa's alleged tardiness, that crippled the ANC after the April election.

In his defence, Ramaphosa points out, quite rightly, that he has had to do other things in the ANC apart from being secretary-general, such as leading the ANC delegation in multi-party talks at the World Trade Centre.

'The criticism [against me], I would say, is valid. At the same time, without being defensive, one has to look at the workload.

'This actually applies to quite a number of people in the organisation. I mean, people like Thabo [Mbeki] – he had to be head of international affairs, he had to be national chairperson and had many other tasks.

'At this conference, obviously, we will want to analyse all that. We will be raising the question of overloading a few people with too much work,' he says.

This notwithstanding, he believes the ANC in Government has 'done very well, and with people who did not have experience in government'.

The major challenges facing the organisation at the congress are 'evolving a clear strategy and settling tactics around that strategy, what the ANC needs to do itself as an organisation, and how we prosecute the next phase of the struggle'.

Complaints from delegates about a perceived Government bias in favour of the white and business communities at the expense of blacks, he acknowledges, will feature prominently.

So how would he, Cyril Matamela Ramaphosa, like to be remembered?

First there is a pregnant pause, which soon gives way to a wide grin on his face.

'Well,' he says, 'it's a difficult one because one is only remembered when one is dead and gone, and I am not yet.

'But maybe as a person who made a small contribution to bringing us where we are, and who got a great deal of satisfaction in seeing us moving from the apartheid matrix into a democratic dispensation.'

ANC's Sweeping Plans

22 December 1994

Bloemfontein – The ANC yesterday ended its 49th national congress here with a ringing endorsement of its new twin-track policy of moving towards delivery to its core black constituency on the Reconstruction and Development Programme (RDP) while also ensuring 'maximum national consensus, stability and peace'.

The policy, which includes a healthy balance between preaching reconciliation and addressing the concerns of the black majority, saw the 3000-strong congress adopt sweeping resolutions on restructuring of the civil service – including the security forces and the judiciary – transformation of the country's economy, and rebuilding of the organisation ahead of next year's local government elections.

A resolution on the constitution-making process committed the ANC to 'democratic majority rule based on a constitution without fetters on our ability to transform South Africa politically, economically and socially and rid South Africa of the legacy of apartheid'.

Delegates to the congress also voted in a delivery-oriented new national executive committee (NEC) with leaders with strong links to grassroots membership such as former ANC Youth League president Peter Mokaba (1824 votes) and Deputy Arts, Culture, Science and Technology Minister Winnie Mandela (1802 votes) placed third and fifth respectively.

However, there were few changes to the overall leadership, with most members of the former NEC members retained.

'We are acutely aware that overwhelming victory is only the beginning of the process of transforming our country. We are conscious of our responsibility to lead the country to reconstruction, reconciliation and nation-building,' the organisation said in a declaration at the end of the congress.

In his closing address yesterday, Mandela said the congress had 'confounded the prophets of doom who had predicted that the leadership would be roasted by delegates for neglecting the concerns of the majority and concentrating on reconciliation.

'Contrary to such predictions, delegates here have shown an unprecedented degree of unity. One of the dreams of every national organiser, and indeed of every member of the ANC, is that from every conference, especially a national conference, the organisation should emerge more motivated, more united than ever before.'

He said it had been clear that during the course of the congress delegates had appreciated 'the historic mission of the ANC, and that the organisation will discharge that mission only if delegates approach issues with a high sense of discipline'.

He said inputs made by new deputy chairman Thabo Mbeki on the 'Strategy and Tactics' document, and secretary-general Cyril Ramaphosa's candid report, had set the tone of the conference.

Delegates, he said, had been concerned with the implementation of the RDP and 'bettering the lives of our people'. The level of debate had been 'very high'.

He said next year's local government elections were of great concern to the ANC, and were 'more important than the April election'. The organisation wanted to win these elections 'at all costs'.

Read by new national chairman Jacob Zuma, the declaration said the ANC's responsibility was to ensure 'maximum national consensus, stability and peace' and reassure all sections of the country's population 'that they have a common and prosperous destiny to share in the land of their birth'.

The declaration reaffirmed the liberation of blacks in general and Africans in particular as 'the main content of our national democratic revolution', reaffirmed the ANC's character as 'a broad-based national liberation movement' and committed the ANC to working with 'other peace-loving South Africans in order to bring safety, security and peace to all communities.

'Further, this is the only way we can secure lasting peace for all our people, including our white compatriots who are beginning to experience real freedom and security under our emerging democracy,' said the declaration.

'We emerge from this conference stronger and more united than ever before, reinforced in our confidence to lead the country to a new and prosperous future. We are fully aware that these tasks are in the interest of the nation as a whole,' the declaration said.

Typical White Over-reaction to ANC Resolution

3 January 1995

The resolution by the ANC's 49th national congress in Bloemfontein two weeks ago that the country's new constitution should make provision for 'ordinary, democratic majority rule', in the words of Water Affairs Minister Professor Kader Asmal, has met with the usual pooh-pooh from some among our compatriots.

That in itself is not surprising, for it was to be expected that those for whose comfort the hybrid Government of National Unity (GNU) was intended would resist the next logical step to full-blooded democracy.

What *is* surprising is the fact that, in their response to the ANC resolution, some white commentators have failed lamentably to rise above their own narrow, selfish interests. Not only did they not declare up-front an interest in the matter, but they also sought to create the impression that theirs was a well-reasoned, objective response.

But before we go on, let us look first at the ANC's decision.

The resolution notes that the organisation's objective of 'a fully democratic South Africa based on majority rule must be achieved by drafting of a new constitution', and confirms the ANC's belief in 'democratic majority rule based on a constitution without fetters on our ability to transform South Africa politically, economically and socially and rid South Africa of the legacy of apartheid'.

That seems to me innocuous enough. Anyone who has closely followed political developments in the country over the past four years, but particularly the multi-party negotiations process at the World Trade Centre (WTC) last year, will know that the ANC made a major compromise by coming up with Joe Slovo's idea of a GNU with a five-year term.

This effectively met the National Party's then loud demand for power-sharing.

But even as this compromise was sold to the smaller parties at the WTC and ultimately drafted into the required legalese in the form of the present Interim Constitution, it was tacitly understood that this was a transitional measure which would not outlive the GNU's term of office.

And so why are some white commentators now shouting murder and suggesting that the GNU should become a permanent feature of our lives? Some of their arguments are even premised on racist stereotypes, to boot!

We can understand NP leader and Second Deputy President F W de Klerk's throwing his hands in the air in desperation and pleading plaintively for the continuation of the forced coalition government system.

Despite his earlier promise as an enlightened reformer, his recent utterances and actions have increasingly shown him to be, after all, no more than a mere tribal leader concerned more about Afrikaans and Afrikaners than he is about the bigger South Africa.

And it is no secret that he wants the present system to continue because he is white and leads a party that represents white interests. Democratic majority rule was fine when it still applied to only the white minority, but now that the black majority is enfranchised it is suddenly inimical to democracy as understood by the 'New NP'.

Following the ANC congress, colleague Graham Linscott argued the case for the maintenance of the status quo. Just as the NP and liberals argued over the years that sanctions would 'hurt most the blacks they were intended to help' and not so much white South Africa, he suggested that real [black] majority rule would harm blacks and the ANC itself.

('Would it better achieve economic upliftment for the disadvantaged? . . . In KwaZulu/Natal the ANC would be shut out from decision-making. Would it be content with that?' he wrote.)

And he went on to churn out the typical stereotypes about how majority rule 'has not been a success in Africa'. Quoth he sagaciously: 'In Africa multi-party adversarial government was divisive and dangerous and the response was often one-party state'.

Yes, but what about Botswana which has had a proud history of full democracy without being a one-party state? And why was majority rule not such a bad thing for NP-ruled white South Africa over the years?

Methinks we are owed answers.

Not a Day for Collective Amnesia

20 March 1995

The past, we are often told, is something that should not be dragged into the present, but should best be left alone and forgotten.

There is a lot of merit in that argument, because a country with the kind of history that ours has can very easily get caught up in that past, drown in its sorrow and bitterness and become prisoner to it. And so we need to move on, for failure to do so would make reconciliation that much more difficult.

But there are things we dare not forget, for even proponents of the 'let bygones be bygones' philosophy would surely not want to wish on us – one hopes – collective amnesia.

Many will accept that we do need to be mindful of whence we have come in order to better appreciate the present and know what pitfalls and temptations to eschew in future.

Many years after the event, a significant percentage of our Afrikaner compatriots have yet to forget the inhumane manner in which they were treated by the British in concentration camps following the Anglo-Boer war. Hence the invitation extended by some right-wing groups to the visiting Queen Elizabeth.

Of course, the right-wing group would have known even as it was discussing the invitation that its chances of being accepted were very slim indeed, if not altogether nonexistent.

Similarly, there are events and days that black South Africans will not be in a mad rush to forget. Apartheid with its attendant barbarism and brutality is one such thing that some of us will not forget quickly, no matter how much some of our white compatriots may want us to do so.

After all, the glaring legacies of that foolish system are there – and will be there for some years to come – for all to see.

Thirty-five years ago tomorrow in a place called Sharpeville in the Vaal Triangle, trigger-happy members of the South African Police callously opened fire on – and brutally murdered – 69 men and women whose twin sins were being black and protesting peacefully against the pass laws.

The world shuddered at this coldblooded assassination of citizens by a country's own security forces. However, the National Party leaders who ruled our lives with an iron fist then responded in the only manner they knew: they moved swiftly to ban the PAC and the ANC and to throw into jail leaders of these organisations.

March 21 will forever stand out as one of those dark days in our history, along with June 16 and a few other days. It is fitting and proper, therefore, that – albeit after much persuasion – President Mandela's Government last year declared the day a public holiday and called it Human Rights Day.

It was the least this country could do to honour the memories of the men and women who were mowed down on that day.

Equally fitting is the name given to the holiday, for tomorrow and on every other March 21 we must reach out to one another across the racial, political and geographic divide harmoniously or, in the words of one sage, 'all perish as fools'.

Although inspired by the evils of apartheid, March 21 is not – and should not be seen as – a 'black holiday'. Neither should it be seen as the PAC's holiday, although that organisation played no small a role in the cataclysmic events of that day 35 years ago. Instead, it is a South African holiday, belonging to all of us, black and white.

Let us, on that day, move even closer to one another in a very real way, and not only cosmetically – as has been the case so far.

Let us remember that those who lost their lives that day, on June 16 1976 and on the many other dark days on our calendar – and indeed on any other day – would not be happy with the situation which obtains in the country today, when nothing more than the colour of our political leaders has changed.

They and the many black South Africans alive today deserve much, much more.

A Long Time Before We Enjoy Freedom's Fruits

27 March 1995

If champagne flowed at the Orlando West, Soweto, home of Winnie Mandela following the court ruling in her favour, the celebration may have been premature.

There is every indication that there is a concerted bid, within and without the ANC, to get rid of her at all costs. She will no doubt come to appreciate fully, as all of us do from time to time, that *omne simile non est idem* – especially in politics.

But Mrs Mandela is merely the primary target, and the campaign to rid the ANC of 'populists and radicals' has just begun.

By the time it has run its full course people who have a history of close association with the black masses, and of consistently articulating the many and varied concerns of these wretched of the earth, will also have become political casualties.

Numbered among them will be Peter Mokaba, Bantu Holomisa, Tony Yengeni and Harry Gwala.

But first Mandela, who some in the ANC fear may have presidential ambitions, must be 'put in her place'. (What did Brutus say of Julius Caesar? 'But 'tis a common proof/ that lowliness is young ambition's ladder... So Caesar may, /Then lest he may, prevent...')

Once she has been dealt with, then, everything else will fall into place – or so hope those who live in a world of make believe. What, dare we ask, is their sin? From officialdom the answer will be that they are 'populists and radicals': that they 'shoot their months off without thinking', that they have proclivity to get into trouble, that they are prone to controversies which embarrass the infallible and beyond-reproach Government of National Unity – and those towering Colossuses who run it – and that they are 'corrupt'.

The real reason, however, is likely to be that these individuals continue to make nuisances of themselves by repeatedly pointing out that the political settlement we have now is so heavily weighted in favour of whites that it will take ages before the people of Mshenguville and Zonk'izizwe in Gauteng, Bhambayi in KwaZulu-Natal and Langa in the Western Cape can feel the concrete material benefits of their supposed freedom.

Now it is not popular to point these things out in this era of putative equality and bending over backwards to accommodate so-called white fears in order to perpetuate the myth of a newly-found racial harmony in South Africa.

Although Mandela may have won her court application against the illegal search of her offices and her home, hers may yet prove to have been a pyrrhic victory. This is but the first round in a long-drawn-out battle for the heart of the ANC.

If, in this era of the much-vaunted reconciliation, it is proper and just to drag Winnie Mandela's past screaming and kicking into the present and to hold it against her, then it must be equally proper and just to do the same to others across the entire political spectrum – even-handedly.

Sitting in President Mandela's multi-party cabinet today are people who have to answer for innumerable things. Are we all supposed to be suffering from selective amnesia?

By all means conduct investigations into allegations of corruption and prosecute where there are grounds to do so, but do not, in the process, launch a witch-hunt against those you do not like.

This purge of so-called 'populists and radicals' in the ANC may yet prove to be a very costly exercise for those involved in it. The targeted individuals all have considerable support in their constituencies, and three of them – Holomisa, Mokaba and Mandela – were placed in the top five during elections for the new national executive committee (NEC) at the ANC's national congress in Bloemfontein in December.

They each have more support on the ground than many of their colleagues on the NEC and in Government. They are more aware of the concerns of the poorest in the black community.

Is it possible to purge the ANC of them without also splitting the organisation down the middle? Are there, perhaps, any echoes here of 1959, when Africanists within the ANC walked out to form the PAC?

History may well repeat itself, but only time will tell. To those in the ANC leadership still amenable to reason: *verbum satis sapienti.*

Coping with the Pressure Drop

NP Leader FW de Klerk Talks About the New South Africa

19 April 1995

His assessment of the Government's performance so far

For all of us who have participated in the Government of National Unity it was a new experience. From the National Party's side a new experience: a coalition government, and for the ANC the first time it is bearing the responsibility of governing. For the IFP also a first time in a government at national level.

I think we succeeded very well in developing a good working relationship, in establishing conventions for the operation of the Cabinet and a system of Cabinet committees reporting back to Cabinet, which works well.

We have succeeded in avoiding party politics to interfere with the ordinary day-to-day decisions and find that there is free flow of discussion and ideas, quite often differences among Cabinet members from the same party on practical issues.

The same does not apply when it comes to a few fundamental issues where parties take up very strong positions, also in public debates. There we have thus far succeeded to bridge our fundamental differences by reaching compromises for joint decisions. Overall, therefore, I think we have performed rather well.

On whether the GNU is delivering

That is another aspect of the public debate. I think that expectations were too high in that regard and would add my voice to all those who caution against the public expecting too much too soon. I think we have made two important breakthroughs which will ensure delivery at a reasonable pace at a reasonable time. The first is that early on we agreed on an economic policy framework which will be investor-friendly, which will ensure that we create the right circumstances for sustained economic growth.

On the RDP

The second breakthrough was that we agreed on what I prefer to call a new Reconstruction and Development Programme, which is a programme of the GNU and not just of one party. The RDP has become the centrepiece of the GNU's delivery programme. It aims to be well co-ordinated, well managed, cost-effective and properly prioritised.

Some time has been spent, but I believe well spent, on a consultative process, because one needs to have wide support for such an ambitious programme.

On affirmative action

Here I would just like to dispel the notion and the perception that has been created from certain quarters that the NP is against affirmative action. It simply isn't true.

We are saying that affirmative action must be implemented in such a way that firstly it doesn't destabilise the career prospects of those who are in service, that secondly it must not result in a reverse form of racial discrimination and thirdly that if one looks at the employment of young South Africans irrespective of their race or colour then one cannot accept a situation where the quality of your results at university, or technikon or school is ignored and you are discriminated against. Therefore, yes, we say there must be an active programme and it must be balanced.

On whether he is happy with the NP's performance

The NP obviously had to go through a period of adaptation immediately after the election. We are proud about the constructive role we are playing in the GNU and the various governments of provincial unity – and politically we experience strong interest from a significant number of people across the country who wouldn't vote for us in the elections.

We believe in our great potential and we are committed as a non-racial party to values to extend our powerbase.

On his adjustment to a new position

As far as my position as deputy president is concerned, I also had to go through a period of adaption. I was psychologically relatively prepared for it. Some stress and strains did arise at time. Fortunately, we have emerged from these incidents a little stronger each time.

There is a good working relationship between the president and the executive deputy presidents. I find fulfilment in what I do within the Government. And what I do is meaningful and almost on a daily basis I am constructively involved with the help also of Cabinet colleagues.

On power-sharing beyond 1999

Yes, we firmly believe that five years is not long enough to effectively stabilise the country and ensure long-term stability and long-term peace.

For many reasons we believe that in some form or another we are not married to the exact present composition of the GNU – we must take the concept of joint decision-making by taking political role-players on fundamental issues at the level of the executive further into the future beyond 1999.

On the possibility of entering into temporary alliances in the constitution-making process

We are not approaching the constitution-writing process from an alliance viewpoint; we're approaching it from the issue viewpoint.

Our attitude is that we would like to identify with all parties on those issues on which we are in agreement so that we can, in a constructive manner, develop proposals which are more inclusive with regard to those specific issues. The issues will differ from party to party.

On SA's final constitution

In the final analysis no constitution can be accepted without the ANC also accepting it. No constitution can be accepted without a two-thirds majority and that is where the balance will have to be struck. The best possible constitution will be one that could be accepted unanimously. That is the ideal and I think that should be the purpose of negotiation.

As to whether that can be achieved is another question. I don't think it's impossible.

On the absence of blacks in top positions in the NP

Black South Africans are in a democratic process establishing themselves in leadership positions within the party structures.

We only have a limited number of Cabinet posts available. We've developed a system of chief spokespersons and there many playing a very good role. They themselves tell us: 'Please stay away from tokenism'.

His assessment of the president's performance so far

Generally speaking I think he has a tremendous task on his shoulders and he carries a tremendous responsibility.

I have very high appreciation for what he is doing to achieve peace and reconciliation and in selling South Africa, and very particularly his maintaining the cohesion within the GNU by adhering to the spirit of consultation and seeking consensus. I am therefore positive. In as much as I have criticism on specific issues I will reserve that for private discussions with him.

On Mbeki as heir-apparent to President Mandela

I don't want to involve myself in the leadership stakes of the ANC. I can say that as the Cabinet system has developed the two of us work very closely and very well together. I didn't know him well beforehand and I've developed a lot of respect for him and we got along fine.

On Chief Buthelezi's performance in the GNU

Because he is not an executive deputy president his role is somewhat different. At times he is specially consulted by the presidency in recognition of his position as the leader of the third biggest party in the GNU.

In that process I have always found him in Government matters to be co-operative, constructive and he is punctual and he is performing well in his role as Minister of Home Affairs.

On the first dismissal of Winnie Mandela

From the GNU's point of view it was a delicate situation. I did not interfere but I am glad that the President took decisive action because the uncertainty was to my mind damaging to the country as a whole.

On whether he has regrets about the course he took for the country

None of the fundamental decisions would I have taken differently. What I now know with hindsight, I might have changed some of the strategies and would have done certain things differently. But the decisions taken on the basis of principle as to where we should be going, or what we should move away from, that would not be different at all and I have no regrets. I would have done it all over again.

A Dream Lives One Year Later

27 April 1995

Here we are, South Africa in 1995. Today, on April 27, it has been a full year since our founding, all-race election was held, yielding a dream result which gave concrete expression to the constitutionally envisaged power-sharing.

The ANC came uncomfortably close to the two-thirds majority which would have enabled it to write the country's final constitution on its own, but fortunately came a few percentages short. The National Party obtained the crucial 20% of the vote, which guaranteed F W de Klerk the second deputy presidency.

The Inkatha Freedom Party confounded political analysts, psychologists and critics when it got 10% of the national vote and emerged as the outright victor in its backyard, KwaZulu-Natal. This assured former KwaZulu Chief Minister Chief Mangosuthu Buthelezi and two of his colleagues of seats in the multi-party Cabinet, and brought South Africa relative peace and stability.

It was as good a foundation to build on as any the Government of National Unity (GNU) could ask for. The priority, it seemed, was merely consolidating the political gains already made, making reconciliation across the racial and political divide a reality and getting down to work on rolling back the legacy of apartheid.

Where are we today? Can we, with all honesty, claim to have succeeded?

One must tread carefully here, for responses to these questions can sometimes have less to do with objective reality and a lot to do with such variants as the race of the respondent and where he/she sits in the political continuum.

Many will agree, however, that the most important achievement of the GNU is its continued existence almost a year after its establishment, especially when one considers that represented in this hybrid creature are parties which only a few years ago would not sit at the same table.

Even now, they still have some fairly strong differences – materially, stylistically and ideologically.

It has not always been smooth sailing, though, for one can enumerate at least three incidents over the past year which have come close to threatening the continued survival of the GNU as we know it.

Ingonyama

The Executive had hardly begun to function when it was revealed that on the eve of the April election, De Klerk had signed into law the Ingonyama Land Trust Act, a piece of legislation initiated by the former homeland into a trust held by Zulu King Goodwill Zwelithini.

It was this 'crisis' that the multi-party Cabinet had to deal with at its inaugural sitting in Cape Town on May 23. A solution was found and the IFP remained in the coalition.

Then there was Buthelezi's 'unauthorised entry' into an SABC 'Agenda' studio in Durban in September last year, while one Prince Sifiso Zulu was being interviewed. Buthelezi offered to resign, but a solution was again found.

In January, the NP leadership went on the defensive when it was revealed that De Klerk's former government had secretly granted indemnity to two former Cabinet Ministers and 3 500 policemen, a mere two days before the election. In a heated Cabinet meeting, President Nelson Mandela and De Klerk differed sharply, with the NP leader threatening he may have to reconsider his position in the GNU.

The two men kissed and made up, talking of 'a new beginning'.

Some may also count as a success the Government's – particularly Mandela's – policy of reconciliation, which some cynics in the townships refer to as the policy of appeasement. It is indeed true that South Africans are today generally much more tolerant towards one another than was the case three or more years ago, and that there are now much fewer racial hang-ups than was the case then.

But that is a simplistic view often preferred by enthusiasts and *aficionados* of the 'new South Africa' – numbering among them recent converts – the majority of whom are to be found in the white community. It ignores the fact that this relaxation in racial tension has been a process which began well before the advent of the GNU, and that for most black South Africans racism – albeit now no longer in the crudest forms – is as much a reality as it ever was.

Among the things most black South Africans resent about the 'new South Africa' is the fact that racism continues to blight their lives and that most racists – both the crude ones and those of a benign type – at the workplace and in almost all other spheres of life go on in pretty much the same way they have done over the years.

Lawlessness

For them President Mandela, who has repeatedly warned people in his core black constituency against lawlessness and crime but has yet to send a similarly strong caveat to racists, is 'a good leader'. They have moved over the past year from being wary and anxious about a black-led South Africa to positively idolising Mandela.

For they are no fools and realise that apart from the colour of our new political leadership, very little else has changed in the country.

But to judge the GNU on its record on delivery – or, more appropriately, its lack thereof – may be harsh. This is because there simply has not been much visible delivery. We have yet to see 'RDP houses' mushrooming in their thousands everywhere, jobs created and houses electrified on a great scale.

But that in itself is not a damning failure. There are at least two reasons for the slowness of change, and they are that Mandela's priority in his first six months in office was, with some good reason, reconciliation and that the necessary groundwork for delivery had to be laid from scratch.

With 60% of the people in the GNU having no prior experience in government, and given the huge legacy of apartheid, this has not been easy.

To be welcomed are indications that there is growing realisation from the GNU, especially from the ranks of the majority ANC, that concrete delivery that goes beyond the provision of free health care to children and pregnant women and the feeding scheme at schools is imperative from now on. A year from now people in townships will no longer be content to be told, as Mandela has done many times, that 'the wheels of government grind very slowly', but will want, with justification, to see real change in their material and living conditions.

The country has done well economically, with positive growth being the reward for a sound fiscal policy. Although political power continues to reside firmly in white hands – and will do so for years to come – a growing black political and professional elite has benefited from the new dispensation.

However, these benefits have yet to trickle down to the masses who need to feel them most.

For a Government not lacking in legitimacy, the GNU's over-arching failure was in cracking down on general lawlessness and rising crime. A year after the April 27 election, the crime rate is not any better than it was then.

Deaf Ears and Blind Eyes don't Change Harsh Realities

2 May 1995

Nobody had ever said it publicly before – at least, nobody had ever put it that strongly and that bluntly. Perhaps that explains the concerns some people in the ANC have expressed, since the publication in this paper last week, of that marathon interview with First Deputy President Thabo Mbeki, who is also deputy president of the organisation. The interview was conducted with him in his dual capacities, and it was with his hat as ANC leader on that he made the statement with which some have since been uncomfortable.

Parasite

Now, many had long speculated about a time in the future when the ANC's long-standing alliance with the South African Communist Party (SACP) might come to an end. The SACP, various commentators often argued, fed off the bigger ANC like a parasite and often – in their view – had a say and influence in the alliance way out of proportion with its numbers.

The SACP's influence in decision-making in the ANC has always been grossly exaggerated, but there is no denying that the party did have a not-so-insignificant influence in the alliance. Key SACP leaders even said as much at the party's national congress outside Johannesburg last month, when they stated publicly that three of the seven ANC provincial premiers, as well as a handful of national Cabinet Ministers and Deputy Ministers, were SACP members. Nobody made a big deal out of that for, thankfully, the shameful era of red-bashing is now over.

This is the reason commentators had long expected the alliance to come apart, and it was generally accepted that this would happen after the country's first all-inclusive election once apartheid had been defeated. That has now been delayed by, among other things, the constitutional provision which bars parliamentarians from crossing the floor and remaining in Parliament.

In the interview with me and colleague Patrick Bulger, Mbeki said time will come when 'the ANC as a broad movement will begin to identify itself in terms of different schools of political thought', and that out of it would come different parties. Does this, or does it not, constitute a 'break-up', a 'disintegration' and a 'splitting' of the ANC?

Some ANC spokespersons think not. Mbeki's point, they say, was that the logical outcome of the 'natural evolution' of the ANC would be a transformation of the organisation, which will culminate in different political groupings and one ANC which will be smaller than the broad church it is now.

I think this is splitting hairs and engaging in semantics, and the ANC spokespersons think otherwise. They argue that the two mean different things.

Let Mbeki speak – yet again – for himself: 'What will happen is that as you get a more normal society this racial divide recedes because of changes you are able to make. Then the ANC as this board movement will begin to identify itself in terms of different schools of political thought.

'Out of the same ANC you will get a social democratic party, you will get a liberal democratic party and so on. As South African society becomes more normal and the further away it moves from the apartheid past, the closer you get to the transformation of the ANC.

'How long this takes depends on the speed with which you transform South Africa. The faster you move to become a normal society the sooner you will arrive at a situation where people in the ANC will say we have always recognised that this is a broad family that has done what it set out to do, and we can now go our separate ways.'

Remembering

Once people in the ANC have gone their 'separate ways', once social democratic and liberal democratic parties 'and so on' have arisen out of the ANC, won't this amount to a 'break-up', a 'disintegration', a 'splitting' of the ANC? You be the judge.

It is worth remembering, however, that although those who founded the PAC in 1959 walked out of the ANC, they object to this day when the PAC is described as a splinter group, and regard themselves as true custodians of the values for which the ANC stood since its formation in 1912, but especially of the Programme of Action pioneered by the ANC Youth League of Anton Lembede, Nelson Mandela and Walter Sisulu in 1949.

Mandela's Great and Good Image is on the Line

8 May 1995

President Nelson Mandela is without doubt a fine person, blessed as he is with so many admirable attributes. In a very real sense it is he, more than any other person, who is responsible for where the country is politically today.

He emerged from almost three decades of imprisonment with a remarkable lack of rancour and bitterness, took the ANC first into meetings with the National Party government and later into multi-party negotiations, the outcome of which is the present interim Constitution in terms of which the country is now being governed.

One would indeed be hard put to find even one person in Mandela's multi-party Cabinet, let alone in the ANC itself, whose commitment to racial reconciliation surpasses the president's. Deservedly, he has grown to be regarded, both here and abroad, as a beacon of hope and a symbol in the fight for justice.

That is how most of us would like to remember him: as a saintly figure, the selfless man who sacrificed so much – including his family life. For that he deserves our gratitude.

(Of course, I know and acknowledge that F W de Klerk also deserves credit for our being where we are now, for he it was who had the courage to normalise politics in the country, enter into negotiations with black leaders and do what no other Afrikaner leader before him had ever dreamt of doing: give up political power and hegemony.)

However, if things continue the way they are going at the moment, there is a danger the president many leave behind a less than flattering image of himself, so that whatever mistakes he makes now end up upstaging the good things he has done all his life.

That would be terrible and must be avoided at all costs.

But only Mandela himself, and those he surrounds himself with, can help prevent this.

As things stand now, it looks increasingly as if the president is either prone to reckless pronouncements or he is getting bad advice. Either way, the cost to himself is almost incalculable in the long run.

His emotional outbursts last week about KwaZulu-Natal, when he threatened first to cut off Government funding for the province and later to amend the Interim Constitution to give himself more powers, must surely take the cake.

They were reckless, potentially dangerous pronouncements unbefitting of the president.

Mandela ought to be reminded that his Government does not do KwaZulu-Natal – or any other province for that matter – a favour by allocating public funds to it. He is constitutionally obliged to do so. And the money comes from us all, tax-paying citizens of this country, including people – a significant number of them IFP members – in KwaZulu-Natal.

He may not realise it, but his uncharacteristic threat to punish IFP-controlled KwaZulu-Natal economically will only strengthen the case of those who, like the IFP, argue that provinces should be given more powers so that they can, among other things, raise their own taxes to lessen their dependence on the central Government.

But it is his threat to amend the Constitution to give himself more powers to deal with the situation in KwaZulu-Natal that is more worrisome. Thankfully, he cannot do this, because his ANC does not have the two-thirds majority he would need to effect such an amendment, but it is a scary thought, nevertheless.

Thus are dictators born. They get into power with good credentials meaning very well indeed, but they begin to tinker with the Constitution, amending it here and there to give themselves more power, eventually suspending it altogether and declaring themselves Presidents-for-life as has happened in some formerly 'independent' homelands in this country, as well as in some countries north of our borders.

We should guard against it. To be sure, the IFP leadership, particularly party leader Chief Mangosuthu Buthelezi, has recently made fairly inflammatory statements about which Mandela is justifiably angry, but these pale into insignificance compared to the president's bluster.

He should heed Buthelezi's warning: 'If he does something unconstitutional, then he must expect people will take a cue from himself and use unconstitutional means to oppose what he's doing.'

We're Facing in the Right Direction

An Interview with Chief Mangosuthu Buthelezi

12 May 1995

His assessment of the GNU's performance in its first year in office

I think that the fact that we are still together after these months is an achievement, and I do believe that as far as the direction of the country is concerned, we have achieved [something and] if we want to meet the expectations of the people we are in the direction we need to face.

On the downside in the past year

We are still wrestling with whether there is real consensus in decision-making because whereas at the level of the executive things are going well, if you come here to Parliament you find that the attitude of the caucus of the ANC for example is that they are the majority party and that their point is that the GNU must exist only at executive level.

And also I think that since we double up as a Constitutional Assembly I would say that even there, there is a downside insofar as every session I've attended I found that the spirit was not a constitution-making spirit insofar as there was booing.

On prospects for long-term peace

The whole thing of the Truth Commission is bound to exacerbate the problem of peace as far as I am concerned and even the behaviour of the ANC [in Parliament]. That's not how we build peace and confidence and reconciliation.

On whether he will encourage IFP members to appear before the Truth and Reconciliation Commission

If it's the law, I suppose they will have to appear. I don't think that there'll be resistance.

On the cause of differences between himself and Zulu King Goodwill Zwelithini

Quite clearly the king was given certain promises. He has been approached by many, many people, clergymen and so on.

On the possibility of a solution to the impasse

My view is that as long as the ANC leadership is doing this, as long as he [the king] is mesmerised by them [it will be difficult to find a solution] ... All these suggestions by some spokespersons of the king where it was said that his emoluments and things should come from the President's Office and so on – as he goes on that way, I cannot see how one can take him away from that kind of alienation which is self-imposed.

On the IFP-aligned chiefs' demand on the king to call an *imbizo*

When we suggest he should call an *imbizo* we are trying to provide him with a dignified way of returning to his people again. We are going to do everything to make sure that that happens.

On the king's opposition to mediation

We are talking about the institution of monarchy here. That is why it is wrong for people to say the king now says he is no longer interested in international mediation. He was never really directly involved in that specific issue.

On difficulties in constitution-making

Constitutions throughout the world and the centuries have been written on the basis of consensus [and] not on the basis of majoritarianism. Those are the constitutions that last. A disaffected majority can destroy a constitution; equally, a disaffected minority can do the same. If you look at the Northern Ireland issue in Britain then you can see what's going to happen; there's not going to be any peace – it won't stick..

On power-sharing beyond 1999

We agree absolutely that the country should be run by the party which wins the election.

On the IFP's preparedness for local government elections

Since those elections will be done on the basis of voters' rolls, I just think that the practicalities of that do not assure me. In any case there has been nowhere in the world where people are registered without the wards being demarcated. I've never heard of it.

On whether the elections will take place on November 1 as scheduled

It's difficult for me to say publicly that it's not possible, but really I'd be pleasantly surprised, purely from the point of view of practicalities.

On how well he thinks the IFP will perform

I have no fears about that. I expect that I will retain majority in KwaZulu-Natal, and I expect that nationwide I will get more than 10 percent. We are a poor party and one wishes one had money for organisers.

On transformation of the IFP away from its Zulu image

Actually, if you look at us in Parliament I don't see why anyone should say we are not a nonracial party.

On his health and perceptions that he is a difficult man

As long as my party wants me I am in fine fettle. I've never been in hospital for more than 30 or 40 years – I haven't been a patient in a hospital. I sometimes praise God for that, knowing the punishing schedules we have.

It doesn't worry me that I'm swimming against the tide. If you look at history generally you find that there are many people who wrestled with the truth who often swam against the tide, were even vilified, but [whom other] people appreciated, even when they were dead, because they were right after all.

On how the IFP plans to influence constitution-making

It's strange. Last year we walked out of Kempton Park. But in a way our influence was there [because] there would be no premiers today without us: there would have been no double ballot if we didn't have the courage to take that stand.

We did not abandon communicating or talking bilaterally. Some people tried to write off our removing ourselves as some sort of petulance.

On whether he is happy and at peace with himself

I would say I am happy because I know that to the best dictates of my conscience I think I'm serving my people and the country, which I think

I'm doing faithfully and loyally. From that point of view I'm quite happy. As Shakespeare said: 'No man can do more than his best.' I believe that I've done my best, whatever the problems I'm having. I do my best.

On whether he is happy with the way the president dealt with the 'Agenda incident'

The president was under pressure from many enemies I have, and the media itself made it a big issue. I've heard from many sources that he was under great pressure to remove me, [which] I had no problem about because when we talked man-to-man I myself offered to resign. Mr Mandela could not have handled it in any other way.

On relations with other people in the Cabinet

There's one minister . . . we don't even greet each other. I won't talk to him. But for the rest – even those who are not, well, friends – we behave towards each other in a civilised way, we share a cup of tea and even jokes, but there is one minister with whom I am not on speaking terms. And I feel very happy about it because I did raise the matter with Mr Mandela in the presence of the Cabinet and he just said we should talk between ourselves, but in fact things have never improved.

His assessment of the president's performance

I think he has done very well. I don't think that he could have done better taking into account that he is inheriting a country like this which has been ravaged by racism and apartheid for a long time.

On whether FW de Klerk has adjusted to being number three

I think he has done very well, really. It's fortunate that he is experienced and that we have him as one of the vice-presidents.

On whether he thinks Thabo Mbeki is fit to be president

I'm not very sure now. The events of March-April [on the mediation issue] disillusioned me. Mr Mbeki is really a very competent person and I feel that he is the right person in the right place as far as his competence is concerned. [But] if that is his style then I'm really worried about the future because I'm very worried about that style. That style of doing things is not reassuring.

On whether he sees a future for himself in KwaZulu-Natal politics

In the 40 years that I've been in politics the truth of the matter is that my politics – although I don't apologise for being a Zulu , an hereditary leader in that area and having a base there, and having been forced to be the chief minister there – has always been national politics.

On whether he has any ambition to become president

I've never gone out to say I want to be president of South Africa. People have written about that but I don't think I have said it to anyone, I've never said so. I'm prepared to serve under anyone who is the choice of the people of South Africa.

On lack of change in people's lives since the election

Even before this country was liberated it was my message that when liberation takes place, that's when the struggle would actually start. That has been my theme right through.

SA Ill-served by Reckless Words and Commentaries

15 June 1995

The political temperature is gradually hotting up over KwaZulu-Natal. As yet there does not appear to be an end in sight to the ongoing political bickering, the consequences of which have often been a growing pile of dead, black bodies.

At issue is no longer just the trilateral April 19 agreement on international mediation, which has yet to be honoured. It is, instead, also political hegemony and control.

The question which is very rarely asked aloud, but which determines the actions of the major political players in the province, is: who calls the tune? Is it the IFP, which won last year's election in the province with a slim majority, or is it the ANC, the majority party in the Government of National Unity (GNU)?

These questions are at the centre of the tug-of-war in that province. The IFP sees KwaZulu-Natal as a base from which it should first launch an aggressive campaign for federalism and then spread its tentacles throughout the country in an effort to become more than just a provincial party.

It is there that the IFP feels entitled to flex its muscles from time to time, especially in its dealings with the ANC-led GNU. This helps explain why the party has now decided to move its secretary-general, Dr Ziba Jiyane, arguably the most effective and eloquent articulator of the IFP's views, from the National Assembly to the KwaZulu-Natal legislature.

The ANC has yet to come to terms with the fact that it lost the election in that province. Although the organisation accepted the outcome of the election 'in the national interest', it still believes that it – and not the IFP – would have won had no irregularities taken place in the area.

It sees itself, then, as the putative majority party and the IFP as a pretender to the throne. As in the Western Cape, the organisation finds it difficult to come to terms with the fact that although it is the majority party in Parliament, it is not in power in KwaZulu-Natal.

The National Party in KwaZulu-Natal finds itself sandwiched between these two bullies, impotent and helpless, and can only look on as the two parties spoil for war and the political temperature rises.

Chief Buthelezi and President Mandela have used words with growing recklessness. Their relationship has been damaged irreparably, and neither appears prepared to back down. Both are proud traditional African men and regard any challenge to their respective positions as an attack on their very manhood.

There can be no winner here. Buthelezi is too firmly entrenched in the politics of rural KwaZulu for any strategy aimed at turning his constituency against him to work, and Mandela is a larger-than-life figure to his legion of followers.

But the situation is not helped by commentators who often rush to pronounce on issues without understanding or contextualising them. South Africa, but KwaZulu-Natal in particular, is ill-served by this disturbing practice.

During the days of multi-party negotiations at the World Trade Centre, readers were confused by headlines screaming 'Breakthrough' one day and 'Deadlock' the next. And three weeks ago, a press briefing by Mandela's advisers and a handshake between him and Buthelezi led to a report the following day saying the president, who had launched his most scathing attack yet on Buthelezi a day earlier, had backed down on his threat to cut off Government funding to KwaZulu-Natal. He had done nothing of the sort.

This week some sections of the press bought ANC propaganda that the IFP's 20-point plan was secessionist. A careful reading of the discussion document – for that is what it is – reveals that, by and large, its author merely wanted the IFP to assert powers which are listed in Schedule 6 of the Interim Constitution as falling within the provinces' competence.

Does He Who Pays the Piper Call the Tune?

19 June 1995

Let us get this out of the way first: I, as regular readers of this column may have long surmised, have no particular affection for men and women who derive their power and influence from accidents of birth. In fact, I loathe them.

It is my belief that so-called traditional leadership as an institution has no place in a modern democracy such as ours, notwithstanding the fact that some of the older Western democracies still have them. For some of us the memory of chiefs supporting and helping with the implementation of the crudest forms of apartheid is still fresh in our minds.

But I am a tolerant person, and know that there are people in some rural parts of this country, a minority though they might be, who still look up to their tribal leaders and would like to see them continue playing some roles of influence in their respective villages.

I return to the subject of traditional leaders today not with gusto but with great reluctance, for it is not at all a subject that is close to my heart. I return to it because it is a topical matter, what with President Nelson Mandela determined to push through Parliament the controversial Remuneration of Traditional Leaders Bill which would enable him to pay chiefs at the national Government level.

It is an open secret in knowledgeable political circles that Mandela has long wanted to centralise the payment of traditional leaders and that his primary motive has been to break the Inkatha Freedom Party's almost asphyxiating stranglehold on chiefs in KwaZulu-Natal. It is all part of the long-simmering feud between Mandela and Mangosuthu Buthelezi, who themselves have some royal blood coursing through their veins.

Mandela's concern is understandable for, in a province where all civil servants – teachers included – employed by the former KwaZulu government were once required to take up IFP membership, chiefs have indeed been politically abused and manipulated. They, in turn, have done the same to their subjects.

On the face of it, therefore, Mandela's proposal appears eminently reasonable. But that's only on the face of it, for almost everything else about it is worrisome. What guarantee is there that the ANC might not later seek to manipulate the traditional leaders in the same manner the IFP did? Does he who pays the piper, after all, not also call the tune? No matter what Mandela and the ANC might say, that danger exists for the ANC is no bunch of angels.

In fact, Mandela's intention to give the estimated 800 traditional leaders the same perks as MPs 'who have uniform salaries, who are provided with official residences, who have official transport, who have secretaries [and] who have drivers' – all of which will be done at the already over-taxed taxpayer's expense, of course – smacks of a crude attempt by the president to bribe the chiefs.

The only thing worthy of support from this proposal is the standardisation of traditional leaders' salaries, so that chiefs in the Northern Province will receive the same, modest stipend as their counterparts in, say, the Eastern Cape or KwaZulu-Natal.

But there is an even bigger problem with Mandela's proposal: it is manifestly unconstitutional and confirms yet again the ANC's deep-seated aversion to federalism. It may also betray a surprising lack of familiarity with some details of the Interim Constitution on the part of some in the ANC – apparently including Mandela's advisors – eager to whittle away at whatever minimal powers the provinces presently enjoy.

As the IFP leadership has pointed out, the payment of traditional leaders is a provincial competence.

Schedule 6 of the Interim Constitution lists both 'cultural affairs' and 'indigenous law and customary law' as provincial competences.

The Constitution is emphatic about something else, as one of the immutable constitutional principles contained in Schedule 4 states: 'The powers and functions of the provinces defined in the Constitution, including the competence of a provincial legislature to adopt a constitution for its province, shall not be substantially less than or substantially inferior to those provided for in this Constitution.'

There is a good chance that the Constitutional Court would rule in favour of the IFP-controlled KwaZulu-Natal if the matter went to court.

'Luister na Jou Goeie Leier'

3 July 1995

Someone really ought to be telling them that their protests amount to nothing more than nonsense, but we are all such nice people – or we try to present ourselves as such – that we will not do this.

We are forever consciously aware of the need for us to be seen to be one, happy nation of 'New South Africans', who do not wash their dirty linen in public and will not dare to do anything that will challenge the perception of South Africa as a new racial haven.

Having graciously allowed bygones to be bygones, we now embrace as ours that anthem of our domination, 'Die Stem'; we jubilate over the conquests of a predominantly white national rugby team in the Rugby World Cup; and we heed calls from our respected political and religious leaders to allow the South African Rugby Football Union to retain the springbok as an emblem.

Is there anything we will not do to advance reconciliation? Why, if we could be persuaded by President Nelson Mandela and Archbishop Desmond Tutu, honourable men both, that for us to give up any claim we have to this country would advance further the course of racial reconciliation we would do it. Gladly.

So enthusiastic are we about making our white compatriots' lives easy – even if we may have to turn again the other cheek in the process.

Having done so much for reconciliation, should we now baulk at doing more? Should we not prove ourselves worthy compatriots and swallow holus-bolus whatever our former political masters, adept at barking instructions and calling the shots, now deem to be our due?

Surely it is not much to ask that we, the black people of this country, should agree to be addressed and receive correspondence in that most important of languages, the *'egte amptelike taal'* of our former political masters, Afrikaans. Why, any man or woman worthy of the citizenship of the 'New South Africa' should prove his or her patriotism through proficiency and fluency in that language.

And so why, we ask earnestly, does Public Service and Administration Minister Dr Zola Skweyiya suddenly issue instructions to National Assembly Speaker Dr Frene Ginwala and Secretary of Parliament Robin Douglas that correspondence to him should be in English, IsiZulu and IsiXhosa only and not in that beautiful, most poetic of languages, Afrikaans?

In letters to Ginwala and Douglas, Skweyiya says valid reasons should be given for failure to comply with this request, and argues that African languages are being neglected in favour of English and Afrikaans. What cheek!

Just who does he think he is? Must he be that uppity just because he is a Cabinet minister? Does he not know that his own President and that once-troublesome cleric, Tutu, speak Afrikaans from time to time to appease us? Damn K...ir – *ag verskoon tog*, for a moment there I forgot the K-word is no longer politically correct.

Now, where was I? Oh yes, even that *verlig* of newspapers, *Beeld*, knows that the Honourable Minister is merely a black racist – and there are many of them, too – who seeks to discriminate against that most blessed language of ours.

What fool is this Skweyiya not to know that, in reality, there are still only two *amptelike tale* in this country, Afrikaans and English, notwithstanding what the interim Constitution says? What does it matter that the Constitution says everybody has a right to be addressed in a language of his/her choice?

Just listen to *Beeld* (June 28, page 10), *ou kerel*: 'Perhaps [Afrikaner] people should write to Dr Skweyiya and let him know what they think of his approach and how they feel about the exclusion of Afrikaans. And they must do it in Afrikaans, so that Dr Skweyiya can see how many people there are who feel strongly about the issue'.

What more can I say? Even the NP (Frik van Heerden), the DP (Kobus Jordaan) and, predictably, the Freedom Front (Corné Mulder) agree with me.

Vir Oom Skweyiya het ek net een ding om te sê: Hierdie is nou ons land. Luister na jou goeie leier, Mandela, ou maat.

SA Needs to Send a Powerful Message to Tin-pot Dictators

24 July 1995

It seems like such a long time ago, but it was a mere five-and-a-half years ago that South Africa – now held up internationally as a model of how a country can transform itself peacefully from a conflict-ridden, race-torn society to a democracy – was a leper among civilised nations of the world. With good reason, too.

Just think about it for a moment. Where was South Africa in January 1990? A state of emergency first imposed by former State President P W Botha in 1985 was still in place, organisations such as the United Democratic Front and the Azanian People's Organisation were restricted, and the ANC, the South African Communism Party and the Pan Africanist Congress were still proscribed. F W de Klerk had just assumed the country's presidency, and had immediately relaxed petty apartheid and allowed protest marches, but racial tension was still rife and we were far from the kind of society we are now. Punitive economic sanctions against Pretoria were biting deeply and the economy itself was bleeding badly. And, of course, we were an isolated country.

Now it is all different. South Africa is perennially the flavour of the month, our political leaders are in great demand abroad and we have been fully embraced as a respected member of the international community. This is all positive but its spin-off is that it confers on us certain obligations and responsibilities.

Nobody in his right mind, I am sure, hankers after the pre-1990 South Africa. Most of us are happy to be citizens of the 'New South Africa', whose newness, like beauty, is in the eye of the beholder.

Although this was the only country in which racism was constitutionally entrenched, it was by no means the only country with racial problems. Indeed, countries like the United States and Britain, like many others, continue to experience racial tensions and divisions. There were dictatorships in some countries in this continent, in the Americas, in Asia and even in Europe.

Given our recent history, we in this country should be concerned about any disregard for human rights shown by some tin-pot dictators anywhere in the world, but especially on this continent. Why are we folding our arms, for instance, while dictators in Mbabane, Swaziland and Abuja, Nigeria, trample with what appears to be impunity on the rights of people in those countries?

Archaic

Not far from our borders, young King Mswati III rules the tiny kingdom as though it were his personal fiefdom, trying in vain to control and stage-manage the democratisation process there. The mind boggles at why a young man like Mswati III, even if he is a king, should show such aversion to democracy, preferring instead to cling tenaciously to archaic views and principles. Political parties are still not officially allowed in that country, and Mswati III has now banned trade unions. He does not appear to be capable of overseeing the on-off democratisation process in Swaziland.

I have news for him: he should change with the times or risk being dumped, together with the institution he represents, into the dustbin of history.

Then there is that military dictator in Nigeria, General Sani Abacha. Although he, like other military dictators before him in that country, which has been plagued by *coups d'état*, claimed upon acquiring power that he was going to pave the way for a civilian government, he has yet to do so. Chief Moshood Abiola, putative winner of the recent presidential election in that country, still languishes in jail.

South Africa can no longer afford to fold its arms and watch as the bizarre political drama unfolds in those countries. Yes, we should respect the sovereignty of other countries – even if, in the case of Swaziland, that country is miniscule and largely dependent on us economically – and I am not about to advocate a military invasion of Swaziland or Nigeria.

That we should never do, but we can send a powerful political message that cannot be misunderstood by the demigods in Mbabane and Abuja. We can, for starters, send their High Commissioners in Pretoria back home to demonstrate in a concrete way our strong disapproval of their modern-day dictatorships. We can take a leaf from the book of the international community and impose our own punitive economic sanctions against the regimes represented by these semi-deities.

We know what it is to be oppressed. We are not impotent – let us do something NOW.

No Need for Selective Harassment in Search for Truth

11 September 1995

Former Bophuthatswana President Lucas Manyano Mangope is not a terribly likeable man. He is an obdurately obstinate fellow not blessed with that most prized of political gifts: the ability to read correctly the situation around him and then act accordingly.

Of the former homeland leaders, he is the one who held most steadfastly on to the illusion of an 'independent state' to the very end. His political naiveté never ceased to amaze. Once, in 1990, he chastised 'my people' – as he called them – for flocking to the First National Bank Stadium south of Johannesburg to listen to a recently released President Nelson Mandela, whom Mangope called a *'bandiet'*, while there was a poor turnout at his own rallies. And early in 1994, as one homeland administration after another tumbled, he swore that Bophuthatswana would never 'in a hundred years' be reincorporated into a united South Africa.

Quite clearly he was dreaming, and this column pointed out then that the fate of that territory was not Mangope's to decide – that decision was for the denizens of the area, the overwhelming majority of whom wanted nothing more than the immediate restoration of their South African citizenship.

But Mangope would not listen. Instead, he dug his head in to the sand and attempted, vainly, to stand in the way of the inexorable winds of change about which former British Prime Minister Harold MacMillan had warned during a visit to this country three-and-a-half decades ago.

Opportunity

Through the multi-party talks at the World Trade Centre, and in numerous bilateral discussions between his regime and the ANC, Mangope had a wonderful opportunity to negotiate honourable terms of surrender for himself.

And he had a few options open to him. He could have thrown his weight behind the ANC to win himself another lease of political life, like many other erstwhile homeland leaders who were opportunists did. Some of these men are today either in Parliament or in one of the nine provincial legislatures as ANC members of the provincial legislatures.

Mangope could also have followed John Gogotya's example and joined forces with the National Party, which would no doubt have loved to have him on board in the hope that he commanded some support in the North West. Had he followed this route he would also be an MP or MPL today.

He could also have shacked up with his former Freedom Alliance colleagues such as Chief Mangosuthu Buthelezi's Inkatha Freedom Party or General Constand Viljoen's Freedom Front. That, too, would have extended his political life.

But no, not Lucas Manyano Mangope. He would have none of that – even when the Freedom Alliance began coming apart and former Ciskei military dictator General Oupa Gqozo (anybody still remember him?), a former ally of Mangope's, threw in the towel. The politically naive Mangope wanted to fight to the bitter end, even though anyone with political savvy must have known that he was fighting a losing battle. He did not even know when it was time to go, and still protested bitterly when former Foreign Affairs Minister Pik Botha and the ANC's Mac Maharaj flew to his hideout in the former Bophuthatswana at night to confront him with a *fait accompli.* He has yet to recover from that humiliation.

Knives

These things, however, do not justify the apparent harassment of Mangope by the North West Government presently going on. A commission has been set up to investigate alleged financial irregularities in the former Bophuthatswana during Mangope's reign, and he was recently summoned to appear before the commission. One cannot help but sense that the knives are out for him.

Now, there is a lot that can be said for clean and responsible government and digging into alleged past corruption must qualify to be seen as responsible government. But surely Mangope is not the only former homeland leader to have been suspected of having had long fingers.

Indeed, the legacy of the chaotic state in which the finances of the former Transkei and Ciskei were in is felt to this day in the Eastern Cape. And the former KaNgwane government was once alleged to have sold government-owned cars to some of its senior staff at ridiculously low prices. And it was not the only one to engage in wholesale financial looting on the eve of its dissolution.

If we want to establish the truth about what happened in the homelands in the dying days of apartheid – and there is no reason why the former NP government should be exempted – then we would have to be even-handed in our approach and not single out for victimisation those homeland leaders we do not like, like poor Chief Lucas Manyano Mangope.

We, the People, Would do Well to Remain Alert

18 September 1995

Now that we have a democratically elected government – we have had it for almost 18 months now – what is expected of us as citizens? Must we go along with everything the Government does, even if we do not think particularly highly of that action's merit or wisdom, or fail to speak out where we believe our new rulers err?

Instinctively, regular readers of this column will know my response to that question. It is my belief democracy is not some fragile entity which needs to be handled with care for fear it might fracture beyond repair.

Instead, I believe it is a self-assured entity which allows – nay, which thrives on – robust debate and comment.

Although now almost one-and-a-half years old, ours is still a fledgling democracy. It has not endured any serious crises and is still far from seeing the country's second and successive all-inclusive general election, as prescribed in our Interim Constitution.

As things stand at the moment, we all hope South Africa will indeed remain a multi-party democracy, with regular general elections.

But what guarantee is there that that will indeed be the case? Apart from the constitution itself and the important institutions it has spawned – such as the Constitutional Court – there really is nothing which guarantees us our next general election will take place in 1999.

History is full of examples of countries which began as shining democracies, but whose rulers later tore up constitutions as good as ours.

And so we rely on two crucial factors for the survival of our democracy as we know it today: the goodwill of our political rulers plus the commitment and resilience of our civil society and the proverbial man-in-the-street.

It is for these reasons we as citizens ought to be concerned about things done today by our political mandarins, as everything they get away with sets a precedent.

That would explain why this column did not mince its words of condemnation when President Nelson Mandela, who is the primary custodian of the constitution after the Constitutional Court, recently threatened to cut off Government funding to the Inkatha Freedom Party-controlled KwaZulu-Natal administration and amend the constitution to give himself more powers 'to save lives'. That was not one of his brightest moves, and it is good that wise counsel prevailed.

Ought we to be concerned about the fact that a constitutional amendment defeated in a joint sitting of the National Assembly and the Senate a fortnight ago was passed, in exactly its original form, a week ago?

I think we should. Not so much because parliamentary rules say a defeated Bill should not be re-introduced in the same session of Parliament unless both Houses approve, which they did in this case.

We should be concerned because it sets a potentially dangerous precedent that all the Government has to do whenever the constitution stands in its way is simply amend it.

I will concede immediately that one of the two amendments was indeed necessary to enable the local government elections to go ahead as scheduled on November 1 in those parts of the country which are ready for the poll, because the constitution decrees the elections had to be held on the same day throughout the country. To get around this provision, it was essential to amend the constitution.

Not so the other amendment, the effect of which was to enable President Mandela to sign the controversial Remuneration of Traditional Leaders Bill, which will enable the Government to pay traditional leaders directly, into law.

Therein lies the problem. Not only does the constitution say 'cultural affairs' is a Schedule 6 provincial competence, it also stipulates that all legislation on traditional matters has to be referred to the as-yet-unestablished Council of Traditional Leaders at the national level and the Houses of Traditional Leaders in the provinces where there are traditional leaders.

This was a flawed amendment which may yet embarrass the Government when the issue is taken up at the Constitutional Court, and we must hope that it does not set a precedent which will see the Government forever amending the constitution where the document stands in the way of any Government intention or action.

Ruling Reaffirms Faith in Top Watchdog Body

22 September 1995

The ruling by the Constitutional Court today that President Mandela's proclamations on the November 1 local government elections arrogating to himself and his Cabinet some powers laid down in the Interim Constitution as belonging to the provinces is important for at least two reasons. It proves much more concretely that South Africa's most important court, which some once believed to be dominated by ANC sympathisers, is capable of rising to the occasion and exercising its responsibilities independently and objectively.

The ruling is, therefore, to be welcomed, because it is vital that citizens and all political parties have confidence in the Constitutional Court, now the only sovereign body in the country.

But it also reminds the ANC-led Government of National Unity, and Mandela in particular, that the era when the country's rulers could make any laws they wanted has passed. Now the constitution is supreme, with Parliament and the Executive all subject to its pronouncements. Although Hernus Kriel's Western Cape government has every right to rejoice about the ruling, the biggest victor in all this is the constitution itself.

The good news, however, is that the country's founding democratic local government elections will go ahead on November 1 as scheduled. The Constitutional Court has given the Government the chance to remedy the defect in the Local Government Transition Act before October 25.

Reminiscent

What will happen now is that an emergency session of Parliament, quite reminiscent of the last session of the former tricameral Parliament a week before the April 27 1994 election, to amend the Interim Constitution to accommodate a last-minute trilateral agreement between the three GNU parties, will now have to take place to amend the Local Government Transition Act accordingly.

It's Open Season on ANC Ministers in the GNU

26 September 1995

It is open season on the Government of National Unity (GNU) or, more specifically, on the ANC component in that Government. Suddenly everybody has an opinion on what is wrong in the country, but not all suggest ways in which the wrongs can be put right.

Apart from President Nelson Mandela, who is the darling of white South Africa, just about every other ANC person in the GNU seems to be fair game.

The solution, the new sceptics will have us believe, is simple. It is encapsulated in by now popular calls for the heads of some people. 'Fire Ministers Naidoo, Zuma, Skweyiya, Bengu, Nzo, Modise . . . 'on and on the chorus goes.

Now even supposedly disinterested commentators like the University of the Witwatersrand's Professor Geoff Hughes seem to have an axe to grind with the new establishment.

In his column – 'Watch Word' it is called – meant to address matters pertaining to English usage and grammar, Hughes has railed against some individuals and institutions.

He has taken cheap shots at Winnie Mandela, aimed a few barbs at SABC Radio chief Govin Reddy, joined the once deafening chorus of SAfm critics and, last week, indirectly added his influential voice to the by now fashionable but nevertheless shallow condemnation of our first democratic Parliament and its functioning.

Lest I am misunderstood – for, make no mistake about it, there are people out there who are only too eager to twist others' arguments and understand them the way they want to – I am all for informed, objective criticism.

However, intellectual probity demands that ideological attacks be presented as such, and not cloaked in supposedly disinterested, academic garb.

I must say I smell a rat here. It seems to me there is a growing tendency in certain quarters to lay the blame for everything at the door of the black-led GNU. There is a drought in the country? Why, it is all the GNU's fault, of course. That seems to be the thinking.

I have argued here before that although crime has now spiralled completely out of hand, it is by no means a problem South Africa has had since April 27 1994. I can recall attending many press conferences in Pretoria, both at the Union Buildings and at police headquarters at Wachthuis well before last year's election, where more wars than I care to remember were declared on crime.

And the result? The crime has kept going up steadily. That is the situation that was inherited by Safety and Security Minister Sydney Mufamadi, and it has now become worse.

Admittedly, matters have not been helped by the GNU's over-eagerness to release prisoners from jail since it took office. But then again, this is a practice started by National Party leader F W de Klerk, well before Mandela's ascendance to power, for political reasons.

What is also often conveniently forgotten whenever the question of crime comes up is the ease with which criminals get bail. It is ironic, is it not, that while we want to be a democratic country giving South Africans the constitutionally entrenched right to bail and a speedy trial, we also want to see these rights taken away from others?

Back to the calls for the dismissals of certain Ministers. In Port Elizabeth last week, Democratic Party leader Tony Leon called on Mandela to embark on a 'thorough house-cleaning of his multi-party Cabinet by sacking "useless" Ministers and abolishing unnecessary portfolios'.

High up on his list of candidates for the chop was, predictably, Naidoo, followed by Chris Fismer (General Services), Ben Ngubane (Arts, Culture, Science and Technology) and Jeff Radebe (Public Works).

You will notice that the Ministers mentioned come from all three GNU parties. (He is smart, our Tony, and does not want to be accused of being yet again on an anti-ANC crusade). Nzo, Modise, Zuma and Skweyiya have often been mentioned in the same breath, although Leon refrained from also mentioning them last week.

Even if one were to make allowance for the fact that there is an election looming (they have a way of getting the worst out of politicians) it still does not make sense to blame one person, Naidoo, for the slowness of Government delivery on the RDP. Although fairly widespread, perceptions of inefficiency on the part of Nzo, Modise,

Zuma and Bengu are only that: perceptions.

Some foreign ambassadors I have spoken to in Pretoria have a healthy respect for Nzo and do not share the view that he is out of his depth in his job and, during a four-hour-long post-dinner discussion in Cape Town early this year, Modise struck me as a man quite on top of his job.

Zuma and Bengu have inherited messes in their departments, and it will take more than 18 months to undo the legacies of apartheid health care and Bantu Education.

President Mandela would be most ill-advised, therefore, to shuffle his cabinet now at the insistence of people with political agendas.

Politics of Desperation is Foolish and Dangerous

9 October 1995

Like their fellow citizens anywhere else in the country, the people of KwaZulu-Natal have a right to security, peace and political stability so that they can give their best to their country. They have all the rights that others enjoy and sometimes take for granted in different parts of the country, such as rights to free political activity and free choice.

But KwaZulu-Natal is the one province in the country where there is an ever-widening chasm between what is and what ought to be. Instead of much-needed peace and political stability, the province has conflict galore. Indeed, tensions are mounting and war drums are beating ever louder. In the past week alone, for instance, since the provincial legislature reconvened in Maritzburg on Tuesday, political tensions have increased tenfold.

And the Inkatha Freedom Party is largely responsible for the recent escalating tensions. As regular readers of this column will recall, I have previously pointed out that neither of the two main political parties in KwaZulu-Natal, namely the IFP and the ANC, was an angel. I have further argued that the chaos in the province was largely attributable, almost in equal measure, to these two parties.

It is common knowledge that the ANC leadership in the province does not believe that the IFP was the legitimate winner of the April election in that province. ANC leaders often remind us of the 'massive fraud and rigging' which allegedly occurred in KwaZulu-Natal during the poll last year, and firmly hold the view that the election result and the consequent balance of power in the province would have been different had there been no fraud as alleged. Like the aggrieved party it believes itself to be, the ANC has therefore not made it easy for the IFP-led provincial government to run the province properly.

The IFP, on the other hand, also believes that the alleged 'massive fraud and rigging' in last year's election drastically reduced the party's provincial majority, and some in its ranks – including leader Chief Mangosuthu Buthelezi – hold the strong view that a freer and fairer fresh election in the province would substantially increase the IFP's majority in the provincial legislature.

But instead of concentrating on governing the province effectively, the IFP has expended a lot of energy on fighting minor battles against the ANC-dominated Government of National Unity. It has opposed just about every move or initiative taken by ANC ministers at the national level, and has even stupidly failed to use Reconstruction and Development Programme funds and implement RDP projects which would benefit the people of the province. Hence the recent row between Department of Public Works director-general Sipho Shezi and KwaZulu-Natal Public Works MEC Senzele Mhlungu.

Whereas, as has already been argued above, both parties were more or less equally culpable for the sorry state of political affairs in the province, in recent weeks it has been the IFP which has upped the political temperatures considerably in that part of the country.

Only last week the party tried to steamroller its controversial Green Paper, which contains the IFP's constitutional proposals for the province, through the provincial legislature by getting it introduced as a Private Member's Bill so that it can be passed with a simple majority and not the two-thirds majority required for constitutional proposals. It also unveiled plans to change the composition of the provincial constitutional committee in order to increase the IFP's representation in the committee.

This is the politics of desperation, and it is as foolish as it is dangerous. It is strange, is it not, that the IFP – which has pulled out of the Constitutional Assembly at the national level and has alleged, wrongly, that the ANC wanted to write the country's final constitution on its own – is now doing precisely what it accused the ANC of doing at the national level.

It has openly sought confrontation with regard to the writing of the provincial constitution, and has made no secret of the fact that it will call an early provincial election if its semi-confederal constitutional proposals are rejected, as indeed they will and should be.

Interestingly, one senses that there is much more accommodation of other parties' views in the constitution-making process at the national level.

Given recent developments in the province and Buthelezi's comments, one is forced to come round to President Mandela's view – expressed during a State visit to Tanzania in June – that Buthelezi is a major stumbling block to peace in the province. For there is no doubt at all in political circles that the IFP's national leadership – especially Buthelezi and IFP deputy national chairman Dr Sipo Mzimela – has been running the province with remote control from Cape Town.

Hence the apparent victimisation of people perceived to be moderates, such as KwaZulu-Natal MPL Arthur Konigkramer who, in his capacity as chairman of the provincial constitutional committee, was much more willing to *negotiate* the province's constitution with other parties instead of presenting them with *fait accompli*. Hence, also, the public censure of Dr Frank Mdlalose's government by the IFP leadership at the party's recent congress.

For the sake of the country, for the sake of peace in KwaZulu-Natal – if these still matter to the IFP leadership – this confrontational attitude in the constitution-writing process should be outgrown as a matter of urgency.

Even ANC Shows Greater Tolerance to 'Enemies'

12 October 1995

About 18 months since the inception of democracy in our country how tolerant is our society today? Are we much more willing now than we were then to hear the other person's point of view, even if it may be anathema to us?

That, surely, must be one of the yardsticks we use to gauge the extent to which a democratic culture has taken root in South Africa, for tolerance is an important indicator of a country's and a people's civilisation. In established democracies, differences – whether political or not – are resolved through dialgoue and not through fisticuffs and other kinds of violence.

Now ours has been a very repressive and violent society, and people who held views different from those of the various political groups were dealt with most harshly. In their attempts to contain dissent, successive National Party governments jailed, banned and even murdered those who dared to oppose apartheid. And so we had Nelson Mandela and Robert Sobukwe and their comrades in their respective organisations removed from their families and imprisoned. We had Steve Biko and others assaulted to death in the country's prisons, while Oliver Tambo, Joe Slovo and others were forced to flee the country to wage war against apartheid from outside.

Ferocious

Within the black communities things were no better. Members of different political organisations once tore into one another with a ferocious viciousness (and, to a certain extent, still do in KwaZulu-Natal); many people have lost their lives for belonging to 'wrong' political parties, and in some townships and communities rival political parties trying to campaign were prevented from doing so.

In the run-up to our first all-inclusive election last year, for instance, there were townships in which the NP and the Democratic Party could not campaign because some politically immmature hotheads belonging to other parties prevented them from doing so.

In KwaZulu-Natal there was no free political activity for the ANC in the hinterlands of the former KwaZulu homeland – remember the gruesome murders of ANC campaign workers in Ulundi? – and for the IFP in some ANC-controlled townships in the urban areas.

With that having been the case, to what extent does the result of last year's election reflect the will of the people? Is it possible, as the NP and the DP have sometimes argued, that these parties could have done slightly better than they did had they been able to campaign freely in the townships? Or, that the balance of power in KwaZulu-Natal would have been different had the two major parties, the ANC and the IFP, had easy access to every nook and cranny of the province?

We will never know, but can only hope that the influence of intimidation was minimal and that the results reflected as closely as possible the will of the people of South Africa.

A number of changes have taken place since last year's founding democratic general election. In some parts of our country a democratic culture is gradually taking root. There is a growing realisation that there is nothing wrong with people belonging to different political parties, and that, in fact, they have a fundamental right to make that choice.

Free and Fair

We must hope, therefore, that the November 1 local government elections will be a lot freer and fairer than last year's general election, that all parties contesting the elections will be able to sell their policies wherever they want, and that voters will be able freely to profess allegiance to parties of their choices and to vote for them.

At a press conference in Johannesburg last week, the ANC announced that President Mandela had written to all ANC candidates in the forthcoming elections to call on them to allow free political activity in their areas. The organisation's Code of Conduct for ANC candidates was also enclosed.

That is commendable. Indeed, of late one has sensed a greater willingness on the part of the ANC to allow other parties to coexist peacefully with it in most parts of the country but not in KwaZulu-Natal, where there are still tensions between the organisation and the IFP. This new maturity on the part of the ANC must have to do with the fact that the organisation is now in government and is, therefore, much more self-assured.

Mandela's move is to be welcomed and it is now up to the other parties to issue similar injunctions to their members and candidates.

If Anything Happens to Me . . .

18 October 1995

At the end of a two-hour long interview with IFP leader and Home Affairs Minister Chief Mangosuthu Buthelezi in his ministerial office in Pretoria on June 16 last year, I thanked him for having agreed to meet me and colleague Shaun Johnson at short notice.

'Well, you know, Mr Nyatsumba, I have many enemies in the media,' he said, turning to look at Johnson before adding as he shook my hand, '*and you are not one of them.*' (During a TV interview on the 'Inkathagate' scandal about four years ago, Buthelezi called Johnson a racist – just because Johnson had dared to ask him a question he did not like!)

At the IFP's national congress in Ulundi in July this year, the same Buthelezi told the party faithful what a wonderful, objective journalist I was. He called me a respected South African journalist who was in no political party's pocket.

Before that he had also singled me out in an address to a meeting of the Conference of Editors in Durban, where he once again sang my praises as a journalist. He did the same when he was my guest at a luncheon at *The Star* on July 10. (He was the first political leader I had invited to a luncheon with *The Star's* political team.)

And then at the weekend Buthelezi, angered by my mild criticism of him in this column last week, viciously tore into me. He accused me of having 'conducted a virulent campaign of denigration' against him over the past two years, alleging that I had indulged in 'cheap propaganda on behalf of a party that is in conflict with the IFP'.

He added: 'I am personally flummoxed by the lengths to which Mr Nyatsumba is prepared to go in his vendetta against me... I am constantly amazed at the extent to which hatred can drive people to such extremes of irrationality – even people one regarded as intelligent.'

(The ANC rushed to my defence, saying I have 'a democratic right to express my views without fear or favour'. That is commendable, but I wish the ANC had said the same when its members in KwaZulu-Natal last week called Durban-based SABC journalists security agents.)

Which is the true Buthelezi speaking? Can the man not make up his mind about me?

Now, I can borrow some of Buthelezi's much-beloved words and say that all this is 'poppycock', 'arrant twaddle', 'claptrap', 'balderdash', 'rubbish' and 'nonsense' – which it is – but I am not going to do so. that would be *infra dignitatem.* I will not stoop to the level of a paranoid, old man.

I repeat, the mess that KwaZulu-Natal finds itself in, including the confusion with regards to the writing of the province's constitution, have a lot to do with Buthelezi. He should concentrate on his national portfolio as Home Affairs Minister and leave the running of the province to his party's chairman, Premier Dr Frank Mdlalose.

The record will show that I have, in fact, always given the IFP a fair hearing. Regular readers of this column will recall that I condemned President Mandela quite harshly for his threat in May to cut off central Government funding to KwaZulu-Natal and to amend the Interim Constitution to give himself more powers to deal with the situation in that province.

They will recall further that I have consistently argued that the international mediation promised to the IFP on April 19 last year had to take place, and that I had pointed out that most of their claims for more provincial powers were legitimate in terms of the Interim Constitution.

Yes, I have criticised Buthelezi, but I have also criticised leaders of other parties. And none of them has ever incited members of his party to assault me, for Buthelezi's tirade at the rally in Empangeni must be seen as such. Should anything happen to me, Buthelezi will be held personally responsible.

Sometimes You Want to Vomit

25 October 1995

Some among our compatriots, especially those from the ranks of the formerly privileged racial elite, have an amazingly short memory. Given half a chance they will gleefully falsify our history and have us remember only their romantic version of it – and all of this done with the straightest of faces.

But the vast majority of us suffer from no amnesia and, backed by personal experience and documentation, still have a fairly accurate recollection of events as they once were.

Picture the scene. You are at a racially mixed lunch or dinner table and, almost inevitably, the discussion veers to crime and 'slipping standards'. Almost without exception, the majority of the people around the table plaintively bemoan the 'ever-escalating' crime rate and the 'inability of the weak-kneed new Government' (a coded reference to the ANC component in the Government) to deal with it.

They nod their heads ruefully and talk not about the problems and challenges facing the Government of National Unity, but rather about the GNU's 'bungling' and 'monumental incompetence'. They say nothing about their individual standards of living, which remain pretty much what they were before last year's general election – among the highest in the world. Instead, they whinge about imaginary falling 'standards' at the workplace, at our tertiary institutions, in the civil service and even in governance.

You look around at the people mouthing these inanities without shame, and you find that it is people who are no fools, people in very senior and responsible positions in society, people for whom you once had some respect. In short, people who should know better. Almost without exception, they all have one thing in common: they are white and, no matter how much they try to deny it, were proud beneficiaries of apartheid.

The table, you soon come to the sad realisation, is dripping with nostalgia for 'the good old days' of apartheid when crime was still a black problem confined to the townships, when whites' apartheid-bequeathed senior jobs were safe and way out of the reach of blacks and when our 'competent' (read white) Government was still in office. The less couth and diplomatic among them will even make bold to say, without any sense of shame: 'Things were better in the olden days.'

Nausea wells up and you want to vomit because of these social dregs, but you refrain from doing so – after all, you are supposed to be in civilised company.

The question has been posed in this column before, but I will pose it again: this reconciliation we have heard so much about, is it supposed to be a unidirectional thing? Why is it that white South Africa has generally received so much goodwill from black South Africa without reciprocating to the same extent? It is just as well that many a person in the black community is gradually waking up to this fraud of our times.

But this aversion to change is not only limited to the closet conservatives who nevertheless believe themselves to be liberals. It would appear to also permeate the ranks of the National Party (NP), whose leadership remains as lily-white today as it was two years ago.

Not only has NP leader and Deputy President F W de Klerk taken exception to the recent statement of fact by President Nelson Mandela that the crime we are experiencing now is a legacy of NP rule, but he has now also taken to hammering the ANC for lack of delivery on the Reconstruction and Development Programme. On his election campaign trails throughout the country, De Klerk has posed a rhetorical question to mostly black audiences: 'Where are the houses the ANC promised you before last year's elections?'

Where, indeed?

Well, there is no denying that delivery on the RDP has been painfully slow, but why was that? Surely the answer is not, as De Klerk will have us believe, that it is because of the 'incompetence' of the blacks who were employed by the ANC ministers, as part of affirmative action, in their ministries?

Not only is this racist and paternalistic, but it is also extremely simplistic. A big part of the problem must surely be the sheer magnitude of the daunting legacy of apartheid.

It is because the previous governments of De Klerk's NP built no houses for blacks – until 1985 blacks were, after all, supposed to be sojourners in white South Africa – and because the Nats' distribution of public resources was so unashamedly skewed in favour of whites that the construction of houses and other manifestations of the RDP have been so slow. It is because De Klerk's NP governments expended so much money and energy on using the country's security forces on enforcing apartheid and fighting against political parties instead of combatting crime that we have the crime problem we have now. These are incontrovertible facts.

Yes, the ANC's record of performance in government is not exactly glittering, and this column has not spared the ANC criticism in that regard. It is essential, however, that such criticism should be informed by history and put in perspective.

The rising crime rate and the slowness on delivery of the RDP are all matters for concern, but they are OUR problems rather than the ANC's.

De Klerk should also accept his part of the blame for them and together with his new partners in Government devise solutions.

The local government elections have come and will soon go, but South Africa and her problems will be forever with us. Let us be responsible.

Don't Force the Worm to Turn

1 November 1995

The picture is redolent with the aura of old South Africa. I am looking at it, as it appeared on the front page of *The Star* on July 31, 1990, as I write this column. I can count at least 10 uniformed policemen – there were about 25 of them – all white, with frightening visages. They walked in twos in the form of a guard of honour, and between another two was a bespectacled Sathyndranath 'Mac' Maharaj.

Now South Africa's Transport Minister, Maharaj was manacled to a black policeman. Detained a week earlier in connection with 'Operation Vula', an alleged SACP plot to seize power in the event of negotiations failing, he had been given permission to attend the cremation service in Brixton, Johannesburg of his 59-year-old sister, Mani Persad, who had died of cancer while he was in detention.

We had been tipped off that Maharaj was going to be at the cremation service and I remember being filled with revulsion as a convoy of police vehicles arrived at the crematorium and many serious-looking policemen got out. And when Maharaj was taken out of one of the cars, manacled to a policeman, there was tension in the air.

Full of dignity even under these conditions, Maharaj maintained his composure and looked right ahead as he was led into the crematorium.

He was not allowed to talk to anyone, including his lawyer, Ismail Ayob. Maharaj remained stoical throughout the service until he was driven away in the same melodramatic fashion after the service.

The ANC had already signed the Groote Schuur Minute with the then National Party government, and followed this up with the Pretoria Minute – in terms of which the organisation suspended its armed struggle – on August 6 that year.

There was a firm agreement in place that all those who had committed crimes in pursuance of a political goal before October 8 1990 were going to be given indemnity.

In a statement on November 5 that year, the ANC said Operation

Vula had been authorised by the organisation's National Executive Committee, and 'as such the entire NEC is responsible' for it.

The ANC went on to say that since all 'so-called offences' in connection with Operation Vula had occurred before the agreed cut-off deadline, the trial had to be suspended and all eight men – including Maharaj – released on bail pending the outcome of their indemnity applications.

Maharaj and his comrades were first released on bail and, on March 22 1991, granted indemnity. The decision ensured not only that negotiations continued, but also that we have the relative political stability we now seem to be taking for granted. Since then many others on all sides of the political spectrum have been indemnified and political prisoners released from jails for political expediency.

Tomorrow General Magnus Malan and 10 senior police and military officers are to be arrested and charged with the murder of 13 people in Kwa-Makhutha, south of Durban, on January 21, 1987. Indictments are to be served on them relating to their alleged role in setting up a paramilitary force for the Inkatha Freedom Party (IFP), which was allegedly responsible for the attack.

Last week President Nelson Mandela turned down Freedom Front leader General Constand Viljoen's request that the indemnity cut-off date be extended from December 6 1993 to the more significant and emotionally imbued May 10 1994, the day on which Mandela was inaugurated as South Africa's first black president.

Now, it is easy to hate Malan and most, if not all, the generals to be charged with him.

After all, politically they are not very likeable chaps, but we would be making a grave mistake to allow our dislike of them to blind us to the dangers inherent in their persecution.

It will create uncertainty anew within the security forces, which have so far showed themselves to be remarkably loyal to the constitution and the new dispensation (perhaps because there has not yet been a real crisis which might have put their loyalty to a test).

As some ANC ministers concede privately, this Government is not yet certain that it enjoys the full loyalty of the SAPS and the SANDF. That is why, at his rally in Soweto on Sunday, Mandela made a pitch at the security forces by publicly praising SAPS Commissioner George Fivaz and SANDF Chief General Georg Meiring as men of integrity.

It will also, as preliminary reaction has already indicated, raise political temperatures unnecessarily and give the almost moribund right wing a cause around which to rally.

The Interim Constitution guarantees political indemnity to all those who can prove their crimes were politically motivated, as long as these occurred before December 6 1993. There is no doubt, therefore, that Malan *et al* will be indemnified by the Truth and Reconciliation Commission. The men's prosecution now is dangerous and politically unwise.

Of course, justice must be done and be seen to be done, but justice and political expediency are mutually exclusive. Just as it was once politically expedient to free our jails of political prisoners and indemnify some people for the sake of negotiations and the consequent political settlement, it is now politically expedient to grant Malan and company temporary immunity from prosecution until they receive full indemnity from the Truth and Reconciliation Commission, for the sake of political stability.

As for the indemnity cut-off date, that should indeed be extended to May 10 1994, the day on which Mandela took a salute from the SANDF and pledged himself to a 'new covenant'. If right-wing pre-election bombers benefit from this – as indeed they will – so be it, but they will not be the only ones. So, too, will members of the PAC, the IFP, Azapo and the ANC itself (there have yet to be prosecutions on the Shell House killings).

Besides, it is important that Viljoen, who by Mandela's own admission has played a very positive and constructive role in the new dispensation, should be given something to show for his efforts. Otherwise he will continue to be ridiculed in extreme right-wing circles and lose the influence he has on the responsible right.

He is a reasonable man: let us not push him to desperate measures. After all, pushed too far, even the meekest worm will turn.

Let Us Not Forget the Jackboot

Beware of Hounding McBride

29 November 1995

Almost two years after news of South Afria's historic peaceful political settlement made headlines here and abroad, the world continues to marvel at the ability of black South Africans to forgive. In a country where they are a majority, and where they have cringed for centuries under the heavy jackboot of white supremacy and apartheid, blacks have been forgiving to a fault.

For years blacks repeatedly stated that although the majority of white South Africans supported apartheid – white voters returned the National Party into office one general election after another, remember? – they (blacks) were against the diabolic system of white supremacy which they wanted to see brought to an end, and not against whites as a group. This view was shared even by men like founding Pan Africanist Congress leader Robert Sobukwe and the late Black Consciousness leader Steve Biko, both of whom are men whose views were sometimes misunderstood to be anti-white.

This country is awash with black people who have suffered insults and all kinds of indignities because of apartheid, people who carry with them emotional and physical scars every day as a result of the NP's policies, and people who have lost loved ones because of the former apartheid governments' security apparatus.

Do these people scream 'revenge' and bay for the blood of the whites in whose name, and for whose benefit, apartheid was practised? Do they espouse the philosophy of an eye for an eye, asking that those who treated black people like dirt in the past should be given a dose of their own medicine now that blacks run the country? Do they, generally, call for the mass arrest and prosecution of those who committed unspeakable human rights violations, including the murder of school children like Hector Peterson and many others?

On the whole, the answer to these questions is 'no'. The majority of black South Africans share President Nelson Mandela's and the

Government's philosophy of reconciliation, provided this reconciliation is not a unidirectional process and does not take place *at the expense of the black majority*.

Why, then, do some among our white compatriots – granted, a minority, perhaps – seem to find it difficult to show the same commitment to reconciliation when they are the ones who are hurting? Why do they conveniently want reconciliation when it suits them and turn their backs on it when it does not?

Consider the case of former ANC MP Robert McBride, for instance. Nine years after the unfortunate Magoo's Bar blast in Durban, some newspapers still find it difficult to write about McBride without labelling him in reference to that June 15 1986 incident.

Why the double standards? Why do these papers not call former State President P W Botha and ex-Defence Minister General Magnus Malan 'the Butchers of Maseru', where many more people died during the infamous cross-border raid than at Magoo's Bar? Why don't they also call NP leader and Deputy President F W de Klerk 'the Butcher of Umtata', where almost a whole family – including young children – was wiped out in one of the most brutal, cowardly and callous raids of our times, ostensibly because the victims were believed to be members of the PAC's military wing, the Azanian People's Liberation Army?

Why are NP leaders not labelled mass murderers, for we cannot begin to enumerate those who died at the hands of that party and its security apparatus, either directly like Biko or indirectly like Sobukwe and many, many others?

Fact is, ours is a very bloody past, hence the need to put it behind us without resorting to Nuremberg-type trials which may bedevil the reconciliation process. It is no exaggeration to say the hands of those who fought on the side of apartheid are far bloodier than those of the people who fought for democracy, and the two sides do not even begin to compare in terms of morality.

Now that McBride has joined the Department of Foreign Affairs, there is a campaign to remove him from his present job and to block his possible appointment as an ambassador.

Victims of the 1986 blast are planning to sue McBride 'for pain and suffering', and are reported to have enlisted the aid of an international lawyer to fight their case.

The group of 30, so say reports, also plans a nationwide campaign to have the ANC member sacked as a deputy director of foreign affairs.

Now, I cannot pretend I know how the 30 and families of the three women who died in that blast feel. I have fortunately not lost a loved one in the violence – including the State violence. The 30, therefore, are entitled to feel the way they do. They, in fact, would find themselves in agreement with the families of Biko and assassinated Durban lawyers Griffiths and Victoria Mxenge, who want to see justice done.

The difference, however, is that in McBride's case justice was done. He was apprehended and prosecuted, and spent eight years in prison, four of which were on Death Row. Like many others, he benefited from the indemnity which was granted to political prisoners. Biko's and the Mxenges' murderers, however, have yet to be prosecuted.

The NP, we are told, is also opposed to McBride's appointment. The party, and those seeking to stigmatise and isolate McBride, should consider very carefully the implications and consequences of their actions.

They may be setting a precedent which many others in the black community may soon follow with glee.

A Government Can't be Held to Ransom

The ANC will have to Break Free From the Unions

20 December 1995

Two weeks before South Africa's founding democratic general election in April last year, I flew to Durban to address senior Portnet managers on the political situation then prevailing in the country, and on the likely future political scenario.

The country was almost on the boil then: political tensions were thick and palpable, the right was spoiling for a civil war, and the IFP was still adamant that it would have nothing to do with an election which would take place in terms of a 'fatally flawed' interim constitution.

We may now take the relative peace and tranquillity for granted, but there was a time 20 months ago when all that most people spoke about was how much violence there was likely to be on election days, whether defeated parties would play by the democratic rules of the game and accept defeat, and whether we were not heading for a civil war. It was in that context, then, that the Portnet management extended the invitation to me.

At the end of my presentation, I was asked to comment on future relations between the ANC and labour federation Cosatu in particular and the future of the broad ANC-led ANC-SACP-Cosatu-Sanco alliance in general.

Understandably, this is a taboo subject to the ANC and its allies. Anyone who dares to suggest that all may not be rosy in the alliance, and that a time may well come when this alliance may come apart altogether, is often considered something of a heretic.

But most political observers know not only that the alliance is on shaky ground at the moment, but also that a time may well come when the different interest groups in the ANC itself – which has been variously described as a 'broad church' or 'a multi-party democracy within itself', and which Chris Hani once described to me as 'an omnibus' – may begin asserting themselves in years to come.

And so I said at that Portnet meeting that once the ANC was in government there would inevitably be a conflict of interests between itself and its labour ally, Cosatu. I said while it would be in the interests of the ANC as government that the country's economy grows much more rapidly, that there are fewer or no strikes and stayaways so that our country can be attractive to foreign investors and more jobs can be created, it would be in Sam Shilowa's interests that workers are paid well, that they benefit from the new dispensation and that they remain in a position to use 'mass action' in its various forms as an important bargaining chip when necessary.

And so, because of these conflicts of interests, I forecast growing tensions between the ANC-led Government of National Unity and Cosatu in particular and between the organisation and its other alliance partners in general. Alliances, of course, function cohesively when they have something which binds them together (in our case, apartheid), but things change the moment that ceases to be the case.

I added, however, that the ANC-SACP-Cosatu alliance would not come apart before the 1999 general election because, among other reasons, of its historical strength on the one hand and of the anti-defection clause in the interim constitution.

The clause makes it impossible for SACP, Cosatu, Sanco and indeed Contralesa (Congress of South African Traditional Leaders) members presently in Parliament on an ANC ticket to cross the floor to another party. The ANC's own code of conduct makes it impossible for these individuals to vote against the organisation in Parliament or the provincial legislatures.

The tensions I forecast in April 1994 have already manifested themselves a number of times in the past 20 months, and will continue to do so again and again in the months and years to come. Let us consider a few examples.

Shortly after becoming president, Nelson Mandela told a Cosatu congress in Johannesburg that the federation's members should not be 'selfish' and demand higher salaries when there is an army of unemployed people in the country. They should, he said, accept lower wage increases so that those who are unemployed could also get jobs. Needless to say, his message was most unpopular with Cosatu.

Other examples of similar tension abound. For instance, while it is generally accepted that Trade and Industry Minister Trevor Manuel is doing a great job, Cosatu has not been entirely pleased with his lowering of protective tariffs with a view to finally dropping them altogether. Some Sanco members in some parts of the country stood as independent candidates and not on ANC tickets for the November 1 local government elections; and Contralesa, which has been vocal in its criticism of the government's handling of legislation affecting traditional leaders, even called for a boycott of the November 1 poll in some parts of the country because of differences with the ANC. And then there was last week's showdown between the Government and Cosatu, over the Government's bold and welcome announcement to proceed with the privatisation of some state assets such as Telkom. This is a far more philosophical difference between the two allies, and is likely to heighten tensions even further, notwithstanding statements to the contrary from some within the two organisations.

If it is not careful, the ANC in Government will find itself held to ransom by its allies, notably the giant federation Cosatu, and ANC ministers will have to keep looking over their shoulders to make sure their moves do not infuriate Shilowa and his colleagues. Like the Labour Party in Britain, sooner or later the ANC will have to break free from the clutches of organised labour.

Laying Down the Law – Gently

Madiba touched on what was obvious

14 February 1996

For at least a week leading up to the opening of the third session of South Africa's first popularly elected Parliament on Friday, political writers and commentators speculated – as is usually the case – about what President Nelson Mandela was likely to say in his state-of-the-nation address. A number of us gave our penny's worth of opinion solicited or unsolicited, in print, on radio or on TV.

Although the degree to which such speculation is informed depends, among other things, on the strength of one's contacts, it is fairly easy to anticipate the things likely to find expression in a speech such as the one Mandela delivered on Friday. The challenges facing the Government in 1996, surely, are obvious: crime, violence in KwaZulu-Natal, the economy, the final constitution and the Truth and Reconciliation Commission.

For, in South Africa today, is it not common cause that crime is the burning issue, that the carnage in KwaZulu-Natal is a terrible blot on our copybook as a nation, that the apparent failure of the steady economic growth to yield jobs is an important concern, that the conclusion of our new constitution is an important milestone and that hearings of the Truth and Reconciliation Commission have the potential of inflaming passions?

These were so obvious that it is not with any pride or gloating that I can reveal that in two radio interviews last week I – like, no doubt, countless other commentators – anticipated correctly that Mandela would pronounce on these challenges. In a sense, then, Mandela's speech, which, as usual, had inputs from a number of his ANC colleagues, notably Deputy President Thabo Mbeki, was scripted for him by prevailing national circumstances. What none of us could forecast with any authority was the precise wording and formulation of the above-listed concerns in the President's presentation.

Having said that, let us now take a critical look at the 14-page speech itself. Commendably, it touches on all the challenges confronting us as a country. Like Mandela's opening-of-Parliament address a year ago, however, this year's was also long on content but short on detail. In fairness to the president, it must be pointed out that he did say that details on some of the things he spoke about would be given later by his ministers, some of whom have already been doing that in parliamentary briefings this week.

Perhaps typically, Mandela had something for everyone in his speech, beginning with the country's sportsmen and women, for whom he was effusive with praise, calling on the nation to emulate them 'to make South Africa a winning nation' in all spheres.

Importantly, Mandela echoed his disappointment, first expressed in his annual January 8 ANC statement, about the failure of some in the white and business communities to embrace fully the new South Africa and its generosity of spirit by reciprocating the goodwill blacks have shown towards them. Before identifying the challenges facing the Government and all South Africans this year, he stressed that all citizens were called upon 'to become builders and healers'.

Such building and healing, he said, could not take place if they were 'perceived as one-way processes, with the victims of past injustices forgiving and the beneficiaries merely content in gratitude' or 'if the rich in our society see the poor as hordes of irritants, or if the poor sit back, expecting charity'.

Such building and healing could not take place 'if we continue to have people in positions of influence and power who, at best, pay lip service to affirmative action, black empowerment and the emancipation of women, or who are, in reality, opposed to these goals'.

It could not take place 'if we have people who continue with blind arrogance to practise racism in the work-places and schools'.

Neither could such building and healing take place 'if – in both the private and public sectors, in the schools and universities, in the hospitals and on the land, in dealing with crime and social dislocation – we continue with business as usual, wallowing in notions of the past'.

Are you listening, white South Africa? Corporate South Africa, are you listening?

It was important that Mandela made these points, although he did not make them strongly enough. Some of us have repeatedly said these things and have invariably been called all sorts of names. It is important that the highest office in the land should now articulate the same sentiments, especially considering the arrogance and racism of some white schools which continue to turn black pupils away in present-day South Africa.

The president went on to give the Government's priorities for the year as education, health delivery, housing policy and implementation as well as land reform. Anyone with the country's interest at heart must agree that these are indeed important.

Unfortunately, we were once again treated to the usual anti-crime rhetoric, without any concrete proposed action to give force to the sentiments outlined. It is only in the case of violence in KwaZulu-Natal that some firm measure – the prohibition of the carrying of dangerous weapons 'in public manifestations' – was announced.

Overall, then, Mandela's speech was carefully balanced and addressed all the issues that needed to be addressed. If there was any disappointment from the ranks of journalists in the Parliamentary Gallery – and there was – it was that it was a fairly bland, undramatic speech in which nothing jumped at you.

Mortality and the Marketplace

The matter of Mandela's successor won't go away

21 February 1996

About 18 months ago, long before it was fashionable to speculate about a post-Mandela South Africa, I had occasion to comment in this column about the legacy President Nelson Mandela would leave behind when he retires and about the competence of the men most likely to succeed him.

I said then that the issue, although a legitimate concern, was often discussed privately, even then in hush-hush tones, both within and without the ANC. I said that instead of discussion of a post-Mandela era being taboo, the matter should be taken out of the privacy of our houses and aired publicly.

Since then, of course, the matter has been talked about countless times, with concerns about a South Africa without Mandela growing almost to a crescendo as we approach 1999, when Mandela will step down as the country's first black president.

The concern has grown, too, both here and abroad, and countless are the times I have found myself called upon, especially by members of the diplomatic community, to respond to questions about the president's health and his likely successor/s.

These concerns are going to be with us at least until 1999 when Mandela officially hands over power to his successor. Although in terms of the ANC's constitution the organisation's 50th national congress is scheduled to take place around December 1997, there are still some imponderables. Nobody, for instance, knows with certainty if Mandela will relinquish the presidency of the ANC at that congress and allow his successor to assume control and stamp his personality, or if he will seek re-election.

Should Mandela relinquish the presidency of the ANC in December 1997, this would leave Thabo Mbeki and Cyril Ramaphosa (with a late challenge from Gauteng Premier Tokyo Sexwale or even maverick Broadcasting, Posts and Telecommunications Minister Dr Pallo Jordan not to be ruled out) to battle it out for the leadership. Although anything is possible, as things stand at the moment Mbeki is the clear favourite.

This would strengthen Mbeki's own position in the ANC even further and clearly establish him as Mandela's heir-apparent. With the president already delegating serious responsibilities to Mbeki, this would ensure that the deputy president begins, even while Mandela is still around, to stamp his authority in government and get South Africa used to the idea of a 'President Thabo Mbeki'.

Mandela, on the other hand, would then be free to play the role he has chosen for himself, the role which has preoccupied him since he ascended to the presidency: reconciliation and nation-building. He is very conscious of his position in history, and wants to be remembered by future generations as the amazing man who emerged from 27 years in prison, absolutely without rancour, to lead SA to racial reconciliation.

Like a man with a premonition, Mandela almost said as much when he addressed students at the University of Potchefstroom. 'I will pass through this world but once,' he said, 'and I do not want to divert my attention from my task – which is to unite the nation.'

Even more revealing was his next sentence: 'I am writing my own testimony because I am nearing my end. I want to be able to sleep till eternity with a broad smile on my face knowing that the youth, opinion-makers and everybody is stretching across the divide, trying to unite the nation.'

What a testament indeed! That should help us all understand Mandela better and always place his words and deeds within the context of that statement.

The president might be advised against relinquishing the leadership of the ANC, perhaps even by people whose intentions might be less than noble. It might be argued that he would need to maintain a direct link with his constituency and that Mbeki, as F W de Klerk did to P W Botha in 1989, might no longer consult with him and effectively cut him off from the grassroots.

But Mandela is not Botha, and no amount of manipulation by anybody will cut him off from the people. It behoves him, for Mbeki's and South Africa's sake, to help make the transition smooth. It would be unfortunate if Mandela were to hang on to the presidency of the ANC beyond 1997, and only hand it over to his successor at the organisation's 52nd national congress in 2000, a year after our next general election.

One must ask, however, how many times one should point out that Mandela's likely successors, Mbeki and Ramaphosa, are both men of exceptional ability who would do a good job in running the country, either jointly or severally, before the Johannesburg Stock Exchange and the markets will believe this. How many times must one point out that both Mbeki and Ramaphosa do not have ideological differences with either Mandela or each other, that they are both committed to the philosophy to which the president is committed, before the markets can believe this?

There was that irresponsible rumour last week, started off by some foreign journalist who misunderstood Mandela's off-the-cuff remarks in Parliament on Thursday to be a valediction to the country, that the president had suffered a heart attack. The markets reacted predictably and the rand plunged.

Now I am no guru on markets, but this much I know: the markets are conservative and do not like change. When Deputy President De Klerk threatened to resign from the Government of National Unity early last year, the markets shivered; when Mandela so much as has 'flu, the markets react. Nobody, except perhaps economists, should worry unduly about the markets' hypersensitivity to political developments, or even if Mandela were to die – God forbid – the markets would normalise once a new incumbent was in office and the situation had stabilised.

Mandela Raps 'Praise Singers'

Hero worship, coupled with denigration of Mbeki, is distasteful

23 February 1996

In an unprecedented move last weekend, President Nelson Mandela took the trouble of writing an article – published in the *Sunday Times* – in response to comments made in that paper's editorial a week earlier.

He opened with reference to his recent address at Potchefstroom University, during which he disclosed that he is now writing his own testament because he is nearing the end of his life. He said further that in his remaining years his determination to pursue his goals of racial reconciliation 'will be even stronger'.

'This,' he wrote, 'I pronounced from the fullness of my conviction.'

Mandela then proceeded to express, at some length, his unease about being singled out by some political commentators who, at the expense of some of his senior ANC colleagues such as Deputy President Thabo Mbeki, liberally shower him with praise.

'It is particularly unacceptable that this train of hero-worshipping should be coupled with a systematic campaign to denigrate other ANC leaders such as Mbeki – a campaign that is beyond any civilised norms of discourse, let alone objectivity. Further, an attempt is made to decide who should be in the leadership of the ANC, and whom I should have in Cabinet. The exaltation of the president, and denigration of other ANC leaders, constitutes praise which I do not accept,' Mandela concluded.

Why, it might be asked, did the president find it necessary to take the most unusual step of personally writing to a newspaper to defend his colleagues? The answer lies in a vicious campaign to discredit Mandela's most likely successor, Mbeki. For almost a year now, some people have systematically targeted Mbeki for denigration. His judgement has been questioned, sometimes without justification, and he has been portrayed as a bumbling man not quite up to his job.

But what triggered Mandela's response was some comment following the shivering of the markets as a result of the unfounded rumour two weeks ago that the president was on his deathbed.

Interpreting the markets' fairly predictable reaction to the rumour, The *Sunday Times* was moved to remind us that 'among investors, faith in this continent is paper-thin, and the spectre of a South Africa torn to shreds by sectional hatreds has not yet been erased'.

Then character assassination: 'More to the point, Deputy President Mbeki, the anointed crown prince, simply does not inspire confidence. His diplomatic skills and his vaunted gift for quiet backroom committee work have given him a mildly discomfiting image.

'Where Mr Mandela projects warmth of spirit and generosity, Mr Mbeki *appears* [emphasis mine] manipulative and calculating. Where Mr Mandela has reached out to nervous minorities, especially Afrikaners and rightwingers, Mr Mbeki has become associated with *the angry Africanist wing of our politics*. Where Mr Mandela inspires affection, even love, Mr Mbeki invokes uncertainty and fear.'

But, dare we ask, in *whom* does Mbeki not inspire confidence: black people in the townships or the whites whose interests the *Sunday Times* represents? To *whom* is Mbeki's image 'mildly discomforting'? What makes him *appear* 'manipulative and calculating'? Is it wrong for Mbeki to be associated with 'the angry Africanist wing of our politics' (whatever that means), especially when Mandela is associated more and more with the white, 'nervous minorities' represented by that paper? In *whom* does Mbeki evoke 'uncertainty and fear': the black people who live in squalid conditions in match-box houses and squatter camps or the rich, Johannesburg northern suburbs-type whites who run the Johannesburg Stock Exchange?

The truth is that although Mbeki shares Mandela's philosophy of reconciliation, he unashamedly represents black interests. It was he, after all, who authored the ANC's Strategy and Tactics document which argues that reconciliation should be balanced with delivery on the RDP. It is he who has been most critical of the maintenance of the status quo in many spheres of our lives, including the private sector.

This, so goes the chop-logic, means that Mbeki is associated with 'the angry Africanist wing of our politics' and therefore rules him out of contention for the presidency. The kind of black president white-controlled markets and 'nervous minorities' can accept is one who is pre-occupied with '(inspiring) affection, even love' among whites.

Some of these quarters nurse the secret hope that Cyril Ramaphosa, of whom many in the white community approve, would be such a president. They forget that Ramaphosa was once a 'radical' trade unionist representing mineworkers, and that he, too, is acutely aware of the need to counterbalance reconciliation with RDP delivery. This would also make him, in their books, 'associated with the angry Africanist wing of our politics', and therefore evoke 'uncertainty and fear'.

Admittedly, Mandela is a major stabilising force in this country, and South Africa will never again have a leader like him. But South Africa does not need another Mandela. Instead, it needs an intelligent leader who will build on the solid foundation laid by Mandela.

For the sake of his successor – whoever it will be – and SA, Mandela should step down as ANC president at his organisation's 50th national congress in December 1997, while serving the rest of his term as the country's president. He should, of course, remain a member of the ANC's NEC, or even the deputy president, even if it means that the ANC's constitution may have to be amended to make room for two deputy presidents, Mandela and Ramaphosa.

That way he would make it possible for those in whom Mbeki 'evokes uncertainty and fear' and to whom 'the idea that Mr Mandela may be replaced by Mr Mbeki inspires great nervousness' to get used to the idea of a 'President Thabo Mbeki', and for Mbeki to take on more responsibilities in the running of the country. Mandela, as state president, would continue to do what he loves best: 'inspire affection, even love' among 'nervous minorities, especially Afrikaners and right-wingers'.

Winnie's Finances will Sink Her

Allow the Mandelas the privacy they still have

28 March 1996

Poor President Nelson Mandela. Poor Winnie Madikizela-Mandela. There they were at the Rand supreme Court in Johannesburg last week, members of the most prominent family in South African politics, battling it out in full view of the general public, with every sordid and prurient piece of detail thrown up in public. They were providing lurid entertainment to a largely puritanical nation starved of titillating political gossip.

It was the divorce case of the decade, pitting Mandela versus Mandela. On the one side was the saintly, grandfatherly Nelson Mandela, first president of a democratic South Africa, on the other a demure Winnie Nomzamo Mandela (now Madikizela-Mandela), the hard-as-nails 'Iron Lady' of South African politics.

There was no love lost between them. The president wanted out of a marriage he said 'exists only on paper', declaring that he would not reconcile with Madikizela-Mandela 'even if the entire universe tried to persuade me'. She proclaimed her undying love for him, albeit unconvincingly, and continued to hold out for a possible reconciliation with her husband, even at that late hour.

A visibly saddened Mandela, who is widely revered here and abroad, was forced – he had tried repeatedly, without success, to have the matter settled out of court and therefore away from the public eye – to divulge things which were even more damaging to Madikizela-Mandela. He revealed that she had not once, during the two years they had lived together following his release from prison on February 11, 1990, entered their bedroom while he was awake.

'The bedroom,' Mandela observed correctly, 'is where a man and a woman discuss the most intimate things. There were so many things I wanted to discuss with her, but she is the type of person who fears confrontation.

'She never responded to my invitations. *I was the loneliest man during the period that I stayed with her.*' (Emphasis mine.)

How sad. How very, very sad.

Things did not have to get to that. The President certainly did not have to be forced, as he was, to appear in court as a witness, let alone to make the kind of disclosures he had to make. Very few of us can imagine the pain he must have felt in that courtroom.

It did not have to end that way. Like the respected members of society they are, the Mandelas should have discussed their differences privately, including agreeing on the division of their marital assets. It is most unfortunate, therefore, that Madikizela-Mandela's handlers and political advisers failed – one assumes they did *try* – to persuade her that forcing the matter to be settled in open court was not the wisest of moves and could boomerang quite badly, as indeed it did.

Now a divorce is an intensely personal matter and the Mandelas should be afforded what little privacy they still have. I will not, therefore, go into the merits and demerits of their respective cases.

Sad as last week's developments were, they are nevertheless unlikely to have any impact on the two Mandelas' respective political lives. The President, who again emerged as a gentleman, is so immensely popular both here and abroad, and across the racial divide, that it would take quite a doing to diminish his image and public standing, both personally and politically.

And this is beside the fact that he came away from the whole thing with his image not only intact but also significantly enhanced, for he was without doubt the legal and moral victor.

Madikizela-Mandela will have to learn that nobody, not even the wife or ex-wife of Nelson Mandela, can stand up to the President and emerge victorious.

What about Madikizela-Mandela? Has she taken the political beating of her life, never again to be a major force in the politics of the country? Although there are many who would wish that were so, that is unlikely to be the case. Madikizela-Mandela has shown herself to be a fierce fighter with more than nine political lives.

She has been embroiled in numerous controversies before, both personal and political, and has always made stunning comebacks. She is likely to do so again.

Personally, she has taken quite a hammering. In the eyes of her many political and personal detractors, she has yet again confirmed herself to be all the terrible things they have always thought she was: a very bitter, callous woman who can be as dangerous as a serpent, and who should never be allowed anywhere near a position of public importance.

Politically, however, Madikizela-Mandela is likely to continue to be a force. As even some of her detractors must grudgingly concede, she emerged from the overbearing shadow of her husband many moons ago and has contributed immensely in the fight against apartheid.

President Mandela was wrong, and may have been blinded by his own resentment of his ex-wife, when he said other women, notably Albertina Sisulu, had suffered more at the hands of apartheid's security apparatus than Madikizela-Mandela did.

Much to the chagrin of her political opponents she still has quite a sizeable constituency in the ANC, which is why she and Bantu Holomisa are among those who have been asked to campaign for the organisation ahead of the May local government elections in KwaZulu-Natal.

It is not Madikizela-Mandela's detractors, therefore, who will drive her out of politics. Instead, it is legal and financial problems, such as being declared insolvent, which could be her political undoing, and here her political handlers and advisers have their work cut out.

NP Federal Executive Split Almost Down the Middle

10 May 1996

Outgoing Deputy President F W de Klerk stunned members of his party's parliamentary caucus when he told them, a few minutes after he had walked into a caucus meeting shortly after 10.35 yesterday morning, that the National Party's federal executive council had decided earlier in the day that the NP should withdraw from the Government of National Unity.

Well-placed NP sources said although the possibility of withdrawal from the GNU had been discussed over the past two weeks, most NP MPs and senators did not expect a decision to be taken on the matter until around August.

'They were shocked. They could not say anything. They were not expecting it,' said the source, a member of the federal executive council, the party's highest decision-making body.

The Star was also told that the NP was divided along racial lines over whether to vote in favour of the final constitution adopted on Wednesday. Most white NP MPs were against it, 'but blacks felt they could not vote against so fundamental a document as the new constitution', said the source. The blacks won out and the NP joined the ANC and the PAC in voting in favour of the constitution. The big decision on the NP's future in the GNU was left in abeyance.

The source said the decision to quit the GNU was taken by the NP's 23-member federal council when it met early yesterday morning, without the knowledge of most NP MPs 'because we did not want to alert the media'.

When De Klerk moved that the NP should leave the GNU, the council was almost divided down the middle, with 10 members – including most of the six ministers and three deputy ministers – opposed. The other 13 members of the council, including De Klerk, favoured a withdrawal.

Once the decision had been taken, De Klerk and his federal executive colleagues went to the caucus meeting, which starts at 10.30 am on Thursdays, the source said.

'When we walked in at about 10.35. Caucus members suspected there was something wrong because we were late, but they knew that withdrawal from the GNU was one of the options being debated. They did not know the decision would be taken so soon, because the federal executive was meant to address the issue at its meeting next Tuesday,' said the source.

'Everybody sat down. When the chairman, Myburgh Streicher, said we were not going to hold a usual caucus meeting and that he was going to call on the party leader to talk to us, people were more tense. De Klerk started explaining that we will have to do it [leave the GNU] now or wait until 1999. He told them about the federal council's decision and there was shock. He said that from the caucus he was going to tell President Mandela about our decision and then hold a press conference.

'Because we did not want a leak, we said everybody should stay there. We waited in the caucus meeting until 12.30, when De Klerk began addressing a press conference,' the source said.